The Reminiscences of

REAR ADMIRAL RALPH KIRK JAMES

U. S. Navy (Retired)

U. S. Naval Institute
Annapolis, Maryland
1972

This manuscript is the result of a series of thirteen tape-recorded interviews with Rear Admiral Ralph Kirk James, U. S. Navy (Retired). The interviews were conducted by John T. Mason, Jr., for the Oral History Office in the U. S. Naval Institute. All of them took place in the home of Admiral James in Providence, Annapolis, Maryland, and cover a period of time from January, 1971 to May, 1972.

Admiral James has made various corrections and emendations to the original typescript. The reader is reminded, of course, that this is a transcript of the spoken word rather than the written word.

An extensive index is affixed for the convenience of the reader. In addition, a copy of the Report on SCAP Progress for 2 July 1962 is included in the appendix because of its great importance in the history of BuShips and of Admiral James' duty as Chief of that Bureau.

DECLARATION OF TRUST

The undersigned does hereby appoint and designate as his (her) Trustee herein, the Secretary-Treasurer and Publisher of the United States Naval Institute to perform and discharge the following duties, powers, and privileges in connection with the possession and use of a certain taped interview between the undersigned and the Oral History Department of the United States Naval Institute.

1. Classification of Transcript.

(X) a. If classified OPEN, the transcript(s) may be read or the recording(s) audited by the qualified personnel upon presentation of proper credentials, as determined by the Secretary-Treasurer of the U. S. Naval Institute.

( ) b. If classified PERMISSION REQUIRED TO CITE OR QUOTE, the user will be required to obtain permission in writing from the interviewee prior to quoting or citing from either the transcript(s) or the recording(s).

( ) c. If classified PERMISSION REQUIRED, permission must be obtained in writing from the interviewee before the transcribed interview(s) can be examined or the tape recording(s) audited.

( ) d. If classified CLOSED, the transcribed interview(s) and the tape recording(s) will be sealed until a time specified by the interviewee. This may be until the death of the interviewee or for any specified number of years.

2. It is expressly understood that in giving this authorization, I am in no way precluded from placing such restrictions as I may desire upon use of the interview at any time during my lifetime, nor does this authorization in any way affect my rights to the copyright of my literary expressions that may be contained in the interview.

Witness my hand and seal this 26th day of MAY 1972.

Ralph K. James
Rear Admiral U.S.N. (Ret)

I hereby accept and consent to the foregoing Declaration of Trust and the powers therein conferred upon me as Trustee:

5/31/72

Interview #1 with Rear Admiral Ralph KIrk James, USN (ret)

Annapolis, Maryland January 5, 1971

Subject: biography by John T. Mason, Jr.

Mr. Mason: It's a delight to meet you. I've been counting on having this series with you and hearing the story of your very significant naval career. Would you begin in a very appropriate way by telling me the date of your birth, the place, something about your family background and your early education?

Rear Admiral James: I was born in Chicago, Illinois, in the year 1906, which makes me a candidate to be sixty-five years of age here this year on the twenty-first of May. My mother was a Canadian born American citizen, my father was an American citizen born of Welsh parents. In fact he was the first in a family of nine to be born in the United States, three brothers having preceded him being born in England, so the family is basically of British background.

My youth was the routine of a young kid in the environs of Chicago that at that time seemed to be urban Chicago but subsequently it has become almost center city.

Q: Was it on the south side?

James: No, I was born on the north side of Chicago in an

area very close to where the old Edgewater Beach Hotel used to be, a well known landmark. I lived a scant half mile from the Edgewater Beach and Lake Michigan which was a delightful place for young people to cavort in the summer time. They even have winter sports, too.

Q: A beautiful section of Chicago. What was your father's business?

James: My dad, at the time that I first remember him, owned two laundries in Chicago. As the proprietor he was a hard working individual. In fact, he labored so hard that it exhausted the rest of us to see him come home of an evening when his boiler would break down or his truck drivers (and I mean wagon drawn trucks) failed to appear. My dad was everything to the laundry and it soon overwhelmed him, so shortly after I was in my early teens he sold out his business and became a member of Armour and Co. in the industrial soap department because of his knowledge in the use of soap in the laundries. The industrial soap department dealt with laundries, hospitals, commercial laundries. Later he became a sales manager with them at which time Swift and Co. employed him, for the same function, at (I presume) a significant increase in his income.

During this time we lived in a home in the north side of the city. My mother was a very fine singer and was a professional to a limited degree that her household duties and her two sons permitted. She was also a director of music in the Summerdale Congregational Church, which was our home church. My brother had been one of the earlier Boy Scouts in the community. He was six years my senior. When I came along and reached Boy Scout age, it was natural that I follow this line of enthusiasm and I became a really dedicated Boy Scout. I joined Troop 805 in Chicago at the age of twelve and didn't leave it until I entered the Naval Academy some six years later. Rather a unique group we were because we had an outstanding Scoutmaster, a bachelor, who was a professor at Northwestern University in accounting and later became a very prominent government accountant. He headed up the TVA in Tennessee and has written many books. The name of this gentleman is Eric Koehler. Koehler had a nack of attracting the older boys to stay on in scouting. Our troop, numbering about thirty-two members, had sixteen eagle scouts --a unique record. In Chicago we used to win the city championships in just about everything conceivable because we were a bunch of relatively old pros and these young kids twelve and thirteen had a tough time competing with sixteen year olds. But we stayed together which is the remarkable thing.

I went to college after graduating from Senn High School in 1923. My ambition was to get into the engineering business and I enrolled at Armour Institute of Technology.

Q: That had quite a reputation in that field.

James: It was considered the M.I.T. of the Middle West by

those of us who knew it. My long term ambition was to become an alumnus of M.I.T. but that's another story and I'll mention that in a moment. Continuing the line of Troop 805, when I was approaching my final year of association with this group of Boy Scouts, of the total of the troop there were about eighteen of us who were college students and still wore Boy Scout uniforms.

Q: It doesn't happen today, does it?

James: No. I emphasize this because I thought it was extremely unusual and I attribute it all to the leadership that one man could give and it was a remarkable lesson to a young fellow and highly important. Participation, understanding, willingness to commit yourself and a stern, but fair, disciplinary approach, which characterized Mr. Koehler.

Q: It probably has a direct bearing on the development of your own character, and career.

James: I remember while I was enrolled at Armour Tech as a very new student, I had no knowledge or aspirations to join the Navy nor to go to the Naval Academy until one Sunday in May, after I had enrolled in Armour but had not yet started, I was reading a Saturday Evening Post article written by Carrol S. Alden, who used to be a professor of English at the Naval Academy. I believe he later became head of the department of English. His story was a fascinating yarn and something caught my eye. It was an explanation of how a graduate of the Naval Academy, who dedicated himself to his work and stood reasonably high in his class could receive post-graduate instruction at M.I.T. and a Master's Degree in whatever particular field the Navy was interested in having him pursue. This is what sparked my interest in the Naval Academy. My dad's finances were not so great that he could afford to put me in M.I.T. for a full four year course. He had promised me, however, that my last two would be there. But here was a way to get there, I thought for certain. So my dad, having some political friends, made contact with our local congressman.

Q: Did he enter into this enthusiastically?

James: He entered into it because he recognized it as a sincere desire on my part which seemed to him to have real justification, not just a whim.

Q: How did your mother react to a proposed naval career?

James: My mother was completely opposed at the outset. Later, bless her, she became the most enthusiastic member of the family because I did enter the Naval Academy. But she was reluctant to see me leave the home nest and barge out into the strange new world. She knew nothing about the Navy. Midwesterners in those days were scarcely well informed. In fact, humorously, on the occasion of a farewell party given to me by one of the church groups, a neighbor who came to say goodbye said, "We often get to Indianapolis and when we next do, we'll come and look you up." That was the degree to which they were aware of where Annapolis was.

Q: And yet the Great Lakes Naval Station was there.

James: It was there but it didn't connote much to the average Middle West citizen. The Navy, as you recall, was slated for being somewhat disassembled as a result of the Washington naval conference, militarily speaking, as follows many post war developments, military comes into disrepute and I think we were suffering a little bit of that in 1923, World War I having ended only a few years earlier.

Q: Yes, I think we were, too. What had your brother done? What was his career?

James: My brother, as I say, preceded me by six years and he was a student at Armour Tech and got a degree in chemistry. At that particular time I'm not sure whether he was employed by International Harvester in their chemistry lab or he was then with the U. S. Gypsum Co., in connection with their chemical purchasing. He was married and his first child was born while I was on my first midshipmen cruise.

This attempt to seek out and gain the political Academy appointment didn't succeed immediately because actually I was asking in May for an appointment to report in June. My congressman hee-hawed the suggestion that these things were that easily available.

Q: Who was the congressman?

James: He was Congressman Carl Chindbloom in the tenth district of Illinois. He had the north side of Chicago and some of the suburbs. Carl Chindbloom did make a commitment to my father that in the succeeding year, 1924, I would be entered as a candidate but that he had already made a commitment to a young chap and the best he could offer me was a first alternate appointment. It happened that the chap that he had already made the commitment to a year in advance for principal appointee, was an old high school classmate of mine and I knew him to be a very bright young fellow. I anticipated no likelihood that he would fail to be accepted mentally. To my surprise, however, after a year, during which time I had literally forgotten about entering the Naval Academy, I got a telegram in April, I believe, from the Naval Academy requesting me to file all the necessary papers and this created a crisis. My friend who had been the principal had failed the physical exam. I was then torn between two ambitions. I was already approaching the year end of my first year at Armour Tech in the civil engineering department doing extremely well and enjoying the work very much. In late May I was slated to proceed to northern Wisconsin with a group of then to be sophomore students to take field work. This sounded like a great summer vacation and the high laced boots and the leather jackets, the transit and rod to create the classic picture of a civil engineer was most appealing to a young eighteen year older. Four of us got together and we bought an old Ford automobile for seventy-five dollars and we were going to drive from Chicago to the point of the summer camp. The day came and no word from the Naval Academy. The day came to proceed to the summer camp and I had left home with my baggage and joined the others at our fraternity house, packed the car, and were headed out of the city when someone said, "Oh, I forgot to get something at the Institute." Back we went to the offices, not too far away from where we discovered his shortcoming, and when we pulled up in front of the Dean's office a young woman who was on the staff and had known me, spotted the car and spotted me and called out and said, "Hey, Mr. James! Your mother and your father both have been calling you at about fifteen minute intervals and want you to call them immediately."

I thought, of course, some terrible disaster had occurred. I reached my mother in minutes and she said, "We have a telegram saying that you're to report to the Naval Academy on the sixteenth of June, 1924." She said, "You're to take a physical exam and if you are accepted you are to be enrolled immediately." There it was. The choice was brutally outlined. She said, "You better call your father. He's been trying to reach you and he's also been doing something to see if you can't get your physical exam in advance of going to Annapolis." She didn't say it but what was in both of my parents' minds was that at the age of eighteen I stood six feet tall, I weighed a hundred and nineteen pounds, and I looked like a walking scarecrow. I'm sure my father believed that I would be incapable of passing the physical exam and being a practical person, his judgment dictated that he attempt to removed this uncertainty before I truly made up my mind as to whether to abandon my work at Armour. By the time I reached him he had succeeded in reaching the Commander of the Naval Station at the Great Lakes and explained my dilemma and my Navy orders. He had gotten a very gracious agreement by this gentleman, whose identity I don't recall, to convene a special medical examining board, and that if I could be there by one-thirty in the afternoon of this same day, I would be given a medical examination that would determine my fitness to enter the Naval Academy.

So I arranged to meet my dad. In those days the old Milwaukee Electric RR was the principal mode of transportation. We met on the railroad platform in downtown Chicago and went out to Great Lakes, found our special medical board had already convened and having gone through the ritual and were awaiting my arrival which was only a moment or two after the scheduled time.

We proceeded immediately into the xamination and for about two hours they listened and pumped and pounded, and looked, measured, and did everything conceivable that I am sure represented a more than normal physical exam, because they too must have taken a look at this figure stripped to his skivvy pants and wondered whether there was a prospective naval officer hidden inside this slim carcas or not. The president of the board was a Capt. Danny Hunt,

Medical Corps, whom I later had the privilege of serving with and who later became a rear admiral in the Medical Corps. He was a very serious and a very delightful person, as I later found out, who told my dad and myself that after their exhaustive examination they found out that I possessed two defects -- one I had a bad case of left scoliosis (neither my dad nor I knew what the hell scoliosis meant) but he said it comes from sitting too much on one cheek of your behind rather than both of them. There apparently was a slight deviation at the base of the spine; also that I was thirty-five pounds underweight and that they could grant a waiver up to thirty pounds but thirty-five pounds was a little beyond their local judgment. While all this was going on, one of them had called the Bureau of Medicine and Surgery in Washington and gotten a thirty-five pound waiver for me.

So there I was. I was physically qualified, I had the appointment, I had a report date, and I had a mental struggle about what to do about my friends, who when we left them in Chicago, proceeded to Great Lakes in our car to see whether I would get in the car and drive on north or bid them farewell. They arrived and I still had to make the decision and when I saw them with all these instruments piled in and the baggage in this old Ford touring car, I had truly had great doubt as to the wisdom of the naval career. But something that my dad said, and I've forgotten what it was, finally made up my mind and with great reluctance I took my baggage out of the Ford. We stood on the spot and exchanged a few bucks which was my share in the seventy-five dollar beauty, and back my dad and I went to Chicago to prepare me for entrance in the Naval Academy, which I did on the sixteenth of June, 1924, one of the most eventful days of my life, and as I review it in retrospect some forty-three years later, it was the greatest day of my life I think of all times. It started me off on a career that has been difficult, exciting, rewarding, and every other appropriate adjective that you might use to describe it.

Q: It's marvelous to be able to say that. You were certainly adequately prepared in an intellectual way, having had one year of college engineering work --you had an advantage over some of the other boys coming in.

James: Yes, I had a very distinct advantage that permitted me to stand well in my class without trying. I think if I had tried hard I might have done better than I did. Plebe year was a breeze because it was largely a repeat of things in mathematics, steam, engineering, and the likes of that that I had taken at Armour. The new subjects, of course, were naval sciences and these aspects of it which didn't come hard either.

The way I found my roommate when I entered was rather interesting and it was the beginning of a life long friendship and it endures to this moment. We were riding down on the old W.B. and A., my dad and I (he was in Washington when I came on and try hard as I could, I couldn't dis-persuade him from coming over to see Annapolis before he turned about). I had a real antipathy about fathers taking their sons into the gates of any college but he wasn't to be denied. As we came down on this train, this ~~one~~ tall dark chap sat directly in front of us and in my father's inimitable manner of speaking to everybody and being as friendly with the world as he could, he inquired of this chap where he was from. This boy, in a very deep southern accent said he was from Freeport. My dad said, "Oh, Freeport. I know that town. I travel there quite often. It's on the Illinois River." This young lad said, "No Sir, I'm from 'Freeport', Louisianna." Dad said, "Yes, I know Freeport but it's not in Louisianna, it's in Illinois." Well, to make a long story short, my southern friend was trying to say Shreveport, Louisianna but his accent was that thick that he had trouble.

When we lined up outside of the main office on the first floor of Bancroft Hall, the afternoon after we had been mustered in, the duty officer came out and announced that now we would select roommates and if we had any friends that we would like to room with we could pick them and fall out in groups of two. I knew no other living soul that was entering the Academy that day and I looked down the line of young men and there was the face of this lad who had sat in front of us on the W.B. and A. and he was looking up in my direction. We nodded and we fell out together. He was Alexander McIntire Leary, Jr. from Shreveport, Louisianna, one of the dearest and finest young men I've ever known. It was only a month and a half ago that he (and his wife) as a member of the Navy Foundation, were here to attend a meeting. We later acquired a third roommate, a Paul Ramseur Anderson from Statesville, North Carolina, and the three of us and our wives who are the first and only wife for each of us, had a nice reunion here in our home.

Our midshipmen days were relatively routine. I was not an athletic type, but I was a joiner and an organizer. Within a few months of entering I was elected one of the two class officers, secretary-treasurer, and retained that post for over forty years. Every time an election would be held, the president, a chap named John Quinn, the secretary-treasurer, myself, would always be put up for nomination and then by the Russian method of closing nominations forthwith we were elected. This went on, as I say, for forty years until John Quinn passed away a matter of three or four years ago, at which time the class voted me to become their president. Having experienced the agonies of directing a group of individualists such as the Naval Academy class, I felt that this burden had to be passed on and succeeded in getting some ground rules enacted within our class to change the office every two years. After forty-one years of service to my class as an officer I finally now am emeritus so that means that now they call me and ask me to do something instead of expecting me to do it.

I also became very interested in Lucky Bag work and proceded to work on the Class of '28 Lucky Bag, only to be elected the editor of the book.

Q: You had obviously, a literary flair.

James: I might say that if I had it it was dormant until it

was developed by becoming editor of the Lucky Bag when it was an essential ingredient to producing a proper Lucky Bag. I might say that when our Lucky Bag was produced for the Class of 1928 (the smallest class then enrolled in over twenty years and which has had none smaller in the forty-two years since we graduated), it posed a real problem because our finances were limited by the anticipation of selling a relatively few Lucky Bags in contrast, for example, to the Class of '27 that preceded us. They numbered over a thousand and fifty entering midshipmen, while my class numbered only a hundred first appointed from civil life and another hundred first appointed from the Navy enlisted ranks. The balance of our class, to a grand total of three hundred and thirty-seven, I believe, were turnbacks from '27 and '26 and even two from the Class of 1925.

Q: Does this reflect the post-war attitude?

James: No. We were the first class to enter the Naval Academy after the number of appointments (which probably reflected the post-war situation) had been reduced for each congressman from four to three. For any congressman to have an appointment at all, in 1924, he had to have two midshipmen that left that year. There were only a hundred so appointed.

So we were a rather unique class. We like to think we were one of the greatest, but we are so very small that too many people are not aware of who are members of the Class of '28. When you mention '28, seldom does anyone respond and say, "Oh yes, I know so-and-so." Today, I guess, we number less than a hundred and fifty alive and perhaps most of those were non-graduates. We've been able to keep our class intimately tied together during this entire period.

Q: Did you also appropriate the title, the Vintage Class, as '27 did?

James: No, because I guess '27 had that title. We sought another one and are known as the BLC, the biggest little class. This was the brainchild of one of our chaps, who is currently the president of our class, Vice Admiral Harry Sears, retired.

As I said earlier, midshipmen days were relatively simple, academically speaking. I had one proclivity that got me into great trouble. I sleep enthusiastically; I'm very difficult to arouse. When I became editor of the Lucky Bag, and as we were approaching the day of publication, the chores became more and more severe, and I sought and received permission from the commandant, Sinclair Gannon, to work until no later than two a.m. on at least three nights a week in the Lucky Bag office doing Lucky Bag business. Four or five others who were on the staff had the same privilege and it was used regularly. So when the six-fifteen reveille came around, I was not ready to leap out of the bunk and head out. I had been appointed the four-striper regimental sub commander in which capacity I had really little to do with the formation so I conceived that it would be a good idea to sleep through the time necessary to dress and march in, and simply join the group for breakfast. That gave me an extra twenty minutes. This became known to the duty officers and after awhile I found that my door was opened promptly at six-fifteen by the duty officer and most of the times I managed to precede him by one bounce but all too often I was found in my bunk and suffered the penalties of being reported. In those days we had accelerated punishment for repeat performance under any given breach of the regulations and I finally reached the point where I was collecting, I believe, twenty-five demerits for a single sleeping after reveille offense.

Q: It was reaching the dangerous point, wasn't it?

James: It reached the dangerous point to the extent that old Thaddeus A. Thompson, who was the executive officer of Bancroft Hall, I think they called him, a commander, was so thoroughly fed up with me and my repeated appearances before the powers that be, especially since I was wearing four stripes as the number two midshipman officer. In those days we started at the beginning and went through the end of the Ac year in the same position. He repeatedly advocated to Sinclair Gannon that I be fired from my position and my stripes taken away. I had been appointed first as battalion commander of the first battalion, that was the first appointment, and Sinclair Gannon, one of the greatest naval officers in my opinion, is the one who promoted me up to be regimental sub commander where I would have no direct duties thinking this might compensate for my extra time given to the Lucky Bag. To a degree it was extremely helpful, so when Thompson was advocating my being broken, Sinclair Gannon refused to do it.

I remember one other not connected with the sleeping bit. I had trod on the toes of a Lieutenant Commander, Rosie Kiernan, an instructor, by being extremely attentive to his wife at Carvel Hall one night. This annoyed him to the point where he sought out every opportunity to find me with some breach of regulation and report me for it. These were all gleefully leapt upon by Cdr. Thompson but when passed into Sinclair Gannon, who apparently had to review all reports against four stripers and the five striper, he basketed these and they weren't applied until finally one came out one Sunday morning after chapel -- a report hand delivered in by Cdr. Kiernan for my failure to wear a white collar under my midshipman dress jacket. Upon the receipt of this one, next morning Sinclair Gannon sent for me. He said, "I don't know what you have done to Cdr. Kiernan but I have a bit of advice. Stay away from him. Don't get anywhere near him. His latest, and this is why I'm destroying all of your reports by him, is the failure to wear a collar in chapel. The first time you sat in front of me," which was my seat in chapel as regimental four striper," he said, "I thought you didn't have a collar on either. During the prayer I leaned over and looked down your neck and I saw that you had simply cut it out and there was the collar and you couldn't be charged with not wearing one, but it sure didn't show." This was a measure of Sinclair Gannon and the reason why, when I graduated, I sought out his ship as my first ship at sea (he went to command the battleship NEW YORK).

The attitude of Admiral Gannon (then Capt. Gannon) preserved my stripes to graduation. However, in the course of my approaching graduation, I had accumulated a hundred and twenty-eight demerits, which was fantastically excessive for a four striper who was supposed to be a pinnacle of propriety. I had only one disappointment. They used to hand out letters of commendation to senior first classmen, principally the battalion commanders and of course the regimental commander and the vice commander. I was the only four striper that received no letter of commendation. They scarcely could have given me this with my outstanding record of demerits. That meant that I only had twenty-two to go before I got the heave-ho.

Q: Tell me about your midshipmen cruises. Was there anything significant?

James: No, there was very little of outstanding significance that I recall. My class was the class that entered when the revulsion abroad to the American foreign policy made it unwise for the midshipmen training squadron to cruise in Europe, so the Class of '28 on our youngster cruise went around to the West Coast and on our second class cruise we made an East Coast cruise. Our first class cruise was a West Coast cruise again. We got to be fairly well acquainted with the coastal cities in the United States but we also felt terribly deprived by not having gone abroad as most midshipmen cruises did.

Q: You were persona non grata because of our attitude toward the League of Nations?

James: Generally speaking, American policy was not embraced enthusiastically abroad after World War II. If you recall there were many actions of the United States that were frowned upon -- the Washington Naval Disarmament Conference was another sore point in international affairs. Actually, it got so bad that naval ships simply didn't enter foreign ports because of the resentment that was found in foreigners. Hard to believe after our contribution to the success of World War I but that's the way it was. Actually, the thing that brought about the thaw was Lindberg's spectacular flight across the Atlantic to Paris, which occurred on the twenty-first of May, 1927. I remember it well because on the bulletin boards on the floor that I lived on in the first battalion in Bancroft Hall there was a great big chalk sign put up on the bulletin board to the effect that Lindberg flies the Atlantic and Jimmy James is twenty-one years old.

Q: The famous couple on the bulletin board. What did you

think in retrospect of the course of studies as they were at the Academy in your time?

James: Well, frankly I didn't think they were too much of a challenge. This, I believe, stemmed largely from my pre-Naval Academy schooling and the fact that in high school I had been a relatively good student. Having an engineering enthusiasm, I believe I sought more of an engineering curricula than the Academy offered. I remember one incident well, a funny little event. It was the summer of entry and I was in the second company of the first battalion. Our company officer was a Lieutenant Russell M. Ihrig. Russ Ihrig had all the new plebes lined up in front of the office one morning and he asked, "Now how many of you have had mechanical drawing?" Perhaps half of the midshipmen held their hands up so he progressively asked how many had more than two years, more than three years, and he got to more than four years, and I looked around and there was my hand the only hand up in the air. I thought, "Oh boy." He asked me what my name was and I told him. He said, "Mr. James, after formation you come and see me in my office." I envisioned that I was suddenly to be launched on some special engineering project that maybe my background of four years of mechanical drawing in high school and one in college would do me extremely well. His first question was one expressing his skepticism that I had had this much drawing. I explained it to him. Then he said, "Well, you're just the man I need to draw some organization charts. I need to fill out these

James # 1 - 21 -

forms and I need somebody who prints well and draws well to do it." So instead of being launched on a special engineering program, I was given the tedious task of doing this homework for him. I later chided him about this as we became good friends in the service and while he didn't remember the initial contact, we used to laugh about it later. He became Commandant of the California State Maritime Academy at the time I was having duty in Vallejo.

Q: He lives outside of San Francisco now. Were you intrigued at all with aviation or anything of a specialized field during your Academy days?

James: My ambition was to enter M.I.T.

Q: That was unswerving?

James: I hewed to this line, I learned more about what the implications were. I learned that it meant that I went into the Naval Construction Corps at the earliest possible moment if I could make it in order to receive an appointment to M.I.T., so I pursued that with great diligence and did everything that I could to enhance my likelihood for selection when I finished at the Naval Academy, after I completed the minimum two years of training at sea as a line ensign. Aviation was a relatively new field in those days although we had what was called an aviation summer which followed our graduation when we were taken up in aircraft and flown around here on the Severn in seaplanes. We expressed our interest in aviation at that time so as a hedge against the possibility of not being appointed to M.I.T. I also indicated my desire to enter aviation. As I explained to you earlier, I had elected, because I was fortunate to have a high choice upon graduation, the USS NEW YORK to which Admiral (then captain) Sinclair Gannon was ordered himself. I've expressed a deep affection and regard and respect for this gentleman and I thought I wanted to follow him to sea for a year or two.

While I was embarked in the NEW YORK, I received orders to what was then known as indoctrinal flight training which was given down at the air station, Norfolk, and that constitutes an interesting anecdote. I was slated to go to a course that was to convene in Norfolk, if I recall correctly, sometime in the middle of June in 1929. Upon leaving the Naval Academy, I went to my home in Chicago enroute to the West Coast to join the NEW YORK and I met this delightful little gal, Virginia Cooper, who was a friend of another girlfriend of mine in Chicago. To make a long story short, in nine days she was wearing my miniature and in nine months we were married. The date of our wedding was planned for the second of June. I was scheduled to leave the NEW YORK for three weeks leave about the twenty-fifth of May to go home to be married. The morning of the twenty-first of May, my orders were suddenly received to proceed to indoctrinal flight training and report on the first of June. This would have fouled up my wedding plans, but good. The invitations were printed, the schedule had been carefully made out, the bride-to-be had accepted. Here suddenly I wasn't going to be at my own wedding. Later I found out there had been a drop out in that earlier course by one George Anderson, who later became CNO, and I was plugged into his vacancy on this particular flight group. Sinclair Gannon went to bat for me but it wasn't until the morning of the twenty-fifth, the day I was to leave for Chicago to attend the pre-wedding festivities and be married, that my orders for that class were cancelled.

Q: It was a close call, wasn't it?

James: It was a close call and I went home with all the physical distress of one who had been under great strain and my mother-in-law to be spoke to her daughter and said, "That green complexioned individual --do you really want to marry him?" The green came from an upset stomach that persisted through the wedding but not through the wedding dinner that followed --I recovered rapidly.

Together and several months later, my new bride and I went to Norfolk and I took the indoctrinal flight training course and soloed and was anticipating orders to Pensacola when suddenly I received my nomination to enter M.I.T. This was to begin in June of 1930.

Q: That really was a signal honor, wasn't it? It was an elite corps.

James: Well, in those days the naval constructors normally

were in the top ten percent of their class. They have been known, however, to possess brains without earthly realism. I don't think the designation is fair but wierdly enough, many of the old naval constructors that I remember used to wear stiff collars and their ties were seldom ever two-blocked. It was a group of -- well in today's market they would be known as the long haired scientist types. In our days doctorates were scarcely heard of and people with master's degrees worked some three years to acquire them. I always considered it a great honor. I always resented and bitterly fought the dissolution of the Construction Corps and its reamalgamation with the line. That's another story.

Q: I hope we'll hear that story when it comes along chronologically. This was an ambition which you finally achieved. How did you react to the course of study at M.I.T.? Was it on a different level from what you had known at the Academy?

James: Oh yes. Extremely higher level. It wasn't all done by rote which was the pattern of many instructors at the Naval Academy. There we had prescribed class instruction and many, and I say this with all possible charity, many of them were completely unqualified to be instructors. I remember a math prof I had, I've forgotten his name, but he knew about one-tenth as much math as I had and yet everybody clamored to get into his class because he used to entertain us as much as he tried to instruct us. One of his little stunts was to have his double breasted uniform blouse fully buttoned and his motorman vest fully buttoned up underneath it. He then proceeded to remove his vest without unbuttoning his jacket.

When I got to M.I.T. it was a serious, determined, well educated group of instructors who did as much to stimulate your thought processes as they did to lead you through factual training type of education.

Q: How many boys were selected in the year you went? Six?

James: In my year there were eleven because there had been a number of vacancies that had accumulated and because we were so small. There were, I believe, six in my class that were appointed. They filled it up again with people from as far back as the classes of '25, '26, '27. So we numbered eleven in all. That was the largest single group then in the naval architectural course at M.I.T. Of course, there was a year earlier group there at the same time and they were about ten or eleven in number, all the Class of '27. Out of that group grew friendships that have endured very strongly over the years. When I went to M.I.T., of course my personal situation was greatly changed from that which I had anticipated when I expressed this ambition. I was married and I was the father of our oldest child. This made for a somewhat different environment. In those days married officers in school were relatively few in number and in the undergraduate school I doubt that there were any married students. My wife was a willing contributor to my school work. She had been a secretary after she had graduated from Northwestern University, at the time I met her, so she did some of my work and helped me out. We enjoyed our little one very much --it was a big nuisance at the time but that's what young people are for, to be young and have children.

Q: Then you as a graduate student at M.I.T. were largely on your own, were you not?

James: Very much so. We had prescribed goals to accomplish and we had all the counsel and advice and text books to acquire that knowledge and, of course, our program was to become naval architects and marine engineers. It was just what I had anticipated it would be and it was just what I had wanted over the years. I might say that my entry into the Construction Corps, however, had been somewhat of a traumatic decision again. Even the filing of my application for consideration as a candidate early in 1929, but after I was married, precipitated objections from my wife, who knew little about the Navy but who heard from many wives of young naval officers, and some senior, that I was making a terrible mistake.

Q: By specializing?

James: By specializing. That the Navy was the sea going officer, the man on the bridge, the man on the conning tower --those were the real naval officers and all these goll-damn naval constructors were just in a new and completely different world. I had, according to my friends, the potential for going far in the sea going line and why would I blow it by going into the engineer specialty?

Q: The intellectual wasn't exactly the acceptable thing, was it?

James: No, it was available to so few that it was resented by many. Then there was a mechanical situation that developed that caused naval constructors to be of rather ill repute. For reasons I've never been quite clear about, classes beginning about '16, '17, '18, and maybe '19 were accelerated in promotion ahead of their regular sea going line counterparts. I recall one officer in the class of '18 who ran with the Class of '16, drew his pay at the higher ranks accordingly. This was resented bitterly by classmate line types and I think was a fundamental reason for the resentment on the part of the line officer, plus the fact that, if you stood higher than about number fifteen in your class you weren't even a hot candidate for the Construction Corps.

Q: Where did you stand in your class?

James: I stood eight. So when you sought advice of

normally enthusiastic line types about going into a specialty corps, the answer was don't -- it's the kiss of death.

Sinclair Gannon was no longer the commanding officer of the NEW YORK when I submitted my request. He was instead the Chief of Staff of the Scouting Force in the Atlantic Fleet at the time and my papers had to go through his boss's command. As soon as he received them, he did me the unusual courtesy of climbing into the staff barge and coming over to the NEW YORK and insisting upon taking me down to a private stateroom where he harangued me for better than an hour and a half about not letting the papers go through. He predicted great things for me in the line if I stayed and predicted nothing but drudgery and unpleasantness and lack of respect from my fellow line associates if I did. Well, my belief was that great that I ignored the advice of Sinclair Gannon and of my wife. I can't say that I might do the same thing again but I never regretted that I did.

Q: It certainly took fortitude at that point, didn't it, to go against your most favorite advisors?

James: Yes, truly it did. My wife has often reminded me of her counsel when I've thought things were unfair. In the course of becoming Chief of the Bureau of Ships, which is the top position in the engineering field, I found more and more feelings of disrespect from line types that resulted in some stupid, if not tragic decisions and I'll talk about that a little later on.

Q: The same thing pertained to men who were interested in ordnance, didn't it?

James: To a lesser degree because the so-called gun cockers were closer to the line types than were the naval constructors. The gun cockers went to sea more often and the gun cockers had therefore a closer liaison. Naval constructors, basically, when they completed the M.I.T. program were land based for the rest of the time.

Q: A few years earlier than your time men who sought a career in aviation were thought badly of, too.

James: By the time I came along, that didn't prevail and I never took the trouble to examine the point you're making so I really don't know.

Q: In your time of going to M.I.T. for graduate work in naval construction, this was the accepted thing, was it not? Prior to that time some men went abroad for their training.

James: That had been necessary in the absence of any school of naval architecture in an accredited college or university in the United States. Constructors used to go to Edinburgh University. However, I don't recall the exact time, but I guess it was about the classes of 1908, '09, or '10 that were first processed through M.I.T. Older naval constructors, on active duty at the time I entered, were essentially alumni of Edinburgh. The program at M.I.T. became an exceptionally fine course. It was started by the Navy.

Q: Was it not subsidized in part by the Navy?

James: I believe it was. Of course, by sending its students and paying their tuition, that was a form of direct subsidy that prevails today. The Institute organized a civilian counterpart of this program shortly after the Navy started to show up there. It is going great guns although the shipbuilding industry is suffering its traditional psychic employment so not too many young men are going into naval architecture today.

The work at M.I.T. was difficult, fascinating, and we managed to survive and graduate with our Master's Degree in 1933, the class that I attended. Later, in my capacity as Chief of the Bureau, I had great responsibility to that program at M.I.T. and became a member of their Board of Visitors (or whatever they call it).

Q: What control did the Navy Department exercise over you while you were there? What contact did they maintain?

James: Practically none. We reported, of course, to the Boston

Naval Shipyard, or the First Naval District, for our logistic support, medical and pay and these routines. We had a Capt. Enright at the time I was at M.I.T. who was the official sponsor of the M.I.T. group but his word was, "Go and do your job at M.I.T. and if you're in difficulty come see me." That was essentially the way it worked.

Q: What would have happened if a man didn't do his job well as a student at M.I.T.?

James: Then the old Burea of C and R, which was really the sponsoring Navy bureau, would have stepped into the situation. There were one or two occasions in the class following me, where two men who had applied for and received an appointment to the M.I.T. program had second thoughts after they were there. The Bureau of C and R had to weigh the question of what to do with these guys. One of them they released forthwith and the other one they had to complete his program and was then released from transfer into the Construction Corps.

Incidentally on that subject I remember another amusing incident. When I received my appointment, I was still aboard the NEW YORK. She was down in Guantanamo Bay in the spring of 1930. It was in the days of the depression and the Navy funds for travel were so limited that I was ordered to M.I.T. by a most circuitous route. This included being transferred to the USS UTAH some three months before I was due at the P.G. school here in Annapolis. That's where I took my first year. I lived in the UTAH, which was to go on the midshipmen cruise, and served in her, anticipating her arrival up here off of Greenberry Point Light to load midshipmen. At that time I would come ashore and report for duty at the P.G. school.

The orders officially designating me as a naval constructor came as a surprise while I was still a line ensign aboard the UTAH. Normally, you went to M.I.T. and finished your first year there and then were transferred from the line into the Construction Corps. However, in 1930 they were having difficulty commissioning all the graduates of the Academy. They were looking for every conceivable vacancy they could find, so all the group that I was with that were to be entered at M.I.T. a year from then were ordered transferred forthwith to the Construction Corps to make eleven more line vacancies. I was on board the UTAH when I was called to Capt. C. R. Train's (the commanding officer) cabin to be sworn in. So I went through the swearing in rigmarole. I had been on the officer of the deck watch list also I had been studying navy regulations that it in effect said a naval constructor was not a qualified type to take an officer of the deck duty on a naval ship. I had been standing these, of course, for months aboard the NEW YORK and later on the UTAH.

Q: And you suddenly lost your qualifications.

James: Suddenly I was not any longer qualified. I went down to the stateroom of the senior watch officer, a Lt. A.W. (Gus) Wellings, a character, and knocked on his door. He called me in and I said, "Ensign James, Mr. Wellings. I just have been transferred from the line of the Navy to the Construction Corps by Capt. Train. According to Navy regulations, I'm no longer qualified to stand a deck watch on board this ship." He said, "Where's the regulation?" So I quoted him the page number and he read it and said, "You're on the watch list now?" "Yes, Sir." He reached in a little slot in his secretary bureau and pulled out the watch list. He ran his finger down to the point where he reached my name and said, "I see you have the eight to twelve watch tonight." I said, "Yes, Sir." He simply said, "Be there." He pushed it back on his desk and that was the end of that. So I have the distinction of being the naval constructor who was officially senior watch officer at sea on the battleship UTAH. I can't believe that the regulation had any merit but it was there. I think it was one that in today's climate maybe we would find a special Z-GRAM on it abolishing it.

Q: I'm sure you would. What about that year at the Academy in post graduate work?

James: That was a very difficult year, I think. The principal purpose of that was a refresher. We came back after varying periods away from the books. In my case only two years but some of

James #1 - 34 -

the other chaps that I mentioned that were out of Class '25 were five years removed from detailed studying. So we were to acquire the ability to study again, to refresh ourselves in some of the subjects and we took one or two additional courses -- under Dinty Cavanaugh, who was one of the profs at the P.G. school, and two or three others who were very stimulating individuals. Thus we were more or less prepared for what we found at M.I.T., real professor types who led you rather than drove you.

Q: So the quality of what you received in that one year was quite different from what you had?

James: Completely different and I think I worked harder at the P.G. school than I ever worked anywhere else because it was quite a transition for a line type. My wife and I and young daughter lived out on West Street in a house that had no insulation. I shoveled thirteen tons of coal in one of the mild winters in Annapolis.

Q: You had had some experience in that on midshipmen cruise, hadn't you? Shoveling coal?

James: Yes. My class made the last year of coal burning cruises and the first year of oil burning cruises. We will always embrace enthusiastically the memory of the coal burning cruise, now. At the time it was sheer drudgery. In retrospect, being the first of the classes to have some of both, we treasure that fact.

Q: There's a bit of color attached to it, isn't there? One more question and I think that might conclude this particular chapter. When you graduated from M.I.T. with your Master's Degree, this was more or less the nadir for the Navy, was it not? It was the height of the depression and there wasn't much of a building program contemplated. Did this affect your spirits and your prospects?

James: No, not at all. Up to now it had all been preparation for getting into the mechanical engineering side of the Navy. The graduation from M.I.T., coming as it did at the height of the depression was certainly an economic problem. But really, as a lieutenant junior grade, we were Economic Royalists because our pay had not yet been cut fifteen percent. We did have a promotion while we were at M.I.T. which raised us from the bare subsistence level of ensign to a higher plane and the cost of living was ridiculously low. I can remember in Boston, actually in Cambridge where we lived, going to the store shopping with my wife on Saturday and spending probably fifty cents to fill all our vegetable and fruit requirements for a week and maybe another three or four dollars to buy all the staple and meats. Pork roasts, ten cents a pound, baked beans and brown bread for two, twenty-five cents -- baked beans and brown bread were a standard Boston Saturday night offering. So there was no unhappiness with the lack of a naval building program at that time because actually none of us expected to be plunged immediately into shipbuilding. We were going through an apprenticeship of ship repairing and we headed out to our various Navy yards and slipped into this pattern. It wasn't long after that that the program initiated by Roosevelt began to take effect and we were building ships again by about 1935, destroyers mostly. We really finished our mechanical apprenticeship and then moved into the higher echelons of ship design and construction which then came along.

Interview # 2 with Rear Admiral Ralph K. James

Annapolis, Maryland   January 26, 1971

Subject: Biography   by John T. Mason, Jr.

Mr. Mason: It's good to see you this morning, Admiral. I know that this chapter has to do with your further education. You graduated, as you recounted last time, from M.I.T. and your next set of orders took you to the Bremerton Navy Yard.

Rear Admiral James: Yes, that's what it was known as in those days. Subsequently, of course, it's been changed to Naval Ship Yard for reasons that aren't too clear. Mrs. James and I proceeded across the country carrying with us our, then, four year old daughter.

Q: I don't think you told me about your marriage.

James: We'll have to go back a few years. This took place in 1929 with a young lady that I hadn't known until after I graduated from the Naval Academy, at which point I had become somewhat involved with a beautiful young girl on Long Island who was extremely anxious to proceed into the marriage ceremony and I was not then prepared to do so. As a result of my efforts at avoidance, I sought a ship on the West Coast for duty and the one to which Admiral (Captain then) Sinclair Gannon was only recently assigned as the commanding officer. I went to the West Coast thinking this would avoid further involvement with this beautiful young lady and immediately upon arrival at my home in Chicago I met a girl who I had not known before and after a whirlwind show of interest over a nine day period, I sent for and received and presented her with a miniature of my class ring. This was somewhat overwhelming to her but we started a very frenzied courtship which ended in marriage nine months later in Chicago.

About a year after our marriage, as I started my post-graduate instruction here at the Naval Academy, we had a young daughter, born in Chicago, who is our pride and joy today. Annapolis in those days was a very delightful town. We had a residence out on West Street in a home that is still in being and still presentable. It was a P.G. student's nightmare, however. We had a very dry and very cold winter and I remember very distinctly having to shovel over thirteen tons of coal into this little tiny bungalow. At the same time we were having a terrible drought throughout the country and Annapolis was suffering from it inordinately more than mos of the surrounding area. I can recall having to come in to the Academy every morning before going to P.G. school with five gallon crocks that were alternately used for making home brew and hauling water, and take water home to Mrs. James to do her daily chores with. That condition lasted most of the summer, as I recall.

Q: The combination of shoveling coal and bringing water was quite stupendous.

James: It made Annapolis a little more primitive than it is today fortunately, but it was sort of a glue that cemented friendships among other people that we might not have met. It made our year in Annapolis a very delightful experience. It was kind of tough to get back to school books but it was worthwhile and it prepared the way for the program at M.I.T. which I was delighted to conclude in 1933 when we were under orders to proceed to Bremerton.

During this period of time at M.I.T. the so-called depression of the 1929-33 period was on. Instead of suffering a pay cut, however, I got a promotion during this period which resulted in a pay increase although at a reduced rate of pay because of the cut. We lived then like Economic Royalists, a condition we have not been able to repeat for generations after.

Q: I guess that's gone forever.

James: It was indeed a delightful period. I failed to mention one thing. While I was at M.I.T. I wrote my thesis on a very pragmatic issue as requested by the Bureau of Construction and Repair. With now Rear Admiral (ret.) William E. Howard, we did a thesis on the holding power of anchors as determined by model anchor tests. The reason I mention this today is because last week I spent two days in M.I.T. and visited again the hydraulic laboratory, which is now a beautiful new facility and not the one we did our testing in. I learned on this occasion that our thesis, and one which followed it up a year later written by now retired Admirals Farrin and Leahy, is still the classic study on model testing of anchors and is being used not only by M.I.T. but by the Navy.

This was very gratifying because this was a graduate student effort and it was almost forty years ago and to learn that its validity is still recognized and used in the commercial design of anchors was most gratifying.

Q: You might say it was a definitive effort then.

James: It was the first effort in fact because the Navy up to that time had done its anchor testing by towing full scale anchors behind tugs and other ships --a very expensive and very tedious process. Bill Howard and I conceived the notion of scaling anchors down and pulling them in various kinds of conditions of bottom mud, clay, sand, gravel, and the likes, under laboratory conditions and extrapolating laboratory results to full scale predictions. It apparently is continuing to do that task.

Q: This is a digression but does your visit to M.I.T. indicate that you are on the board or have some official connection?

James: No. I was invited to come to M.I.T. last week to address a student seminar on hovercraft, which is one of my present preoccupations.

Q: For rescue operations and that kind of thing?

James: For many things. We are hopeful that they will be

applied to build commercial ships that carry high value cargoes at high speed, and to warships. We're actually building one now for the Navy and hope to build more. That's a phase of my career that began after some seven years of retirement from active service. I think it would be more appropriate to gointo that after a while but the answer to your question was this was the invitation of the Institute to bring this new technology to the attention of the graduate student group who were studying urban transportation problems. It was extremely gratifying to be received and go through the various departments and divisions that I had worked in as a student. Some years ago when I was Chief of the Bureau of Ships, I was on the board of visitors, as we call it here at the Naval Academy (I've forgotten what they call it) up there) for a four year period and enjoyed that assocation thoroughly, but it did not put me in touch with the student body which this latest experience did.

Going back to 1933, my wife and I proceeded to Bremerton with our small child by car which was the routine in those days. Upon arrival at Bremerton we were able quickly to find suitable housing and proceeded to adapt ourselves to the new environment of the Pacific Northwest which we found very delightful. My duties in the Navy Yard, as it was then known, consisted of being an assistant in the Planning Division of the Naval Shipyard, as it is now called. Another phase of my education really started. It was an amazingly delightful experience to associate with ships and materials and review problems of commanding officers of ships scheduled in the yard for overhaul, and find the means and facilities necessary to undertake satisfactory repairs and to return them to active service ~~generally~~, as was the pattern in those days, in a period of about three months.

Q: Was that the scope of the Planning division?

James: As the term implies, the Planning division planned for the overhaul of ships in advance, brought in materials to accomplish the repairs, did the assembly of any special tools and equipment, scheduled the work in the various shops in the Navy Yard and then provided the funding to make possible the accomplishment of the repairs. All of this in anticipation of the arrival of the ship and after the arrival of the ship it was simply a task of verification of advance planning and the continued support of work as it proceeded which oftentimes turned up additional work that was masked and unknown at the time of the arrival of the ship and which became apparent as we proceeded to tear things apart.

Q: How closely did you work with the skipper of the ship that was in for a refitting?

James: In my junior capacity I simply was acquainted with the skipper of the ship and wasn't too intimate with them except as the skippers themselves sought to establish intimacy by their constant appearance in the planning division. Later contact with the individuals on the ship became more active as I transferred out of the Planning division to the Production division of the Ship Yard which actually carried on the work that was programmed.

Q: Were most of the skippers truly concerned about the operation?

James: Oh yes. Every captain that brought a ship in, brought in what monies his type commander could provide him and then sought to extend this by means, fair or foul, to give him more than he was scheduled to receive - cumshaw, is the word.

Q: What leeway did he have in altering your plans?

James: Actually, the commanding officer of the ship was the customer. He could modify work to the extent that he felt it necessary. Seldom, however, did the commanding officers of ships challenge the technical aspects, because in those days, the captains of ships were more navigators and gun cockers and pilots, than they were technical types. This was not true in the engineering department where they had many capable people who debated at long length the approaches to various problem solving efforts. As a rule, the ships worked in close harmony with the ship yard people and there was very pleasant rapport.

I can remember a skipper of one battleship, I think it was the old NEW YORK. The skipper was Captain Taffender. At this time I was what was known as the ship superintendent. I was in the Production Department and the direct liaison between the ship and the yard on the actual accomplishment of the work. I was also the supervisor of the various trades that came aboard -- the scheduler and liaison with Ships Company. We were doing a repair job on the teak deck of his ship. It was Navy Yard policy to not permit anything removed from the ship to be taken to the home of any individual officer or workman for his personal use, even though it was discarded material. I think probably the reason behind this policy was that some people found it desirable to declare as unsuitable for use, things that they could use even though they had many years of continued service. The old wood ripped up from this deck that had been scheduled for replacement fell in this category. Taffender was a next door neighbor of mine during his temporary visit to Bremerton and in the course of talking over the fense we discussed the fact that all this wonderful old teak, with the pitch and tar and oakum, was being sent to the incinerator and "wouldn't it make nice fireplace wood?" About two days later my wife called me from home and said, "There's a station wagon here with sailors and a whole load of pieces of wood. What am I to do with it?" I was taken completely by surprise and I rushed home (only a half mile distance) to find that Captain Taffender had ordered these sailors to load his station wagon with pieces of this teak and deliver them to me for use rather than see them go to the incinerator. I think this indicates rather clearly that the rapport between commanding officers and ship yard people could be delightfully warm. In this case it certainly was.

Many other problems came along which were more-or-less generated by the over-enthusiastic younger officers on the ship trying to make character with their commanding officer. But by and large, I think that most ship officers enjoyed having their ships under overhaul and the ship yard generally enjoyed having the ship people in the yard. It was the one major contact that junior ranks had with the operating officers of the fleet. Many people we had known at the Academy came into the Yard. It was a delightful type of duty for me.

Q: Did you gain any knowledge of the use of new materials?

James: Yes. Of course, in the nature of the work we were doing we brought into being many new things in the early days I am describing -- aluminum, for example, was a rather new structural material and was being introduced rather generously in new Navy ships and was being applied to some degree in existing ships. Bremerton was largely an overhaul yard for the bigger ships, the battleships and aircraft carriers. We had a very broad variety of things to have to repair. Bremerton, also, was building ships. As I arrived, the cruiser ASTORIA was finishing up and later there were a series of destroyers of the 366 Class that were being built there -- the CUSHING and PERKINS, to name two. Later it was my privilege to be an assistant for new construction in the construction of these ships in Bremerton. That began a period of education on the new ship construction problems that has served me well over the many years.

Q: Did you get involved with the designing of new ships?

James: No, this was largely a function of the (then) Bureau of C and R and the Bureau of Engineering. There was much additional development design work done at the Navy Yard but as I moved out of the planning division, which had this design function, I moved into the production division and it was only in kibitzing design details that we then continued our association with the development of the design.

Q: How closely did C and R work with you on any modifications of the design?

James: Any modification of a design that was of any major character had to be referred back to the Bureau for review and possible application to other ships of the class. There weren't many ships being built in those days. If you recall, the Washington Disarmament Treaty had kept our Navy from building many new ships and it wasn't until the Roosevelt era came along that any new construction was really initiated ~~at all~~.

Q: It wasn't only the Treaty but also the lack of funds, wasn't it? It was the height of the Depression.

James: Yes. The Depression was in full bloom although, I guess, it was beginning to taper off in 1933. We built four destroyers in Bremerton which was a generous slice of the new then construction underway in the Navy.

Q: There was one activity I think which was a part of that time --the breaking up of old vessels, old ships. Did Bremerton--?

James: Bremerton didn't take part in any ship breaking operation. This was largely done in commercial areas. The Navy would dispose of ships and have them sold off to ship breakers who salvaged many significant pieces of hardware and equipment and oftentimes hold them for a few years and sold them back to the Navy at amazingly high prices.

Q: Sometimes sold the scrap iron to the Japanese, too.

James: We were shipping ship loads of scrap to the Japanese as late as 1941. These were lean days for the Navy; our naval forces were limited in number and were all rapidly aging but Roosevelt had far-sighted capabilities and started the construction program for the Navy, which expanded rapidly when we approached the entry into World War II. Bremerton was marked by another personal event of great importance --our son was born in Bremerton as the whistle blew for eight o'clock on a Monday or Tuesday morning. I thought he was very prompt in arriving precisely at eight a.m. as he did. He and our daughter are our two major joys in the James family. They were here just before Christmas time. Our son is a banker in Pittsburg with the Mellon National Bank. Our daughter is the wife of a former West Point graduate who is now a real estate broker in Santa Rosa, California.

Her marriage, here at the Naval Academy, was a tribute to unification. She married an Air Force officer in the Naval Academy, had attendants from Army officer ranks, our son from the midshipman ranks, and they even had a Coast Guard officer as a groomsman. At that time, in 1951, we thought that was an amazing contribution to unification which was, then, a very hot political subject.

Bremerton duty was of four years duration and extremely valuable for preparing for a further career in this wierd and wonderful world.

Q: Did you have any experience with shop maintenance while you were there?

James: No, I really wasn't involved in shop maintenance. This was a new field and it had an officer and staff in direct charge of this kind of work, and I was not personally involved. My work was either in planning or in production.

Q: Did you have any experience as a docking officer?

James: Yes, of course. All production junior officers are docking officers at one time or another. I had two or three rather amazing experiences.

The cruiser, CHICAGO, came into Bremerton's smaller dry-dock at the time, and as we brought her into the dock we were conscious that we were also bringing in a school of fish. It turned out to be a school of smelt. The size of this school we didn't appreciate until after we closed the gate and started pumping the dock down, only to find we couldn't run the pumps after we had gone down a few feet. We stopped to review the problem and discovered that we had a dock full of smelt, and I say full in the literal sense. We had to flush the pumps backwards, flood the dock again, and kept this up until we got the ship almost dry but by this time we had a layer of smelt that measured at least six feet in depth over the whole floor of the dock. Bremerton is largely a Scandinavian area and the word got out in nothing flat about this event, and literally hundreds of "Scandihoovians" from Bremerton with buckets, bags, basket, and pails, and every conceivable conveyance, came charging into the ship yard --in those days our security was not the greatest and they were permitted in-- and went into the dry dock and scooped up buckets, and pails, and boxes of smelt which they took home and pickled and otherwise enjoyed. We had to shovel smelt out of there by the clam shell for several days, then those fish that got caught in the interstices of the blocks of concrete began to warm up and invade the whole of the Bremerton area with a *foul* smell that was really fantastic.

Another one of the features of the dry dock officers' responsibility was to inspect the ship as soon as it had grounded and the water was pumped down so you could walk into the dock. The dock master would proceed into the dock even though there were two or three feet of water still left and quickly inspect the set-up of the blocks to be sure we were not subjecting the ship to damage.

Bremerton, as you know, is up in the Pacific Northwest where salmon were prolific. I always used to go down into the drydock carrying one of these iron spikes, known as a dry dock dog, a sharpened U-shaped instrument that held wooden blocks together in a stack. Then we tried to capture a good sized salmon. Seldom was I defeated as these salmon would be swimming around in what amounted to six or eight inches of water and were trapped between drydock block bearers about twelve to twenty feet apart so it wasn't much of a fishing chore to hook one with a drydock dog and take it home. However, I caught a beautiful King salmon one day. It weighed about twenty-nine pounds -- that's big even for the Kings. I was anticipating sharing this with our neighbors when I got a preemptory call from the manager of the shipyard, then Captain Albert T. Church, who said, "I hear you've got a beautiful fish." -- which I acknowledged. He said, "Mrs. Church and I would like to have it for dinner soon. Would you have it delivered to my quarters?" It was his property and his shipyard so there was no quarrel with this at all. Capt. Church was one of my good friends. In fact, he latched onto my imprefect skill with the written word to make me his ghost writer for his speeches. This became somewhat of a chore because it all had to be done out of hours as we were quite busy in the working day.

One day, quite unexpectedly, he called to say he was tagged to fill in to make a speech at some affair and he wanted a speech from me by the afternoon of that same day. I was generally a lot more dedicated to speech writing than to whip it up in that short a time. In this instance all I did was look through my sheaf of earlier speeches and clip out some interesting paragraphs and put it into what I thought was a cohesive presentation and delivered it, on schedule. Capt. Church was always very gratifyingly appreciative of my effort and every time after he had delivered a speech, he'd call me on the phone, or intercept me in the hall, or otherwise let me know how the speech went. In this particular case he neglected to do so. Having a slightly guilty conscience I was more anxious to know how it went than any other of my previous efforts, finally about a week or ten days later I bumped into him in the hallway and was brash enough to ask him how the speech went on this occasion. He said, "Look, James, I had already complimented you on that speech. You don't get two compliments for the same effort." So my deception was quickly seen through by a very fine gentleman.

Q: Did the Navy Yard engage in any salvage operations while you were there?

James: No. We had no salvage problem. My first exposure to salvage was out in the war. Speaking not of James' education, but of James' development, there was another interesting situation in Bremerton. When I graduated from the Naval Academy, although I stood six foot tall, I weighed a great big one hundred and twenty-nine pounds. I scarcely cast a wide enough shadow to be noticed. When I got to Bremerton, some five years later, I only weighed a hundred and thirty-four pounds, which wasn't much of a change. I had as a planning officer out there, an old line naval constructor, Comdr. Ralph T. Hanson, who deplored my physical structure and concluded that if others couldn't help me, he would. He decided that the treatment I needed was to consume a pint of half milk and half cream twice a day, he used to make quite a point of calling me from the outer office to his inner office where this milk was stored on the shelf, which he had arranged to have delivered although I had to pay for it. Then he supervised me drinking this glass of half-and-half twice a day. I felt absolutely ridiculous because oftentimes people would bust in and there I'd be swilling a glass of milk under his eagle eye. At one time he concluded that milk wasn't good enough, that goat's milk had to be the answer and he went to the trouble of finding a supply of this and plying me with it, much against my will. It didn't do any good --I continued at a hundred and thirty-four until I left Bremerton. It wasn't until I went to sea and when the family traditional weight increase occurred, I went up fifty pounds in one year completely without any effort on the part of any of my associates.

Q: Did you get involved with labor relations in any way there?

James: No, labor relations were scarcely worthy of the name at that time. The ship yard force was relatively small; the people had close intimacy and there was a rapport between the labor side and the officer supervisory side of the yard that I don't think I have witnessed again in any establishment, be it military or commercial.

Q: Was that due to the efforts of any one officer?

James: No, I think it was due to the environment. Bremerton, in those days, was a somewhat off the beaten track; the people were dedicated Americans --they were hard working. As I mentioned earlier, there were many of Scandinavian extraction and they were thrifty people. They conserved the working hour as much as they conserved their own personal assets. Occasionally we'd get into situations, and you raised a point that suddenly brings to mind a time when I found a workman sleeping in one of the lower compartments of some ship and reported him to his supervisor. The supervisor then put him under report. This chap was brought up before a board to review the incident and his record. I gather he was a rather poor performer in general and this seemed to be the device to unseat him from his job. However, when I went before this board as the principal complaining witness, I had an exposure to labor relations that I've never forgotten. I became the focal point of attack rather than the individual that I had reported asleep. I had a most unpleasant experience for an hour in which my veracity was challenged and my knowledge of what this man's work was to be. The implication was that I was a dastardly villian trying to take the bread out of the mouth of a good honest workman, who in sheer exhaustion had fallen to the tank top in this compartment to take a nap to recover so he could perform admirably from then on. That was the nature of the defense. It was rather a penetratable defense I might say because the man was later dismissed. That was my only real exposure to a labor problem at Bremerton, although we had an officer who handled not only shop maintenance but was known as the Shop Superintendent and handled labor matters. In 1933 to 1937 they were vastly different than we would have to confront today.

I think that's a general review of my four years at Bremerton. I was a reasonably good golfer in those days and Bremerton provided the facility. I was not a fisherman and I've long regretted that I didn't take advantage of the natural opportunities in the Seattle Washington-Bremerton area to become an avid fisherman as I subsequently did.

Q: When you concluded your duty at Bremerton you went aboard the USS WHITNEY which was a further piece of education, was it not?

James: At this point we were more-or-less on the firing line in having to deliver from our background instead of having a staff of people all experienced and supporting every effort. We were more or less on our own. I became the hull repair superintendent on the WHITNEY and was the only technically qualified engineer on board.

Q: Where was she stationed?

James: She operated out of San Diego servicing the destroyers in Destroyer Flotilla One, commanded by Rear Admiral William S. Pye. Among my ancillary duties was as staff member on Admiral Pye's Flotilla staff for ship repairs. I had a classmate, son of his, who was a very fine young man so there was a personal rapport with Admiral Pye.

The work on the WHITNEY was often times making bricks without straw because you had to improvise, you had to innovate; when ships came alongside for treatment of problems without advance warning, you had to size them up on the spot, determine what to do, and instruct your generally very competent articifer members of the crew in how to proceed. You were exercising all of your skill and knowledge that you acquired in prior associations and it was a delightful experience. You got into design matters where you had to sit down in your own stateroom and draw out a design solution to a problem, and improvise materials because often material to replace given parts weren't available on the repair ships. You couldn't defer the repair until the material could be received so you had to improvise from that which was at hand. You had to also stock aboard the repair ship in its supply department, those things which you thought you might need. In effect, you were in a little repair activity of your own and it was extremely gratifying. It was not too time consuming because the fleet was out as much as it was in and during the periods when the felet was not in the harbor there wasn't too much going on, so while I was aboard the WHITNEY we undertook to do more or less of an internal rebuilding of the ship -- a highly illegal process.

Q:	Do you mean not authorized from Washington?

James:	Because it was not authorized from Washington, but yet which added immeasurably to the ship and its facilities for the crew and the repair operation. I remember one rather interesting experience. We were building this rather large deck house on the upper deck of the WHITNEY to house a crew's library and recreation room. In my design I had laid out a number of conventional air ports to be fitted but yet hadn't found the source of those air ports. One day one of my ship fitter petty officers came to me and said he had noticed in the destroyer repair base in San Diego a whole stack of air ports that had been taken out of destroyers that had been laid up in the destroyer reserve fleet there. So I went ashore, cased the joint, so to speak, and found indeed there was literally stacks of these things, hundreds of them; my need was for about thirty odd air ports so I scheduled a help yourself operation after I had run into an initial rebuff at a relatively low level in the repair organization ashore. So we had received on board about twenty-odd of these and were sending a working party ashore with a wheelbarrow to bring off the last of those we needed when the sailor, with a wheelbarrow-load of these air ports trundling them from the storage yard down to the boat landing where our boat was waiting, had the great misfortune of running into the commanding officer of the destroyer base -- old Captain Byron McCandless-- who immediately wanted to know what was going on. All this young sailor could say was that he had been sent by Lt. James to get the air ports and he was taking them down to the boat. Questions followed: "Who's Lt. James? What's his authority?" The young sailor knew none of the answers except to identify me as the hull repair officer on the WHITNEY. He was told to return the air ports to the place he had picked them up, get the Hell back to the WHITNEY in a hurry, and tell Lt. James to appear before Capt. McCandless in nothing flat.

So I promptly presented myself to Capt. McCandless and stood straight up for about an hour lecture on the reserve fleet and importance of the destroyer repair base maintaining fifty destroyers in readiness for any future possible conflagration, and that I was showing complete lack of appreciation of the broad picture in my rather selfish action and to get those other air ports that we had stolen back ashore as fast as I could.

Q: You had to admit that you had them?

James: Yes. Or else suffer the pangs of a court-martial proceeding, ~~which I promptly proceeded to do.~~ I found later it was possible to negotiate with Capt. McCandless for a reduced number of these air ports, which he knew at the time he was chewing me out, and I knew, he had no need for, but he was maintaining a policy position which I can find no quarrel with. But I later got I think, a dozen air ports for my project --not what I had in mind, but completely adequate.

Q: Tell me about some of your experiences in repairing destroyers.

James: I can't think of any situations which were unique. We did have what was known as the gold plater Navy in those days. This began with the Farragut Class destroyer, the PD3-48, which were the first of the so-called Roosevelt ship building program. By the time I got into the WHITNEY there were several squadrons of these destroyers in service. They presented many unique problems because the supply system of the Navy at that time was not geared to the new materials that were present in these so-called gold plated destroyers --the aluminum of various sizes and compositions and the fiberglass, stainless steel, copper-nickel alloys, and various other things that had been introduced into the new ships that had not penetrated the supply system and weren't immediately available for work.

Q: These new things together constituted the reason for calling it gold plated?

James: Yes. That was a nick-name that the fleet gave to these ships, gold platers, because they were so vastly superior to the old twenty-one, twenty-two hundred ton destroyers, the old four-piper Navy which was the greater part of our destroyer force at that time. So this generated a lot of procurement problems and also developing techniques and experience with these new materials.

Q: Their value wasn't completely known, I suppose.

James: And there had been very little work done with them in the repair forces of the Navy up to that time. So I came into the fleet just about the time when these ships were coming in and it was a delightful experience to have.

Q: When the ships were fitted with aluminum in various capacities, was there any contact with the manufacturer?

James: Oh yes. We made great use of the Alcoa representative in San Diego in short-circuiting Navy supply circuits to get essentially needed materials delivered for certain jobs, and to a degree we were responsible for building up by these suppliers local warehouse stocks that were helpful in maintaining the new ships. These items later came into full supply in the Navy supply system but it was a matter of a year or two delay to get the distribution necessary so we did a great deal of improvising, but to good effect. I can't think of any important problems on the destroyers. I can think of one unimportant problem that became a major issue.

I think it was the CLARK, one of the destroyer leaders, commanded by Cdr. Rafe Bates. Rafe Bates was a very meticulous naval officer and he decided that the small awnings around his cabin level should be replaced -- one of the jobs that we did on the WHITNEY was make canvas for gun covers, instrument covers, awnings, boat covers and all sorts of things. Our sail loft was generally the busiest of divisions in the repair department. They always had a backlog and could seldom see when they would come out of the overload condition. So when this order for a complete set of new awnings up on the 0-1 deck came from the CLARK, the sailmaker, after having sized up the job, came to me and said, "They don't need new awnings. They're in perfect shape. All they are is a little soiled and if they'd take a scrub brush and scrub them, they'd look as good as anything I could deliver to them." I went over to verify his judgment and concurred in it. I passed the word back through the first lieutenant, who was then Lt. j.g. Horacio Rivero (now a four-star admiral who commands NATO forces in southern Europe) and told him that we weren't going to replace his canvas because they didn't need it. The next act in the play was a violent blast from Capt. Bates who insisted on seeing me to review the matter in person. I was steadfast in my position and he was bombastic in his. We didn't get anywhere except that I told him I was not going to do anything about this and it was his privilege to see my commanding officer, Capt. Alexander, which he did immediately. Capt. Alexander got into the act and went over with me later to examine the awnings. He concurred with me, whereupon somebody made a remark in Cdr. Bates presence, but not knowing he was overhearing, that a lot of people thought Bates was nuts anyhow, whereupon Bates, with a great roar, opened up his wallet and produced a very wrinkled and very stained letter from the Navy Department. The substance of what it said that after complete psychiatric examination it had been determined that (then) Lt. Cdr. Bates was possessed of all of his mental facilities. This, of course, only confirmed the opinion that many of us had that in order to have to have such a letter, he must have been suspect by many who didn't believe he did have all his buttons. Well, Rafe Bates later became a tradition in the Navy; he's an author of some merit and served until retirement as a commodore in active duty and did extremely well in the war. He didn't get his suit of awnings, as requested, because my captain backed me up completely.

Q: Tell me about Admiral Pye.

James: Admiral Pye was commander, Destroyer Flotilla One, the group of ships that I was attached to. He lived on board the WHITNEY with his staff -- a very fine gentleman. I think his widow is still alive. His son was killed in a tragic accident while we were there in San Diego. He was an aviator and was flying a fighter unit out of North Island Air Base, and in a collision at sea his plane went down and his body was never recovered. A curious sidelight on the commanding officer of the naval air station at the time, then Capt. Ernie King, developed out of that accident. There was a memorial service conducted in the chapel on the air station which many of the friends of Bill Pye, Jr., were attending. The remnant group of flyers in his air squadron decided that during the services they would honor Bill Pye by flying low over the chapel and make dipped wing salute. Ernie King was in the congregation at this service. When the planes came flying in and made their dive over the chapel, he started, turned about, and signaled his Marine orderly that was standing in the back of the chapel to come forward. We didn't know at the time what was happening but we knew that he was annoyed because I'm sure there was a regulation that prohibited low flying over the island. The next day the word came out that all of these aviators that had participated in this fly-over salute to young Bill Pye were put in hack for ten days, grounded of course, I'm sure I don't know who they were. It was a matter of record that they had been so disciplined by Ernie King and many of us thought this was a reflection of the flint hearted individual that he was. As you will recall, when he became Com-Inch, or the senior naval officer during World War II, he made the observation that "When the going gets tough they send for a bastard to run the show." -- or words to that effect.

Q: I think maybe a little stronger than that.

James: I think that covers my recollection of a two year pleasant experience in San Diego, which was a fairly sleepy little town in those days.

Q: You were able to have your family out there?

James: Yes. Our daughter was then in grammar school and our son was approaching kindergarten age when we left San Diego to return to Washington, D.C. for duty in the (then) Bureau of C & R, with

Admiral George Rock as the chief naval constructor and the head of the Bureau. I was in a very small office with a group of other naval constructors. I think there were five of us. We were responsible for the maintenance and operation of shipyard work in connection with all ship types. My task was destroyers. There was then a Comdr. Marrin, a Cmdr. Christmas and myself. Christmas later became captain and Marrin later became a commodore. A curious situation -- a young lady named Gladys Train was secretary to all of us. Our stenographic requirements were relatively simple in those days. Gladys Train later went on to be the secretary to the chief of Bureau of Ships and when I became the chief in 1959, there she was again.

Q: With all that continuity and knowledge.

James: A very wonderful person she was. It was my great misfortune, however, to have to speed her to her retirement and bring in another extremely capable young lady. Gladys Train served a number of bosses and went on up the ladder to become the number one gal in the technical bureau for many, many years.

Q: In this destroyer maintenance desk, did this put you in touch with machine tool people, and so on?

James: No. Again, this was a separate function. The work of the destroyer type desk, and all type desks as they were known, was extremely involved with maintaining the fleet, repairing, getting funds, developing alteration changes to the ships that had been urged upon us by commanding officers and type commanders, reviewing the projected changes against the value returned for the value expended. Machine tools were a sideline and generally were handled by civilians although I think they always had a naval officer in charge. We, ourselves, developed little knowledge of the intricacies of machine tool development. It was a specialty of its own and they had some extremely fine people in Washington, whom I later came to know better as Chief of Bureau than I did when I was on a type desk.

Perhaps the major development at that time was the activity to merge the Bureau of Engineering and the Bureau of C and R into a single entity. This started early in 1940.

Q: Who's instigation was it?

James: I'm not ever sure. I believe it was as much the instigation of the naval constructor group who were staff officers and who had a numerical limitation on the prospect of achieving flag rank. There were never more than two admiral constructors, and two only if the one permanent admiral, which the corps was entitled to, was not then the chief of the Bureau of C and R. Who then held the temporary rank of admiral. The constructors fretted under this limit to their promotion, and sought some broadening of opportunity. I think as much as anything, this desire, plus the very obvious fact that there was a great deal of merit to combining two separate bureaus dealing with the operations of ships into a single entity motivated the study. Actually, in my judgment, there was justification for combining three bureaus into a single Bureau of Ships -- the Bureaus of Ordnance, Engineering, and Hull (C&R). This then would constitute the almost complete ship; electronics was part of Engineering in those days. The program got off the ground with support from practically everybody in both the Bureau of Engineering and the Bureau of Construction and Repair. I think that even though I was a young officer and not completely aware of all the details at the time, there was no lack of support for the projected merger that I witnessed. We brought the consulting firm, Booz, Allen & Hamilton, who sent in a very large team of very competent management specialists. After months of walking about, talking, interviewing, and reading, being reasonably aware of the various technical responsibilities of each of the two bureaus they urged the merger into an entity which became known as the Bureau of Ships. At the same time, they suggested the merger of the Naval Construction Corps with the Engineering Duty Only officer the latter who wore a star of the line officer, but who by experience and by education had qualified as an engineering specialist. The proposal was to merge these two groups into a single corps. However, the engineer officers who had worn the star and who had had many more years at sea than the average naval constructors (whose sea duty came primarily before transfer to the Construction Corps) wanted to preserve that star. In doing so, they forced the constructor group who were engineering this merger to agree to abolishing the Construction Corps thus bringing the naval constructors (almost all of who were former line officers of limited experience sea service) back into the line. This suggestion met with great opposition from the younger naval constructors. We who had been line officers, cherished the fact that we had given up the line to pursue our technical specialty. We very proudly wore the oak leaf that distinguished us as being a rather select group of ex-line officers who had chosen to go this other route. A group of us organized to present our feelings to the Chief of the Bureau of C and R and to protest this projected amalgamation, but we didn't get anywhere -- in fact we were given a rather rough time.

Q: On what premise?

James: That we didn't know enough about the problem, that we should accept the belief that our superiors were better qualified to judge what was best for the Construction Corps -- really, "just don't bother us." We were more-or-less brushed off. This irritated a group of us so we formed a hard-core committee that I called the Young Turk's revolution. We had about nine officers, mostly lieutenants, all of whom were then on duty in the Bureau of C and R, who began to prepare our arguments for presentation on the hill, where a bill to bring about this merger was pending. We had intercepted the House of Representatives action on this merger bill, not only the merger of the bureaus but of the personnel, at a time when the thing had been pretty well progressed through the Congress but a congressman from Minnesota, who later became blind, Melvin Maas, became interested in our case and decided that the young officers' position had a proper attitude toward this thing so he was very willing to receive and introduce our material, which was largely instrumental in blocking the passage of this bill in the House.

Q: Was this not a dangerous operation on the part of some young lieutenants?

James: There were nine young lieutenants and one lieutenant commander who were called to the front carpet and literally chewed out by the then acting chief. First, let me say that the physical merger of the bureaus proceeded a pace. First it was done by simply moving us physically together with our counterparts in the Bureau of Engineering into a single space, and then later the title of the so-called Bu-Eng, BuC&R combination was changed to BuShips, a very proper new organizational entity.

Q: What was the basis for the Boos-Allen recommendation in this regard?

James: The overlapping responsibilities for varying parts of ship building, ship maintenance and operation which would be simplified by the joint efforts of the two bureaus rather than the individual effort of each that required passing questions one to another for review and position. It was a very necessary and worthwhile change to consolidate, to simplify, and to improve the operations of these two separate bureaus. It was brought off physically, as I say, by simply moving us together. In my area, the destroyer operations of the Bureau of Engineering were handled by Oley Sharp, who later became Commander-in-Chief of the Pacific and who only recently retired. Oley and I ran destroyers for a period of months under our separate bureau hats but while sitting across the desk from each other. A very warm and effective personal relationship developed out of that merger.

Getting back to the personnel thing, we were achieving a degree of success that perhaps overstimulated us as neophytes in congressional tactics. We were able to prevent the dissolution of the Contruction Corps for the time being. As I said earlier, the reasons for our position were largely that we had elected to go this route, that we had a tremendous corps esprit, and that we thought would be lost if we became "psuedo line" officers again. It gave us no point to rally our technical specialty as we would be absorbed into and under the direct review of line officers that we believed to be less technically qualified than ourselves. We found that through most of the officers in our group to the rank of commander there was a general feeling that indeed our position was right. But even the older officers, lieutenant commanders and commanders, generally were pleased to see the young squirts try it and if heads would fall, it would be the expendable lieutenants rather than the senior commanders.

Q: It was a rather unprecedented action, wasn't it?

James: I believe it was. We were called into the office of the (then) chief of this amalgam of Engineering and C&R. The Admiral S.S. Robinson, who is still living in San Antonio, Texas. I've called on him and received letters from him repeatedly when I became Chief of Buships. He lined nine young officers up in front of his desk one day and urged us to reconsider our action, stating all of his reasons why he felt this merger should go through. I might add that he was an ED officer of long standing and had not had the association as a staff corps member of the Construction Corps so we didn't exactly consider his arguments to be descriptive of our problem although I'm sure he endeavored to be as objective as he could. He could not have been motivated by the desire to achieve flag rank because he already wore it. He dealth with us in a paternal way as a father might with an intelligent child who had erred. He tried to reason with us and finally concluded by inviting us to go off and reconsider our position and come back after we had and restate our position. Nine of us trooped out. Some of us were chagrined, some began to waver. We met extensively on the issue with a few of the organizers --
Charlie Tooke, myself, Bobby Snyder (whose father was Admiral

Peck Snyder), Bill Leahy, deciding to hold to our initial position. Included was John Ellison, who was our spokesman by virtue of being the senior officer of the group who very recently had made lieutenant commander. There were two or three who decided that we had erred and wanted to disassociate, which they did. The rest of us remained steadfast. We were really the organizational brains of the revolutionary group, anyhow, and the others were more-or-less hangers-on. We went back and met with Admiral Robinson. He, in anticipation of our having seen the light as he had turned it on, was prepared to hear a report of our willingness to drop our efforts on the hill and to take our positions as good little boys in the club, taking what our seniors had decided was good for us rather than what we wanted. I think he was completely flabbergasted when we re-iterated our position and our determination to present our case to the Congress and fight to the bitter end the amalgamation of the constructors and the EDOs into the restricted line status. Then in a moment of pique, and I can see it as though it were happening this very moment -- he walked down the line of us that were standing in front of his desk --

Q: How many of you were left?

James: I guess we were about six. There had been two defectors. He put his long, bony finger out and began to wave it up and down under our noses as he marched down the line. His words are just as clear today as they were then. He said, "In a military organization, there are no dissenting opinions and I can assure you gentlemen present that in this military organization, there will be no dissenters." That was a clear call to failure of selection to our next and higher ranks. Needless to say, it shook us all. We didn't believe that he could take that violent a position but we were now prepared that he might.

The composition of our group was such that the next selection board, which met just months after this event, there were two of our number who came up for selection, both in the Class of '27. One was Charlie Tooke and the other was Bobbie S-yder. When the selection board announced its findings, Charlie Tooke had not been selected, Bobbie Snyder was. Both were very brilliant young naval constructors. Charlie Tooke was a most academically qualified and extremely capable officer; he was passed over. Bobbie Snyder's father, as I mentioned before, was Admiral Peck Snyder, one of the few four star admirals at that time. It wasn't a surprise that the father's influence might have carried the day for Bobbie Snyder, although I'm sure he was marked for extermination. This was in the fall of 1940.

The next year I came up for selection with Bill Howard, who also had been on the Young Turk's Revolution governing body. We anticipated that our heads would roll with the selection in November of 1941. The worsening situation with the Japanese at that time undoubtedly was the reason why all selection for that year became more-or-less perfunctory. Instead of being a full out examination of record, every member of my class in the Construction Corps was eligible for promotion to lieutenant commander achieved it by virtue of the fact that all of us were badly needed and thereby promoted. So my goose was saved by the advent of World War II.

Going back to the event that we were trying to forestall. The action that we had taken in the House through Melvin Maas was completely adequate to stop the merger bill.

Q: That was the Naval Affairs Committee?

James: I assume it was that committee -- it must have been. We were not learned in the ways of the Congress and what our superiors (who were pushing this merger thing) did was immediately take the same bill to the Senate, had it introduced by a Senator, presented to the Naval Affairs Committee, and passed out of the Committee to the floor in a matter of a twenty-four hour period -- a very effective way to circumvent opposition.

Q: Senator Walsh was very amenable. David I. Walsh was the chairman of the Committee at the time.

James: It went through like greased lightening. It was all done before our revolutionary council knew what was happening to us and when it came back into the House, introduced as a Senate bill, it didn't go through committee. It simply went onto the floor of the House, was passed in jig time, and the Construction Corps was dissolved. The merger of engineering limited duty officers and naval constructors as restricted line officers was ordered, and we took our lineal position where we had it at time of our graduation, and the time of initial entry into the unrestricted line. From then on it was no longer any matter of fighting the issue -- we were dead ducks and we just buckled on the responsibilities of the star and all implications of it and went on to carry on our work. That sowed the seed (I can talk about it at length later on) of how come the Construction Corps officers, after they became restricted line officers, began to perceive less and less respect for their abilities and capabilities, and engineering specialists, in general, became regarded with less and less approbation. I attribute it all to that completely unnecessary officer merger into the line. Merging of the individuals was a good idea, but our proposal had been, and I believe should have been accepted, to merge the restricted engineer line officer into a staff corps that we could give a new title to, and have, indeed, a separate group of technical specialists as do the Civil Engineers, the Supply officers, the Medical officers.

Interview # 3 with Rear Admiral R. K. James

Annapolis, Maryland

February 16, 1971

Subject: Biography

by John T. Mason, Jr.

Mr. Mason: We're ready for chapter three today. Last time you concluded by talking about your tour of duty in the Navy Department. Now, I believe, you were detached and sent to French West Africa, which must have been a very interesting and colorful phase of your career.

Rear Admiral James: That was one of the more exciting phases of my career because up to that time my participation in the preparation for, and fighting of the war in its early stages was limited to desk work in the combined bureaus of C&R and Engineering in Washington. For one who aspired to do a little more in the war effort, this was a rather dull, although necessary assignment, so when Admiral Broshek, who was my senior officer at the time, called me in late November of '42 to announce that I had been selected to go on a special joint State Department, Navy mission to Africa of which he knew very little about the nature of it except to say it seemed like it would be about a three week tour of duty. It turned out later to be more nearly a three months tour.

Q: Why were your special talents needed for this particular mission?

James: At the time I wasn't any better aware of that fact than was Admiral Broshek, who was able to convey little or no information to me. He knew practically nothing of the nature of this mission. He did know the composition was to include a naval architect, a naval engineer, and a naval aviator with Rear Admiral William Glassford, who was recently returned from the Philippines and was at the moment the Commandant of the Charleston Naval District, to be the head of the mission.

It was a few days later that we met with Admiral Glassford and other members that were to become our mission group. He could then explain that we were going into French West Africa, specifically into Dakar. His description of our purpose was very limited. It became apparent later on as things began to unfold, that the reason was the launching of Operation TORCH, a landing on the beaches in North Africa. Ours was the major supporting side function.

Q: But Glassford didn't talk about TORCH?

James: Glassford probably knew about TORCH but he conveyed nothing in specific details to us because it had not been started. When it did we had left the United States by air and had proceeded with stops at each point we touched down which included San Juan, Trinidad, Belem, Brazil and later Natal, Brazil.

Q: When you went through Puerto Rico were you guests of Admiral Hoover?

James: No. When we went through Puerto Rico I don't recall that Admiral Hoover was there. I knew who was in command but now I don't recall. We were there only two nights, as I recall it, and devoted our time to seeing San Juan. We stayed at the Geronimo BOQ which was a rather attractive hotel the Navy had acquired for officer accommodations. The same was true when we sat down in Trinidad. We moved into the Naval Base at Maqueripe where we waited several more days. All this time we were carrying two very large and very heavy boxes that were the official responsibility of the two aides -- the Army aide for General Kibbler, who was in our mission, and the naval aide to Admiral Glassford. They had to carry these around like the man with the box that triggers the bomb does today. The reasons weren't known until we finally received the message that told us that we might open up these boxes and pass the material contained in them around to the members of the mission. Then it became crystal clear what our function was -- the invasion of North Africa had already started. Our mission was to go into French West Africa with the objective of bringing the French forces there under the banner of allied forces attacking North Africa. To achieve this we had fountain pens and .45 caliber revolvers as our sole instruments for bringing about such a result.

Q: The boxes contained the orders?

James: The boxes contained the full and complete story of the invasion of North Africa, the forces involved, the schedule dates of the several landings, who was in command, what the French opposing forces (if indeed there was opposition) were expected to be, and a very comprehensive examination of the French West African areas and of the headquarters of the French located in Dakar.

We were expected, as I say, to get a treaty with these Free French forces, if indeed they proved to be Free French after the invasion started, and not hewing to the Vichy French line. Our mission included a gentleman from the State Department, a Mr. Maynard Barnes, who later became the Consul General at Dakar, and subsequently rose to ambassador level on other assignments after the war. We were to be joined in Dakar by a Colonel Julius Holmes, who was a member of the State Department but was in the uniform of a colonel serving General Eisenhower as his counselor along with Ambassador Robert Murphy. We were also to be joined by Air Force Brigadier General Cyrus R. Smith, president of American Airlines, later its chairman and subsequently, the Secretary of Commerce in the Johnson administration. The group, as I mentioned earlier, contained three technical types. My particular assignment along with that of Capt. Benny Haven, who was the engineer member, was to make a survey of all French naval units in the harbor at Dakar and to do what we could to ready them for participation in the war, assuming we succeeded in negotiating a treaty.

I also had the task of reviewing the merchant ships in the harbor. When we arrived, we found, as I recall, about sixty naval ships including the battleship, RICHELIEU, as the largest and newest although not yet finished, sixteen inch gun battleship which the French had just built.

Q: Was she a sister ship of the BART?

James: As long as you've raised the question, let's dispose of the RICHELIEU. The RICHELIEU and JEAN BART were built in St. Nazaire, as I recall. When the Germans came into and occupied all of France, the French sent many of their naval units in service out of the harbor at Toulon in southern France over to Oran on the North African coast, under the command of Vice Admiral Collinet. The JEAN BART and the RICHELIEU were about sixty percent and about ninety percent finished, respectively. The French were able to get up steam on both of them and they fled the building shipyard in France, the JEAN BART going into Casablanca and the RICHELIEU going to Dakar. Both were laid up for some considerable time, but represented to our people in Washington a sizable asset if they might be readied for operation.

So Benny Haven and I were the principals to review the readiness of these ships and make specific recommendations as to their ultimate use. There were over eighty merchant ships that had been interned in Dakar, largely French, but they included ships of at least ten other nationalities. These ships had all been deprived of one or more key pieces of equipment by the Germans who occupied Dakar so they were stranded in the harbor. This was done to frustrate any exuberance on the part of the crews should they try to break the barrier and take the ships to sea.

Q: When had they been interned?

James: They had been interned with the beginning of the war in Europe in 1939 and the number had been building up gradually. As I recall there were no American ships there but there were a number of Norwegians, a few Greeks, a large number of British, and other allied nations.

Q: That was a great prize, wasn't it?

James: Yes. The word from our government was to get these ships back into the allied shipping pool with all dispatch possible. Let me go back to the JEAN BART and the RICHELIEU. These two ships were truly magnificent new war ships of the era. The RICHELIEU in Dakar was completely crewed and Capt. DeRaymond was its commanding officer. He was a very delightful person with whom we had immediate and continuous associations. The beginning of our mission in Dakar started off with the usual amenities where we met first the Governor, General Pierre Boisson. He was an old retired Army general who had served with distinction at the battle at Verdun, during which he suffered grevious injuries including loss of much of his hearing. This he tried to improve by one of the most antiquated hearing aids I've ever seen. His desk was wired to a large box containing battery cells, large size battery cells of the type almost large enough to ring the doorbell in the olden days. Our OSS people had learned that Gen. Boisson was kaput because the batteries were defunct. Amongst other things on our trip from the United States, we carried a set of replacement batteries which were presented to the General immediately upon our arrival.

Q: Apple polishing?

James: Well, it was part of our function to win over the French who were still under surveillance by Germans who were in Dakar as we arrived were there. On this point, as the seaplane which flew us from Natal to Dakar non-stop and made the first landing of allied planes at the French seaplane ramp there, another seaplane was departing two or three ramps away from us and it was being filled with German officers who were evacuating Dakar.

Q: How did this coincide time wise with the landing at Casablanca?

James: The landing in Casablanca took place, as I recall, in mid-November. We arrived in Dakar on Saturday, the nineteenth of December. The greatest part of this delay, in our arrival, was because we had been dallying, as I mentioned earlier with these different stops enroute to Natal, while awaiting French approval for our arrival in Dakar with a guarantee of not being attacked when we came in for our landing. We went over in a PB2M, a completely unarmed aircraft -- the total weaponry on board consisted of a .45 caliber pistol in each of our briefcases.

Q: But you were all in uniform?

James: We were all in uniform.

Q: Who negotiated with the French at Dakar to effectuate your arrival?

James: I don't know that for certain. I would assume that it might have been part of the forces that had gone into North Africa. As you recall, there was quite a bit of cooperation with the Free French for that landing and we had anticipated that a French general was going to take command of the operation after our landing, but certain events came along to foul that up. Our one exposure to the enemy was on that occasion of glaring across a hundred yards of open water at the handful of Germans who were embarking at Dakar as the handful of Americans disembarked there.

As we settled down into the city of Dakar, there was no official social contact with the French because the influence of the Germans was still very strong and people were still fearful that the Germans would succeed in war and they would be headed for extermination if they were seen fraternizing with the Americans. One of the interesting memories I have is as we walked along the street at night (there was no automotive transportation available for us except when we made strictly official visits) people would pop out of the shadows and come up and give us in French an affectionate greeting to reflect that, in Dakar, notwithstanding the presence and the influence of the Germans, there were still many French who were very eager to see the triumph of allied arms in Africa and the restoration of a Free France.

Q: There were no official overtures at all?

James: None whatsoever. In fact we were pointedly excluded from the social contacts with people we met on official business -- our official contacts developed immediately after we arrived. Through General Boisson we were put in touch with all the Navy and Army commanders. The Navy commander was Vice Admiral Collinet who had taken the French naval forces out of Toulon to Oran in North Africa. Here the British later came and bombarded the base and ships but were rather brutally handled by the French. This Collinet was a very fine type of warrior admiral whom I held in extremely high regard. The general commanding the Army was a General Barrau. These officers made available all their staff and their various other functionaries, but denied us any contact with them socially. We were given very pleasant quarters in what was known as the Governor's Guest House right beside the Governor's Palace but we were more-or-less isolated here and I don't doubt but what we were under constant surveillance while we were there.

Q: As newcomers you had to be in quarantine for awhile.

James: Yes. But then on Christmas Day we had a rather eventful occurrence take place when Admiral Darlan, the premier of the Vichy French was assassinated in Algiers. This occasioned much speculation as to what our own future might be. Darlan, to review the history a bit, had been the head of the French Navy, before occupation of France by the Germans. He had been picked by old General Petain, who was the head of the French Vichy government, to be the Premier. He had been considered as the likely person to become the head of Free French forces in Africa after the allied invasion but, of course, he didn't qualify by virtue of being the premier and being unable to be counted upon. His presence in Algiers was brought about by a strange event. His son, a young naval officer, was stricken with polio and the father felt it desirable to see the son and he visited him under a cloak of secrecy. His presence in North Africa after the Allied invasion occurred had become bruited about and he was shot down in the streets of Algiers by Free French, who considered him a traitor to the French nation. That caused a complete change of alignment of French loyalties in French Africa. Up to that very moment, there had been a distinct loyalty to the Vichy government in

Dakar and also a distinct belief that maybe the American force of arms would fail. The French in West Africa felt therefore that they had better play it cozy and not be caught out on a limb by lending support too much to our activities.

The situation became very serious as far as we were concerned on Christmas Day 1942 because if the pendulum had swung to a revulsion by the French to the assassination of Darlan, we could have been considered interlopers and dealt with accordingly.

Q: You were the hostages.

James: Right. The American Vice Consul who had been in Dakar during the period of the German occupation had been interned in a place that has always been a legendary site to me, Timbuctou. We later flew over Timbuctou and discovered it to be a reality, a real scruffy village in the central part of equatorial Africa where this young fellow named Dumont had been interned with a few other American staff members. He had been released only a matter of days before our group arrived in Dakar. So he was all filled with the fact that we had better get our bags packed, pack as much loot as we could for our own survival and be ready to go anytime Christmas Day when the gendarmes came around to collect us.

As it turned out, the death of Darlan apparently freed a lot of the inhibitions of the French in Africa and greater support for the allied effort was immediately apparent in North Africa as it became in Dakar. As I mentioned, we had been excluded earlier from all social contacts with the French, of Dakar having our contacts limited to the very essential business developments of examining their naval ships, their merchant ships, their dockyard, and the other military installations.

Q: And yet they knew the reason for your being there?

James: Yes, there was no question of this. The Governor General received us immediately after we arrived, and it was made quite clear by Admiral Glassford, but the assassination in Algiers caused a complete turn around of attitude. Almost immediately after there was a tremendous effort on the part of the French in Dakar to embrace us socially. Invitations were sent to the group to appear at the French Naval Club, and the Naval Officer's Club, the Army Club, the Diplomatic Club, and all such places that we had been denied.

Q: This was a result of a decision made at the top in the command there.

James: Obviously. We were not a party to it but we were the benefactors of it -- the recipients of their beneficence, I guess is a better way to express it. The day that this ice jam began to move out, messenger after messenger came to our quarters in the Governor's guest quarters bearing invitations to this affair and that affair. Admiral Glassford, whom I considered to be a consummate diplomat, received all of these invitations and we chuckled about the fact that things were now completely different than before. He returned all invitations unopened with the same flourish and flair that they had been delivered, using his two aides to do this. Among the invitations was one from the Rotary Club, as there was one from the Governor General, the commander of the naval forces, the commander of the air forces, commander of the Army. Admiral Glassford returned all of these but sent an acceptance to the president of the Rotary Club of Dakar stating that he and his staff would be pleased to attend their dinner meeting in downtown Dakar.

Q: Why was that? Because it was Rotary International?

James: He undoubtedly meant it pointedly to make clear to all who had ignored us that he too was capable of the same game. We had not been ignored by Rotary -- it had no military connotation and therefore he felt that accepting he showed our desire to communicate and fraternize but that we weren't going to let the slights of the previous days that we had been in the city go unremarked.

Q: The others were declined then?

James: The others were declined. The night of this Rotary occasion, we dressed in a completely non-reg uniform of white trousers and blue coats, all looking very spiffy in this outfit. We walked together to the hotel where this affair was to be held, not using cars or transport which had suddenly become available. I guess we walked a good three miles down through the city of Dakar in loose formation but in formation nonetheless. As we proceeded there were more and more cries of "viva l'France" and "viva l'Americaine" from the populace. The dinner at the Rotary Club must have overwhelmed the local membership whom I don't believe were ever visited by such a curious or spectacularly garbed group. We each were assigned to one or more of their members. Very few of us spoke French, which was to our great regret, but we nonetheless participated in the meeting and Admiral Glassford, who spoke impeccable French, commented upon our pleasure and delight in being there.

Then we had to sit and listen to the lecturer who spoke on "Impressions Gained While Inside the Lip of an Active Volcano," all in French. It was an experience, that I'm sure, because the turning point because from then on we were overwhelmed by people wanting to be nice to us whereas before they had virtually ignored us previously.

Q: What about official invitations?

James: Official invitations continued to flow at a great rate and after the first rejection of all of them we accepted others.

Q: Who was paying for your board and keep?

James: That's an interesting question. The room was provided by the government of French West Africa. Our meals we had to pretty well scrounge ourselves. After we had been there about a week, the merchant ship JOHN PAGE came into port and we were able to preempt a lot of their stores. We set up a mess of our own in a local hotel, the Metropole Hotel. We had a yeoman with our group and he became mess treasurer and chief scrounger. We brought these stores ashore and then began to eat rather well. Our breakfasts we generally had up at our sleeping quarters but this was generally toast and tea. We set up this mess facility shortly after we arrived. It was on the twenty-seventh of December that we opened up a better mess on board a French merchant ship. It was American food, all canned but it tasted delicious -- jam, peanut butter, corned beef, canned beans, beets, butter, coffee, cocoa. The waiters were the French staff on board. I never saw corned beef served in such style before. Our board then was essentially provided by our own government.

The fundamental job that I had to do was to examine all of the ships of the French Navy and determine the extent of the damage that had been suffered by them, especially the RICHELIEU, which, if you recall was attacked by a Free French force aboard British ships on the twenty-fifth of September, 1940. The history behind that is important. DeGaulle, as you know, had gone to England with the fall of France and had tried to become the rallying point for the Free French under the allied banner. He had apparently succeeded in convincing the British that if they mounted an operation into French West Africa with him on board and a large number of Free French volunteers, that the mere presence of this British naval squadron off the port of Dakar would cause the French in Dakar to come along and join the allied cause. I know nothing of the circumstances that completely thwarted this ambition of his but when they arrived off the harbor of Dakar, in September of 1940, instead of being greeted by a friendly group, they were indeed brought under fire by the French ships then in the harbor, which included the battleship, RICHELIEU.

She had been completely outfitted with her main battery and her secondary battery but it had never been test fired. The sixteen inch guns were completely a new design, a wire wound type of barrell, and the ammunition was completely untried and new design. But the ammunition was on board so after the attack opened up, the RICHELIEU got into the act by loading and firing her sixteen inch guns. It was tragic that there had been no real preparation of these guns before firing and before long they had tremendous explosions on board the RICHELIEU from her own powder, which exploded in the barrels of these guns because there apparently was too thin a wall between the powder charge, the propellant, and detonating charge within the sixteen inch shell. The explosive charge in the shell was detonated by the propellant charge and blew up inside the barrel of the gun. Before they could control this, they had blown over the side the outboard two-thirds length of at least three, maybe five, of their sixteen inch gun batteries and there they were completely crippled. The battle raged on and the British attacked the harbor in general and did quite a bit of damage to the shipping and the naval ships in the harbor. I believe the French did sortie from the harbor with some of their destroyers but only after the British had gone. The battle essentially was concluded right there in Dakar harbor.

The RICHELIEU became a completely ineffectual ship as a result of this experience. Of course, Darlan's name became mud. This is the reason why the Free French that still remained had to more-or-less remain completely out of sight because there was not only the German domination of French authorities there in Dakar, but the Vichy French themselves were a real hazard to the Free French. Although you could see the Cross of Lorraine painted on the walls of alleyways and abandoned buildings, there was damned little evidence for any support for De Gaulle until the event of the assassination of Darlan.

The RICHELIEU was so badly damaged that they very cleverly disguised her incapacity by carving out of tree trunks, replacement barrels for the guns that had been blown over the side, the gun barrels, and in a matter of a very short time, to all appearances, at least air surveillance, the RICHELIEU was still in full fighting trim. When we came aboard and had our meetings with the officers of the ship, we quickly had it pointed out to us she had limited capabilities. They wanted us to get her over to the United States along with the other ships and it was obvious that she had great potential if we could replace her main battery. Remember this is in the days of the old battleship and the heavy artillery of the battleship was still a major factor in naval warfare.

Q: You had said previously that she was ninety percent completed?

James: Approximately ninety percent. Her machinery spaces were in beautiful shape and her battery, except for this major casualty, was otherwise in good shape. Her fire control was not completely installed but basically she was a very impressive and important naval unit. I'll get to the JEAN BART in later recommendations to our own Commander-in-Chief of the naval forces, Admiral King, a little later on.

Looking at the other naval units, there were cruisers -- the GEORGES LEYGUEZ was the flag ship of the French naval forces under the command of Admiral Longaud. There were two other cruisers in the harbor. There were destroyers. There were submarines, there were the smaller craft --minesweepers, auxillary craft, support ships and supply ships. Between Haven and I, we toured every ship that was in the harbor. We talked with the captains of each ship and learned of their problems to get them back in full service.

Q: Were they fully cooperative?

James: They were officially cooperative. There were one or two captains that we met that were anything but cooperative but after performing the prefunctory purpose of meeting us, they turned the discussions over to American speaking assistants and disappeared.

We completed our examination of all the ships after a month and a half and prepared a rather extensive list of things to be done to these ships, assuming that a number of them would be returned to the United States to have the work performed.

Just to reflect on this question you raised about cooperation, early in our stay there, we called on the commander of the dockyard, or as we then knew it -- naval shipyard. He was an old crotchety vngineer type Frenchman who was completely in support of the Vichy French. In fact when Capt. Haven and I were introduced we were taken to his rather meager little office, sat down, and he proceeded to deliver us a lecture on how the French had had their honor destroyed when the Germans took over their country for a second time in his lifetime. How it was a tragedy to be sure, but how after a couple of years the people in

France had learned to live with the German invader and how he as a dedicated naval type was permitted to send little packages to his family in the France, packages of food, peanut butter, which was a major staple, peanuts, sugar, soap. These were a great supplement to the family's welfare. But he said, "Now you have come in and landed on the coast of North Africa. You have told us you are going to free the French. I, for one, am free and don't want your kind of freedom. You are meddling, you have no business coming and your presence is very unwelcome."

With that sort of a tirade after we had come in preaching our dedication to the French people and our desire to liberate them, it was a rather large pill to swallow, but we did get on with our work in reviewing the requirements of the shipyard who operate as a major naval facility and perhaps in support of our own naval ships in and around that part of the world. As we were entering the dock yard on the morning of our first visit with this gentleman, a very unpleasant personal experience occurred. A truckload of French soldiers came out of the dock yard just at the moment that the Vice Consul Dumont and myself were entering the dock yard gate. This truck spotted me in my uniform and apparently identified Dumont as being an American also, and as the truck passed with the load of soldiers, many of them the black Sengalese soldiers, someone spat a large wad of spit that hit me right smack in the chest of my uniform. It was an obvious attempt to reflect their personal feelings about the Americans. Happily, my instincts were controlled enough so that instead of acknowledging this insult, I was able to keep my head high and was able to walk in and only after I had entered the gate did I make an effort to remove the stain of this bastard's spittle. That was a reflection of attitudes of many of the people in Dakar. I found it to be even more bitter when I later went up to Casablanca.

To finish the story in Dakar, the previously interned merchant shipping was a very impressive group of relatively modern ships of varying tonnages, varying types of dry cargo ships, bulk carriers and tankers. They had been immobilized by one means or another, by the French Navy. I was given the task of getting these ships back into service and into the allied shipping pool at the earliest possible date. I learned that they had a senior captain who periodically met with the captains of the other ships. I scheduled a meeting for all of these men -- in fact it was the beginning of a series of meetings. As I said earlier, they were all nationalities and spoke all kinds of languages but mostly they had a smattering of English so we were able to get on with the listing of the things they needed to get out of the harbor. They included such things as rocker arms on diesel engines that had been deliberately taken out, life boats that were a requirement, crews that had been interned in Tinbuctou along with other non-French nationals. All sorts of things that were essential to a ship going to sea.

Working between this group and the French Navy I was able

to get the parts removed put back on board, the crews to rejoin their respective ships and the manpower to make essential ship repairs. We were working up to a likelihood of soon being able to get at least a half a dozen ships immediately released and shortly thereafter increasing numbers until finally in a couple of months, I expected all of the ships would have been out of the harbor.

Q: What was the spirit of the personnel on these merchant ships?

James: All were eager to get out of Dakar and all were eager to get back to their own homes. If it meant, incidentally, to join up with the allied forces, they were prepared to do that, too, accepting the fact that their return to their home ports would not be immediate.

A chap by the name of Ivar Strand was their senior captain and a very capable guy. He and I spent endless hours with these other captains. Soon it became too much of a burden for me because my other work was also to review all of the naval ships. The work was just beginning to pile up.

We had direct communications with our own Joint Chiefs of Staff through certain circuits that we had brought into Dakar. Admiral Glassford sent off a request to get assistance from the War Shipping Board for somebody who was experienced in merchant ship problems of insurance, licensing, crew sizes, cargo booking, and all of those aspects.

Q: Does this imply that our intelligence didn't know that there were that many merchant vessels there?

James: No. But at the time we went in there was the belief that the naval engineer and naval constructor could handle this task but it was a greater task than had been appreciated. After about a week or so, maybe ten days, a chap by the name of White, a Britisher, came out of England, and he had been a member of the Joint Allied Shipping Board. His qualifications for the job were impeccable. With great pleasure I took him down to meet the foreign merchant ship captains and introduced them to him and said I was now concentrating on other work and would be, therefore, interested but not in direct contact with them. I thought that the program would proceed extremely well.

However, about a week later I ran into this Captain Strand, by coincidence, on the street. We stopped and talked and I raised the question how things were going. I assumed everything had been accelerated but to my utter dismay I learned that practically nothing had been done except that this chap had met with ship people every day of the week, not as I had met with them about twice a week, and his basic purpose was to get them all signed up with insurance from British Maritime Insurers.

Q: Lloyds of London?

James: Lloyds of London, among others. I learned that he was, himself, a member of that fine group. This was rather shattering and to be sure that I thoroughly understood what was being talked about I went to the next of these meetings. Sure enough, there this guy White was sitting with application forms and he was talking with each skipper. It took him an hour or two or three with each one. He had some eighty ships to go through so nothing was being done to move the ships out of the harbor.

I reported this right back to Admiral Glassford and made a recommendation that we get someone else to replace this guy immediately. He sent off another message to the Joint Chiefs and outlined the situation. Very shortly we were advised that a new American representative of this industry would be sent out. He arrived toward the end of January. He was Chalmers Graham, who, as I later learned, was a maritime attorney and a very capable guy. He arrived about the seventeenth of January and then began another period of accelerated effort to get these ships back into service.

While we were in Dakar, the intent of our President to meet in Casablance was relayed to Admiral Glassford. Others of us had guessed as much because we had a message that said, "Prepare a ramp of such and such specifications and have it available on the air field at Dakar on such and such a day." The specifications of this ramp were something I had just dealt with before I left the Bureau of C & R, in building a ramp for a destroyer for the visit at sea of President Roosevelt. So when I read this, I said, "The President is coming to Dakar."

Everybody poo-pooed this. I

said, "No. He's coming to Dakar, or at least they think he will because they want a Roosevelt ramp built to get him off the airplane."

I went around and told Admiral Glassford. I said, "I've just read this message and I can tell you that I'm sure that is a ramp to accommodate President Roosevelt and his infirmity. We can expect him to be here on or after such and such a date." Glassford knew this all along and he said, "You big nosey type. You shouldn't be so damned smart. That's supposed to be a super secret matter." He then told me, also, that I was to join him in a flight to Algiers and later to Casablanca to join in the Casablanca Conference and to present the report on the French ships in Dakar, Algiers and Casablanca.

I was a lieutenant commander in those days and this was just flying in super elevated circles of grandeur. I couldn't have been happier with the opportunity to go. Captain Haven, who later became Rear Admiral (one of the EDO admirals) was burned up that I was to make the trip instead of him but nonetheless that is the way Glassford rigged it. Glassford and I and one of his aides flew out of Dakar early in January and proceeded immediately to Casablanca where we stayed for a few days and then flew into Algiers.

Q: What was your purpose in Algiers?

James: We took off on the 7th of January for Algiers. Our purpose was to meet with General Eisenhower to outline the character of the work being done by the Glassford mission, the development of the treaty relationship, Admiral Glassford's judgment of the forces and the effectiveness of the Free French, or now the total French forces in Dakar, and the over-all war effort. My particular job was to present the status of the French naval forces and to examine into the situation on American naval ships in Casablanca that had been brought in after their attack on Casablanca. Also I was to judge what to do with a few of our American naval ships that had been rather badly damaged in the attack, and to continue the work that I was doing down in Dakar for the French ships in the harbors at Algiers and Casablanca.

Our first stay in Casablanca was relatively short because our basic objective was to get to Algiers. Nonetheless we did have a day or two there when I met with a number of the French naval officers and prepared for my return and visit aboard their ships. When I got to Casablanca I found one of my old friends, a naval constructor, Capt. Bill Sullivan, who was the salvage officer trying to raise the ships that were sunk in the harbor and to open the port up to full and unrestricted use.

We went on to Algiers and were quartered in the Hotel Aletti right on the waterfront. While we were there we had the questionable pleasure of seeing German air raids in the harbor. I recall one of them had bombed the room that I was in -- not at the time I was in it but bomb fragments messed the hell out of my room. That was about as close as

I've come in the entire war to any personal exposure to the enemy. We immediately met with Bedell Smith, who was General Eisenhower's Chief of Staff and a Lieutenant Commander Butcher, who was a PR type more than any naval warrior type, and presented the story that I had prepared on the status of the French ships. Then we met with General Eisenhower himself and submitted our recommendations as to treatment of French ships.

I had tried to see the JEAN BART before I left for Algiers and had not succeeded. I was to see it on my return. At that time the major recommendation was for the RICHELIEU and to try and find some means of replacing her main battery by having the guns built in the United States. Knowing a little about the ordnance problem I realized I was proposing a very long term undertaking but nonetheless it seemed about the only thing we could do. We didn't know how long the war would take.

Q: How did the General receive this recommendation?

James: I think he was less than completely interested in this sort of a side issue that dealt more with naval than army matters, but he was extremely courteous and attentive. He knew that we were soon to meet with Admiral Ernie King so he really didn't express himself as to whether he thought what we were proposing was good or bad. He more or less just soaked it up as peripheral information.

While we were there, and we were there for about five days, we met with a number of the Frnech who had been in

The plotting of the invasion with Americans and anticipating their roles when the Americans and the allies actually landed. One was Admiral Fenard. I met him and his family and was told that he soon was to come to Washington to be the head of the French Naval Mission here. It was being restored as a result of our joint purpose now. He spent a great deal of time pumping me about his accommodations in Washington. We became very friendly and it developed further after I returned to Washington and he had arrived over here. I also met some of the senior members of the Eisenhower staff - Admiral Cunningham, who was the commander of Allied Naval Forces in Africa; our Admiral Kent Hewitt who served him as the American commander. We sat and heard all of the story of Mark Clark and Jerry Wright's landing on the beaches of North Africa ahead of the troops, and how Mark Clark lost his trousers as they disembarked into a small rubber boat. Also about Admiral (then Captain) Jerry Wright's being designated commander of a British submarine that would bring off General Henri Giraud, who had been finally accepted as the head of French forces in Africa. He had been in a German prison and they had somehow or other managed to get him out of there and got him aboard the British submarine to bring him to Africa. But he refused to sail under the British flag and they promptly decommissioned the British submarine, recommissioned it an American submarine, but Jerry Wright in command and with all the British crew, took General Giraud from France to Algiers.

Later, when we returned to Dakar, Giraud came down and they had quite a hoopla and hurrah for him in Dakar. That is really when the log jam of French sentiment broke. When Giraud arrived in Dakar he solidified the French to support the Allied Forces.

We saw, and visited with, Bob Murphy in his villa in Algiers. We were in the Hotel St. George, which was the headquarters of the American military officers in Algiers at a time when a rather interesting event took place. The Germans had been particularly active in the Mediterranean and had blown the hell out of American ships and all kinds of merchant ships in the harbor. One of them they got was an American ship that had a large group of American woemn on board coming overseas as nurses or as WACS. They had had a real rough time because the ship was sunk out from under them and they were brought into Algiers in the most outlandish assortment of cothing you ever did see. I can quote you from my earlier written recollections - "we had our final meal at the officer's mess in the Army Allied Forces headquarters. There we saw a bunch of sorry looking American females. They were WACS and Army nurses. They had lost all their clothing and uniforms. They were all decked out in British battle dress - a sort of heavy woolen coverall which does nothing to enhance the female beauty. They sure weren't glamorous but plenty spirited. It takes plenty of nerve after such an experience to settle down less than four hundred miles from the front. They received a standing ovation from all the personnel who were there at the Hotel St. George."

Then we were told to get ready. We were to depart for Casablanca aboard a B-17 plane that had been commandeered from an Army Air Force Recon Squadron. The plane commander was Lieutenant Colonel Elliot Roosevelt. Up to this time nobody had said that we were going to Casablanca to find our President there. We knew we were going to find Ernie King but his presence confirmed what I had believed ever since that message about this Roosevelt ramp - that, indeed, we were going to see the President in Casablanca.

Q: And Glassford knew this.

James: Glassford knew this. So we set out by plane. There was Jerry Wright, Julius Holmes who had been part of our group down in Dakar, Admiral Glassford, myself, and one or two other hitch-hikers, I guess. We flew in to Casablanca but on the way we hit a nasty bump in the air that dropped us about three hundred feet and to within fifty feet of the top of one of the Atlas Mountain peaks that were in Spanish Morocco. We had come along the Mediterranean coast and avoided flying right out over the Sahara desert. We had taken this course and gotten ourselves into bad weather. Inside the cockpit of the airplane we were all scrambled about but it wasn't until about three hours later when we landed in Casablanca that we realized how close we had come to not making it at all. In the under carriage of our airplane were branches of a tree top we had hit.

Admiral Glassford, being the senior officer on board, was privileged to sit down in the greenhouse, as they call it in the B-17, the bombardiers cockpit. I think he was still shaking from the experience because he and the pilot were the only two who saw what had happened. It was perhaps my closest call during the war.

The return to Casablanca started the inspection of certain of the French ships and particularly the JEAN BART. Before this visit I had called at the naval headquarters and there, flanking the stairway into the Naval Headquarters, were a number of sixteen inch shells from the American battleship MASSACHUSETTS that had been fired at French installations in Casablanca harbor and had not detonated. The French had defanged them and mounted them on the stairway; they made quite a point of the fact that our armament and our artillery was pretty sad. Of course, I had witnessed what had happened to their own in the RICHELIEU so I could exchange insults in a friendly way with them about our respective short comings.

Q: Incidentally, quite a point was made in the White House and the Ordnance Bureau too about those shells from the MASSACHUSETTS.

James: It was something I saw evern more graphically when I got aboard the JEAN BART. The captain of the ship met me when I came on board and was downright insulting because he had been under attack less than three weeks, or a month, before by the

Americans, and here was a young pipsqueak Lieutenant Commander running loose on the bases. I was supposed to be given the freedom of his ship, which he resented greatly but he carried out his orders. After acknowledging my presence aboard and refusing my extended hand shake, he departed and from then on I was taken on a tour by officers of the ship. I was shown how these shells had penetrated the armour of the JEAN BART and had traveled from virtually the bow to the stern opening great holes enroute but failing to detonate and failing to set off any ammunition aboard the ship causing casualties to be sure and damage to the ship but all of them of minor order in magnitude. The French were rather tickled with this, if one could be happy about anything when being attacked. They had taken, I believe, a dozen or more large sixteen inch shells and not a single one of them detonated.

The visit aboard the JEAN BART, however, generated, in my mind, the obvious solution to the RICHELIEU and her defunct main battery. They were sister ships and had identical artillery. Those on the JEAN BART were undamaged and she was only about sixty to sixty-five pcercent completed. There was a great deal of work that would have to be done to the ship as a whole to bring her into useful service. I speculated it couldn't be done in anything short of about five or six years because of the difference in the metric system used by their designers and our own who used the decimal system. We, therefore, had quite extensive and soon rather acrimonious debates, the French and I, about my suggestion that we take the guns off the JEAN BART, ship the guns to New York and then outfit the RICHELIEU that would steam from Dakar to New York with the JEAN BART'S guns aboard. That way we would put one French battleship into service and I estimated in less than a year's time. I was speculating it could even be considerably less.

The French saw in JEAN BART and RICHELIEU the epitomy of their own naval ship design and were completely unwilling to see either ship ignored. Admiral Fenard made quite an issue of it. He was the one who later came to Washington. In the course of our meetings in Casablanca, Admiral Glassford proposed to Admiral King that the plan to move RICHELIEU to New York and strip JEAN BART of her battery was the only way to get us one ship in a reasonable hurry. Admiral King embraced this suggestion. He presented it and succeeded in this program before the Joint Allied Conference that was going on. I lived to hear that one every time the French were introduced to me after I returned to Washington - "Oh, yes, you are the gentleman who torpedoed the French desire to have the two new battle ships put into service." Admiral Fenard went so far as to offer me the number one French decoration if I would change my recommendation and get both JEAN BART and RICHELIEU repaired. I didn't yield and the French have been rather critical of me ever since because that apparently was a great blow to their naval pride.

Q: This is fairly typical of their reactions to the whole thing, isn't it? Pride gets in the way of over-all objectives.

James: Yes. It was a matter of pride because actually to fight the war (and we were guessing it might go on for four or five years) we would have one ship and if we tried to do both of them we would have none. We would have had the RICHELIEU ahead of the JEAN BART but it would still be two or three years to get those replacement guns built.

Q: What about the problem of supplying the guns with ammunition?

James: That was no problem because our ordnance people seemed to think they could do this relatively quickly. Remember that both ships had come out with their full suit of ammunition on board so until they had expended that they were capable of operating.

To make a long story short, the RICHELIEU did come to New York; she did get the JEAN BART's guns and she went back out in service. I can't recall how quickly we did it because by that time I was out in the Pacific but she went back in and fought the war for at least two and a half years. I guess they took the JEAN BART back in to St. Nazaire after the war and finished her themselves.

The Casablanca Conference, itself, was a delightful experience for a young kid, (I might now judge myself then to have been). In our first approach to Casablanca we stopped a night in Marrakdsh at the

Mamounikin Hotel. The Germans had just evacuated the hotel property only a matter of a week or two before we got there. While we were there, the entire British empire, the entire American government, descended on Marrakesh for a one night stand prior to convening at the Hotel Anfa in Casablanca.

Q: Of course, that's one of Churchill's favorite spots.

James: When Glassford, his aide Allen Morris, and I arrived, Glassford said, "Now clean up and take a bath. We're going out and have cocktails with the British vice consul." I had taken sick on the trip in, not bad sick, just miserable sick, so I thought the opportunity to sleep on a decent bed instead of on a straw pad which had been my lot at the Governor's Palace in Dakar, that I would skip it. So I begged off. Glassford didn't debate too hard with me, or didn't clue me in on what he knew. There was to be a party for Roosevelt and Churchill in a completely informal environment at the Consulate. I could have broken my arm the next morning when the aide, Allen Morris, told me what had happened that night.

Several days later, after having been to Algiers and returned, when we arrived at the Anfa Hotel in Casablanca, I met the entire British empire. Glassford and I and Morris walked into an ante-room waiting to be received by Admiral King just as the doors opened from a meeting room. Out stalked a couple of aides, followed by Winnie Churchill and all the rest of the brass of the Royal Navy, the Royal Army and the Air Force. The ante-room in nothing flat was a shambles of people having tea - this was the place for a little relaxation. There were candy bars by the dozens - it was the place where they convened for their social relaxation from their conferences. As soon as the word was out, in fact the instant the door opened, they knew that Admiral Glassford was in the room so the Premier and his people surrounded Glassford and stood around while he talked. He told them all of what he had been doing. They were primarily interested in the development of the treaty with the French in Dakar.

I was standing off at the side, generally being ignored by the group who were so eager to see Glassford and talk to him until a very handsome, tall captain in the Royal navy came sidling up and stood beside me. He introduced himself but I didn't get his name. We started chatting about various things and in nothing flat this man made me feel that I, too, belonged to this conference, which indeed I did but I was then Mr. Small-fry at the garden party. Later I said to him, " I didn't get your name?" He said, "Louie Mountbatten." Then I realized it was Lord Louis Mountbatten, who had been captain of the KELLY. It was the story of his escape from the KELLY that I had read in some of the damage reports that made me realize that this was just not an ordinary Navy captain - this was Lord Louie, himself.

He was the most gracious, intelligent, delightful person I met in my entire war time experience amongst our allies. He had particularly gone out of his way to see that this young lieutenant commander was embraced within the warmth of the group. He saw to it personally that I shook Winnie's hand that of Dudley Pound, the head of the Navy, and the Air Marshal, Portel, the chief of the Air Forces, Sir John Dill the head of the Army -- I had a field day. Also the Admiral Cunningham. There was a General Cunningham and an Admiral Cunningham, as I recall it. They were brothers. One was Army and the other was Navy. We had a wonderful experience on that moment.

Shortly afterwards we were called in to see Admiral King and others of his staff. We presented the recommendations and I will read another little statement from my recollections prepared earlier:

"Admiral Glassford was delighted with the results of the conference, especially as he had sold the complete bill of goods to Admiral King. He paid me an extremely fine compliment when he said, 'I'll never mention this again in your (Admiral King's) presence, but Jimmy did it all and I want to give him the full credit.'"

Well, that didn't hurt a lieutenant commander one iota, believe me. That was the decision to send certain ships from Dakar to various U. S. Navy yards -- to Charleston, to Philadelphia, to New York, to Boston. I think we had the cruisers in Philadelphia, the destroyers in Charleston and Boston. The RICHELIEU went to New York. We didn't bring back any French submarines, at that time.

Q: That was no small feat because our Navy yards were

crowded to the gills, weren't they?

James: Yes, but it was necessary to work out schedules for their arrival based on, first, their availability and capability of moving, and second, whether the Navy yards could handle them and the acquisition of parts and materials in our own Navy yards to deal with their repair problems, design changes, and the conversion of drawings. It was a thrilling experience for an engineer type because seldom do you get in to such a high level of political-military operational responsibility that it was then my extremely delightful pleasure to enjoy.

After I came back, as a side light here, I found life in Washington very dull. I was looking for another way to get out which I managed to generate in about two or three months after I returned. Then I went to the Pacific theater for two years.

Q: Perhaps at this point it would be well to include a paragraph about Admiral Glassford himself.

James: Admiral Glassford was a polished naval officer, impeccable in dress and manner. He used to affect a little winch-like arrangement on a pair of eye glasses. The winch would curl up the cord that held them suspended while they were on his nose - a sort of pinch type set of glasses. He looked every inch what a polished naval diplomat should be, and he was that in fact. His brother is General Pelham Glassford who had been the Chief of

Police during the bonus marchers assault on Washington back in 1932. So the name of Glassford was a household word, although Bill Glassford had been out in the Philippines at the outset of the war. I believe he was deputy to Admiral Hart out there. He was brought out of the Philippines in a submarine. He had commanded the naval forces over there but, of course, they had been blasted to bits and scattered around. He was brought back to the States and, for reasons that I don't know, he was ordered to the Sixth Naval District rather than any sea command. There are people who never did hold him in very high regard as a tactician but as a diplomat he was perhaps the greatest that I have ever known in the Navy. He was a practical diplomat and I'm sure this is the reason he very wisely was selected for this mission because it was a diplomatic effort. He succeeded in getting the treaty signed and he did all these other things that I've emphasized more because they were in my own sphere, but he did everything he was sent over there to do and then he was returned to West Africa after the so-called Glassford Mission concluded its business, about 1943. He was returned to be sort of a naval commander of forces operating in and around Dakar. With his entree that he had earned during the Glassford Mission phases, I'm sure he was a very capable one. He later took his wife with him, who was a British woman, a very delightful person whom later, unfortunately he divorced. He remarried a younger person whom he had met who is still alive today — she is a charming individual.

Q: Had you known him prior to this?

James: I had never laid an eye on Admiral Glassford until the day in November when we were told to meet with him in a small room in the Main Navy Building to learn what this mission was all about. It was a delightful experience. We maintained contact thereafter, always very pleasant. I always held him in extremely high regard.

Q: During your visit to Algiers and Casablanca did you have an opportunity to witness the tremendous operation that Sully (RADM Wm. A. Sullivan) performed?

James: As I mentioned when I was in Casablanca I stayed with Sullivan in his own apartment. Yes, I saw the work there in Casablanca. He had not moved into personal command of the operation in Algiers. I wish I could think of the other harbor that he did considerable work on - the one that the French Navy retreated to from Toulon at the outset of the war - oh yes, Oran. Sully did a fabulous job and raised ships in a hurry that were seemingly going to take years to clear out of the harbor. Some of them he even had headed back for service in very short order. He had a very fine group of hard fishted boatswain mate type sailor salvage experts with him. He did a fantastic job.

From Admiral James' diary:

"Our arrival in Casablanca was most inauspicious. We had been expected the previous day so a lunch had been planned that day in our honor. All hands were attending the luncheon and none were on hand to greet us. I'm getting rank spoiled, traveling in the reflected glory of the admiral. It does make matters simpler, though. I'm quartered in the hotel apartment of Captain Bill Sullivan from the Bureau of Ships. This is a very pleasant break for me. We had many pleasant conversations about his work salvaging the sunken ships in the harbor."

I note in my diary that I mention throughout my stay in Casablanca that there was very severe shortage of the kind of food we expect for dinner at home. Sully was then working on a merchant ship that had been sunk off the entrance to the harbor in Casablanca. It carried a number of hundred and five howitzer cannons that he was attempting to recover. One day he had an idea that he had found that in addition to guns and ammunition there was a lot of still usable food stuffs on board, so the salvage crews managed to roust out things like butter, canned meats, sugar, and things that were hard to get. He had found an old French chef who had been the head chef and teacher for young chefs on the French line passenger ships, named Papa Gouin. Sully dredged up all the food for a special affair and took it out to "Papa's" place, to be prepared by this expert chef. There were twelve of us including Jerry Wright, a couple of American girls and one French girl. We had the time of our life and a gourmet dinner on that occasion. In my diary I wrote,"the Americans present were Capt. Sullivan, Capt. Wright, Col. Holmes, Allen Morris, Chalmers Graham, and myself. Lt. and Mrs. Salbaing were present. They had just been informed he was to go to the United States as a member of the French mission. He can thank me for that as I had asked Admiral Michelier (Commander, French Navy), to send him. They were planning to send a naval constructor from Dakar whom I did not hold in very high regard and who spoke no English. I pointed out the importance of English speaking officers on a mission so Admiral Michelier concurred and this was Salbaing's prize. They gasped in amazement at seeing him. After dinner we had a pleasant time singing French-American songs. The whole restaurant caught the spirit of our party and it turned out to be quite an American-French love feast."

That was one of the bits of magic that your friend Sully was able to promote out there. I think the name of the ship that was sunk was the HERMITAGE, from which he not only recovered the guns, but he recovered these canned hams, canned butter, and things that Papa Gouin had not seen in Dakar in a year or more.

Q: And that had a more immediate application.

Interview #4 with Rear Admiral Ralph K. James
Annapolis, Maryland   April 6, 1971
Subject: Biography   by John T. Mason, Jr.

Mr. Mason: It's good to see you this morning, Admiral. I think you want to talk about the aftermath to the Casablanca Conference and the return journey.

Rear Admiral James: Yes, I would like to do that, Dr. Mason. There are certain little incidents in connection with our return to Dakar and ultimately to the United States that I think are of some considerable interest although certainly of no historical significance. The party of which I was a part, including Admiral Glassford and his military aide, and myself returned to Dakar by aircraft leaving Casablanca the sixteenth of January, 1943. We proceeded across the Atlas Mountains. Our plane was a DC-3 with short legs so it became necessary to stop at a desert refueling station, a place called Atar.

Q: Did you, during that return journey, suffer from any apprehension because of the experience on the way up?

James: No, not at all. We had, of course, seen the change in the attitude of the people in Dakar and we didn't anticipate any further difficulty. In fact when we landed at Atar we were warmly greeted by the officers of the French Camel Corps, for which this was an outpost. That experience is one I shan't forget. I think the best I might do is read from some correspondence that I prepared at that time to describe the experience. "We are guests of the French Camel Corps for lunch. They are composed of a handful of officers who are virtually sentenced to live in this remote location. They seem all to have gone native. The uniform they wear is a blouse with big baggy pantaloons and sandals. They look like tramps. At lunch we were in direct competition with the flies for every morsel of food on our plate. I've never seen them so thick. We had to keep brushing at each forkful of food as it passed to your mouth to keep from swallowing a few flies that had perched there. My wine glass was filled, and as I reached for it, two flies nosedived for a bath before I could touch it. Food is even more scarce here than in Dakar. We had the unique experience of eating camel steak. It really was quite good but the idea was a little strange and one of our number, who learned that it was camel and remembering that camels are never slaughtered but rather permitted only to die of old age or disease before they are eaten, became quite ill during the experience."

We returned to Dakar and found by this time (several weeks had elapsed since our departure) the Americans had arrived in full force. There were Army troops in charge of constructing a large base there in Dakar and the air field which, incidentally, still remains. We saw it this past winter when we went through Dakar on our around the world cruise. As soon as we returned to Dakar, Admiral Glassford made it clear that the information we had acquired about the situation in the French fleet both in Casablanca, Algiers as well as in Dakar needed to be returned immediately to the United States. Three of us were peeled off from the mission and directed to return, which we did by way of Liberia where Pan American Airways had a station. Their big old Clipper aircraft were being used to carry in Americans and ferry out raw rubber to add to the meager supply that was entering the United States during the war.

Our plane was reconfigured at the airport in Liberia so as to become a cargo plane but they quickly put aboard six seats for the three officers returning, which included Captains Harris and Haven and myself.

Q: What was the status of the merchant vessels there in the harbor at that point?

James: I had little enough time after our return to Dakar and before our departure for the United States to inquire into the state of the Merchant Marine. Through an American chap who had taken over for the War Shipping Board, Mr. Chalmers Graham, I did learn that in the few days that he was on board he had succeeded in actually moving the first ships out of Dakar. That was noticeable progress but the extent of it I really did not learn.

Q: Ultimately they all were . . .

James: Ultimately they all were returned to service with the Allied forces, either under their original nation of registry or under flags of Britain or the United States. You recall that I was rather critical of the gentleman, Mr. Hoyt by name, who had been sent out earlier from Great Britain by Lloyds of London from the insurance elements of our ally. His successor Mr. Graham was surprised, if not non-plussed, to be suddenly thrust in the middle of this African environment. I remember divesting myself of all of the soap and foodstuffs that I had squirreled when I was in Dakar or up north. I turned them over to him with great regret as I wasn't sure if we could get proper meals where we were headed for. Mr. Graham, incidentally, was an Admiralty attorney from San Francisco. He returned there after the war and became rather well established in the merchant marine industry.

On our return from Liberia, we landed first in Natal, Brazil. Our plane was largely a cargo plane but the Pan American officials (contrary to the rules that governed these flights) placed aboard six bottles of liquor for the three naval officers that were returning. The lack of anything to do but sit and enjoy the liquor on the long trip across the Atlantic was a little too much for one of our number. It became necessary for the Pan Am steward, Capt. Harris, and myself literally to physically restrain Capt. Benny Haven, who seemed possessed with the idea of wanting to take the airplane apart while in mid-air over the Atlantic.

Q: As a precursor of a high-jacker.

James: No, this was not with the intent of diverting our landing site but rather to show what inspiration a belly full of booze can give a person who wants to fight the war but forgot which side he was on. It was quite a hairy experience until we finally and deliberately, by giving him more booze, knocked him out that we were able to proceed in peace. We arrived in Natal shortly after midnight of the day we departed from Dakar, the twentieth of January.

We transferred to a new plane, a Clipper again, which still had passenger configuration. It was interesting that some of the passengers being placed aboard the airplane were survivors of a tanker that had burned off Natal while we were there on our outbound trip. The survivors were brought to the same hospital where we were billeted and the staff despaired of their survival because of the serious burns that about three crewmen had. We were able to recognize one individual, through masses of bandages, had an interesting conversation with him on our way back to Miami.

That was the end of the journey except, of course, for the return to Washington which took place on the twenty-third of January. We had one diversion, when we landed in Miami. Our first objective was to get a good square American meal. We arrived very early in the morning and we went to the Columbus Hotel, freshened up and went down to the dining room. They brought us the menu, there were four in the party by this time. We proceeded to order bacon, eggs, ham, sausage, pancakes, fresh milk. The waitress looked at us in utter amazement and said, "Don't you men know there's a war on?" This triggered our rather short fused Capt. Lenny Haven who climbed aboard this poor girl and demanded to see the manager. He reported this unintentional insult to the manager and said, "Where do you think we've just come from?" With this, they broke out the bacon, and the ham, and the sausage which was not to have been served that day because it was a meatless day. This was our first exposure to the restrictions our civilian population was suffering from.

Return to Washington began a rather prosaic period after the exciting experience of being reasonably close to the center of power in the European and African theater as a part of the Glassford Mission. I began to make noises about trying again to move out of the Bureau and Washington. I was told that I was desperately needed to run the Aircraft Carrier Desk because of the many serious casualties that had occurred to our aircraft carrier fleet at the beginning of the war. I was saved however by the visit from the South Pacific of (then) Capt. Roy T. Cowdrey, EDO, who was on the staff of Admiral Halsey and Admiral Cobb in Noumea, New Caldonia where the Third Fleet was then headquartered. Cowdrey needed a naval constructor assistant and asked for my services. Admiral Cochrane was Chief of the Bureau of Ships at the time. I guess I had made enough unpleasant noises about being unhappy being back in Washington so he interposed no objection to my release from Bureau after a five month turn over period. That was a long five month period. Finally in June I was given my orders and proceeded to the South Pacific.

Q: What was happening on the aircraft desk at that time? Were you involved with the jeep carriers?

James: Oh yes. We were deeply involved with the jeep carriers. An incident that perhaps isn't too generally known about the jeep carrier is the important role President Roosevelt had in the creation of that idea. I had only recently been on the desk, and this was before the Dakar affair, when I was summoned to the White House along with one of my senior officers. We met with a naval aide and presented with a very simple little pencil sketch on what had to be a scrap of paper, which I was told President Roosevelt had sketched his idea of how the Jeep carriers should look. He had heard of how our Navy had begun to embroider upon the original British design trying to make these ships more like a conventional aircraft carrier rather than like a converted merchantman. He wanted to initiate a project to convert available tankers which he thought should serve, not as aircraft carriers but as aircraft transport ships.

Q: Just for carrying the planes?

James: Right. With some ability to fly planes on and off but primarily more for the purpose of transporting planes to the war front. He had just sketched on a scrap of paper, what he thought the ship ought to look like.

Q: This coincided with the difficulty in transporting fighters across the North Atlantic.

James: Yes. The legs on the fighter aircraft were too short to make the flight on a single fueling. Roosevelt's little thoughts and notes were handed us and I was simply the instrument of transmitting them back to the Bureau whereupon we proceeded with what is now known as Commencment Bay or the CVS-105 class, largely a Roosevelt concept. As historians have reported, Roosevelt was an avid naval buff having once served as Assistant Secretary of Navy so his interests in naval matters were very great. During the time I was in Africa, we had begun the delivery of new attack aircraft carriers. I think we had seven at the outset of the war -- three were immediately lost or severely damaged and our aircraft carrier strength at one time was down to four carriers.

On my way to Noumea I went through Pearl Harbor. While I was there I had the great thrill of seeing three brand new aircraft carriers at the Pearl Harbor Naval Base. They had just arrived. These were ships of the ESSEX class. The aircraft carrier strength was picking up in the Pacific.

Q: It was the ESSEX and the BUNKER HILL and . . .

James: I don't recall the sequence of the ships but the ESSEX was the lead ship and gave the name to the class. While I was enroute to the South Pacific my family and I drove across country. It became necessary to place them in residence in Los Angeles. I was able to remain there for a scant week to see them located in a house without furniture -- our furniture being enroute. My wife's mother and father were resident in Los Angeles which is why we chose that place. It was a real wrench to leave them in such an unfinished state, things were very crude. We had bought one table and a set of chairs from Sears and Roebuck. We used boxes and crates and a few borrowed beds to make it possible to exist, emptied our suitcases, and that's the way I had to leave them.

The trip out to the South Pacific was rather uneventful, all by air. Over the Pacific we lost an engine and had to go into Johnston Island and sit down for about five days while they flew in a new engine. We proceeded from there to Noumea where I was quickly made a member of the fleet maintenance staff of commander Service Squadron South Pacific, under Admiral Granny Cobb. Cobb was a member of Admiral Halsey's staff of the Third Fleet.

Q: Your branch of the operation was based on Noumea?

James: Yes, where Cowdrey had set up the usual quonset hut type of headquarters. He had a number of younger engineering officers whose job was to coordinate the work on the damaged ships and perform the regular maintenance and overhaul of the ships of the Third Fleet which were in and out of Noumea. Our area extended up through the Solomons to the bases at Tulagi and Guadalcanal. The big base, of course, was the one at Espiritu Santo but it had only limited repair facilities at the time of my arrival.

Q: Did you have a graving dock?

James: No. The Navy moved in the first of the hundred thousand ton sectional floating dry docks, the ABSD-1. Building up of the base to accommodate the repairs on ships in that dock had begun. Capt. Eddie Craig (EDO) was there doing the preliminary work.

One of the first tasks I was given by Admiral Cowdrey was to develop the requirements of that base for use as a major repair facility, the major advanced repair facility in the Pacific. I devoted a number of months and quite a bit of travel reviewing the requirements with the fleet commands inventorying the available assets and beginning ordering of needed materials and equipment from stateside. After about five or six months these things began to flow into Espiritu by which time Capt. Craig had moved on to Tulagi where the fleet focal point was at that particular stage of the war.

Q: I suppose that was a problem in your planning, too, the fact that the hope for advance would make that not a forward base very soon.

James: It was a forward base in the sense of being in the far Pacific but it was really a rear base in the sense of its size and capability. It was intended to be a place to which the ships would return after more advanced operations. This they continued to do even as our forces moved well up and until we took another forward base at Manus in the Admiralty Islands.

Q: Did you also, then, have to think in terms of recreation

and so forth?

James: No. Those facilities were already well established. A commodore, Jimmy Boak, who had command of the base at Espiritu Santo and had begun the development of the facilities there that supported the entire fleet, this included recreational facilities, large clubs for enlisted and officer personnel -- in fact we had the most beautiful officers' club I've ever seen in anybody's country in any circumstance. It was created by the Seabees using Quonset huts, palm trees and was located on a high point overlooking the bay at Espiritu Santo. It was very, very popular with visiting ships personnel.

My part was the planning for the expansion of ship repair facilities at this base in collaboration with Captain Cowdrey. He was reluctant to put me in charge of the new repair base, as he felt that I was quite junior. I was then just a fresh caught three striper. Even though I had done a major portion of planning for the repair base, Capt. Craig anticipated that he would receive the command assignment, and was quite distressed when it was finally agreed that I would go and take charge.

Q: Admiral, perhaps at this stage it would be fitting to comment on the problem of getting supplies from the States directed toward the Pacific.

James: I think this is an essential ingredient to our conversation but if you will bear with me I'll come to it when I think it is the appropriate time.

When I arrived in Espiritu we had begun the ship repair build up. We had not one, but three, floating dry docks, the major one being the ABSD-1. It was capable of taking anything afloat. It had a hundred thousand ton lift capacity. It could lift our largest aircraft carriers and our battleships. We had also had moved in a number of repair ships. Santo previously had had only the USS DIXIE.

I elected to be based ashore. We had a ship repair unit on the beach and about six repair ships were ultimately assigned to this area, so we began the overhaul of major ships. One of the major crisis that we had to face early in my tenure was a collision between the battleships TENNESSEE and CALIFORNIA. It took place just outside the harbor of Espiritu Santo when the fleet was staging there before an assault up in the Central Pacific. The TENNESSEE and the CALIFORNIA were two of the major units that were in the Op plan for the action.

Q: It was probably for the assault on Makin.

James: It might have been. The TENNESSEE rammed the CALIFORNIA and tore its whole bow section to shreds. There were quite a number of casualties as the chief petty officers' quarters were located up forward in the damaged area. I was asked to do my very damnedest to get these ships back on the line at the earliest possible minute which meant four days after the collision, the period of time planned for staging in Espiritu. We concentrated our forces on these two ships. We had to put the TENNESSEE in the drydock and began the repair of the CALIFORNIA afloat because hers was the lesser damage. I was able to get her out in four days with some real jury-rigging which we had to invent. One of our bigger problems at Espiritu was the non-availability of materials and parts, particularly for repairing shipboard equipments. Working around the clock, we succeeded and got the CALIFORNIA out when the fleet sortied. That was a great relief to her commander and the commander of the Task Force. The TENNESSEE, however, was a different story. We had to rip out all the damaged material and remove a few bodies that had been trapped below decks and below the water line. We got her out in twenty-one days doing a repair job that in the shipyard at home normally would have taken about two months to do. We had just smothered her with manpower and again had to jury-rig material because here we had many parts and many equipments that were damaged that were not in the local supplies. We cannibalized ships that were going to be around for a longer period of time, including our own repair ships, removing fans, pumps, switchboards, and the like.

There were a couple of sunken ships in the harbor that we used to send divers in to remove items to supplement our meager supplies. I used to refer to the repair job in a forward base as learning to make bricks without straw because you had to innovate all the time.

Perhaps one of the greatest innovators was a classmate of

mine, Bill Alderman. He had a destroyer that had its stern blown off during the height of the operations up The Slot near the Tulagi, Guadalcanal area. He tied up his badly damaged ship in Tulagi Harbor, camouflaged it and went ashore where he found enemy telephone poles. They jury-rigged a rudder with these poles and were able to proceed to safety with this rig, long before our repair base was established. This was typical of the type of innovating you had to do in the forward areas to move the ships back to home bases for permanent repairs or to repair them adequately locally to continue operations.

Q: You mentioned the fact there were a couple of sunken ships at Espiritu. Was Espiritu subject to Japanese air attack at that time?

James: No. These had been there since the invasion of Espiritu by American forces when the Japanese contested our entrance. One was an American ship, I believe the PRESIDENT WILSON, that hit a mine in our own mine field while entering port. It was a transport. The captain very wisely beached her as soon as it happened because he was in a hundred and fifty feet of water at the time. He rammed her into the shore at full speed. People leapt to safety over the bow although the ship finally slid off the bank and sank in a hundred and fifty feet of water only yards off the beach. She had a wealth of material on board. We were so short of the essential items of shipboard hardware that I organized a regular diving school to train divers and at the same time to recover many items which we used in many applications.

Q: Where had you acquired your salvage technique?

James: Salvage is always, of course, an item of training for a naval constructor. In those days we did a little diving ourselves and knew how to work under water. We had to do this sometimes for the more prosaic things of simply repairing or replacing propellers.

Also while I was in Noumea we had a tremendous storm at a time when a large number of the Third Fleet ships were in the harbor. Several ships tried to sally forth out of the harbor but the route was tortuous and long and about a dozen of them wound up grounded on the coral reefs. Then and there I had a postgraduate course in ship salvage before I had been in the South Pacific more than a few months. Admiral Cowdrey was the chief salvage officer for the South Pacific and we learned fast.

Off Efati I had a little salvage job on a small mine sweeper that had gotten fouled up in the channel and gone aground on the coral. After flying over it and surveying it, and going out to it by boat, and realizing how badly she was damaged, we decided to abandon her, not, however, until we had stripped her of everything that had potential use. We were only one leap ahead of the local natives, I might add, who were doing the same thing.

Speaking of spare parts, which were a constant headache, I had a rather funny incident that occurred when we had great need for valve inserts on some diesel engines. Two small diesel engined subchasers were immobilized for lack of these particular parts and no amount of pleading with the Naval Supply Depot at Mechanicsburg would produce the necessary parts by air or any other means. It was getting to the point where these ships were an embarrassment to the force commander and to our repair forces. One day while lamenting the absence of these particular pieces, one of my sailors came to me and said, "Commander, do you know there are two brand new complete engines of the same type on this island and of course they've got valve inserts inside them. Would you consider taking the engines apart to get the valve inserts?" I replied vigorously and affirmatively. I said, "Where are they?" He said, "The Army owns them. They're in a compound up on the Army base." I said, "Well, that ought to be simple. I'll just call the commanding general (whom I knew quite well) and proposition him." The general said, "Of course you may have them but let me first identify who is in charge and I'll call you back."

Instead, I got a call from a colonel who said, "Commander, you got the wrong dope. There's no complete diesel engine on the inventory of the Army at any post on this island. At the insistence of the commanding general I have scoured every possible Army activity." I said, "My people tell me differently." He said, "No, I'm sure there are not."

So I called the sailor back in and I said, "Where are they?" He told me and I said, "I'll call the colonel back." I did and I repeated my urgent need and I got a refusal again, as there "was just no such engine available." Finally I was driven up to the Army compound and saw what looked like boxes of engines behind high chain link fences.

Q: They were not being used in any way, then?

James: No. So rather than try again to get them out of the Army's hands, I decided we would handle this little maneuver ourselves, but at night. We developed a conceived plan of night riders with points and counter points to attack these two boxes inside this fence, placing some of our jeeps outside to provide illumination for the work to be done. The operation went off without a hitch. We took the boxes apart and got into the engines, pulled the heads, and removed the needed valve inserts. We were highly elated. So back we went and very quickly we started the repair work on the two sub chasers.

The next morning I had to rub it in to the Army so I called them and told them that we had not only violated their security undetected, but had found the engines and taken the parts that we needed. And no thanks to them, the repairs on the ship were going on. This irritated the colonel who said, "I still don't believe it." We then arranged that I should show him where these engines were, which were still in need of being tidied up and boxed up again. We went up to his compound and walked up to these boxes. As I did, I noticed the shipping designator stenciled on the side of the box was FRAY 94, my own activity. These crates had been misdirected when they arrived at Espiritu Santo and somehow had gotten into the Army's compound and were not taken up in Army inventory. We had gone to all this trouble to purloin parts from our own diesel engines. But that, to a degree, gives evidence of the extent one had to go to to find the pieces and parts to make it possible to put our ships back in full service.

Q: When you say all the importunings possible to Mechanicsburg didn't produce any results, was it because they could not comply or was it because they were just a little lax in complying?

James: This is part of my history that comes along at a later date. Suffice it to say that being of a rather violent nature, and being frustrated by what I thought was the inadequacies of a shoreside supply station, I fired numerous and less than restrained telegrams back to Mechanicsburg to the Bureau of Ships and to the Bureau of Supplies and Accounts, protesting the poor repair parts supply situation in the forward areas. I didn't know as I was doing this, that these messages were being accumulated and were to become an embarrassing experience that affected an assignment of mine two years later. We'll get to that in due course.

The work at Espiritu Santo was a fabulously exciting job. We handled everything from merchant ship repairs to the CALIFORNIA and TENNESSEE collision damage, and many other battle damaged ships.

Q: Was Espiritu subject to air attacks at this point?

James: We had one air attack. No bombs ever fell in the areas where my repair facilities were located. We were virtually outside the range of Jap aircraft.

Q: That certainly was a plus to the progress of your plans.

James: Yes. We were not harassed by that problem at all. In fact it was a very pleasant experience in addition to being a very rewarding experience. I remember one battle damaged repair job, the NASHVILLE, then commanded by Capt. Yen Coney. Yen, incidentally, now Admiral Coney, is retired and living here in Annapolis. We got the NASHVILLE because she had suffered several near miss bomb explosions at the after end of the ship. She was a composite ship, meaning that she was of both welded and riveted construction. Her armor plate, special treatment steel in the after end of the ship around the steering room, was riveted. She had been built at a time we were not too sure of techniques for building composite ships. I was loath to do a weld job in repairing her damage, because I was fearful that we might adversely affect the strength of the armor and the watertightness of the ship. So I put out a call to my repair activities for riveters. By this time I believe we had eight repair ships present. In response to my signal, I got exactly three people who admitted of being riveters. I sent for them and to my dismay I learned that they were all aircraft aluminum riveters. There wasn't a steel ship riveter on the entire base and I didn't know what we were going to do. Finally I raised this issue with the warrant officer who had been on the ABSD-1 as assistant docking officer, a Mr. Landry. I learned that he had been a steel riveter during his earlier days. He was the only person I could find who knew how to really heat, handle and drive rivets. So around him I started a training program of anyone who had ever riveted at all or who thought he might want to learn to rivet. We started this at the beginning of tearing out damaged structure from the NASHVILLE so we weren't in desperate need of qualified riveters until maybe a week or two later.

Q: Did you yourself have some special knowledge in this?

James: I had riveted and knew enough how to proceed. I was not a riveter. I couldn't have done this job but at least I knew how to tell people to do it and others were quick to catch on to the technique. In the short time we had three or four riveters and before long we had about a dozen and that took care of our armor plate problem.

I can remember Capt. Coney having grave doubts whether we were ever going to finish his ship, but we did. I had not seen him again until he drove around the corner of our home right here in Providence one day recently. I recognized him and hollered so he stopped and we reminisced about it. He said, "You know we never had a leak or a groan, or a creak in that area from that time on." That, again, was an example of improvisation.

Q: What percentage of the ships you worked on were you able to complete the repairs entirely and what percent had to be sent back to the States?

James: The percentage that went back to the states was extremely low but they were the ones that were badly damaged. The majority were not damaged but were in simply for routine repair and overhaul in anticipation of continued operations. I think the ones that had to be sent back Stateside could have been numbered on the fingers of two hands. We'll get to some of these as we go further along with our interviews. From Espiritu Santo I know of sending one ship back because of inability to make repairs locally. It was the FOOTE, a destroyer, under Capt. Alton Ramsey. She had almost had her whole stern blown off. The best thing we could do was to make limited repairs and send her back to the States. We didn't want to clutter up the facilities with long term battle damage repairs because the docks and manpower were needed for the operating forces.

Q: You couldn't afford to do that.

James: No. If we couldn't anticipate a full and complete repair on the ship by say in a maximum time of thirty days, we wouldn't attempt it. We would do a minimum work needed to get her out and get her back home safely. One of the reasons why Admiral Cochrane was so pleased that I was going out to the Pacific was there had been a couple of ships that had been lost while returning to the U.S. They'd been given a lick and a promise and kissed on the stern and told to proceed. One of them, commanded by now Admiral Tommy Burrowes, didn't make it. This was that sort of thing we wanted to avoid. We always gave the worst battle damaged ships that were to return to the States the lowest priority and hence their stay dragged on and on. It seemed indefinitely in some cases before they were ready to proceed home.

In my experience at Espiritu there were practically no ships that returned Stateside for a full repair through that base. When I went to Manus later, there were a number that we had to return Stateside.

I stayed in Espiritu until about October of '44.

Q: Did you handle any Allied naval ships?

James: Yes, we handled Australians and we had a few French ships that came in. I remember the CAP DE PALM a French frigate, because the skipper was very generous in his praise and in his sharing of his wine locker with those of us ashore.

Q: Did this add to your headaches in terms of parts, and so forth?

James: Generally when you get into a French or an Australian ship you just were incapable of making routine repairs to worn equipment. You would have to build up parts such as worn crank shafts or do what else you could to put them back in service but we had no French replacement parts whatsoever. We began building up a sizable repair parts supply for our own ships in Espiritu Santo.

We also used to read with great interest the manifest on ships transiting Espiritu Santo for the Southwest Pacific then under MacArthur. Admiral Durward Leggett, who later became a chief of the Bureau of Ships, was in charge of the ship repair operations in the Seventh Fleet with headquarters at Brisbane, Australia. He charged (something I have never admitted but it could be true) that we would study ship manifests to see what was coming from Stateside which we could use and then we would intercept these parts in Espiritu Santo.

Q: You were adept at cannibalization so I suppose this is a varient on that.

James: The Statute of Limitations might still not have elapsed so I remain mute. Suffice to say that we had the first opportunity to see what was available on those ships passing through.

We repaired merchant ships on a number of occasions. I remember an innovation that developed in a merchant ship repair and another one on a destroyer repair, both of which have become standard repair practice. We had a destroyer in that had experienced a near miss explosion of a bomb that wrecked its stern tube so that water was leaking badly into the shaft alley and the steering room. We had no dock available at the time and this ship had to get out in a hurry. I reasoned that we could put a pressure on this after compartment that had the leakage and maintain a higher pressure than was causing the water to flow into the ship and proceed with the repairs. It turned out to be very successful although at first my sailors were apprehensive about going in to work under pressure. I had to go in and sit with them and hold their hands but it worked out beautifully and the ship was able to proceed with a full repair. The practice of doing this in lieu of putting ships in dry dock became routine and saved tremendously on the available dry dock time.

Q: Were the things that you learned in that fashion through experimentation passed on to other repair bases?

James: We used to write up the interesting repairs. There was a division created in the Bureau of Ships headed up by Capt. Ernie Holtzworth who came out to the forward bases to interview all the people responsible for repairs to battle damaged ships. He made a full record including photographs and the sketches. So a record was established, maintained, and used in all repair areas.

The other rather interesting repair was to a merchant ship. The ship had a badly leaking condenser. The engineer officer, an old Scotchman, came to me and said, "Laddie, I want some horse manure." I said, "Horse manure -- what for?" He siad, "I've got a bad condenser." I said, "Yes, but why don't we go in and see if we can make a repair by rolling the tubes?" He said, "Oh, no. I've rolled the tubes that I can get to and I continue to have leaks. I need horse manure." I said, "You've got to tell me why." He said, "You know horses, they eat all the oats and the meal. This stuff is never fully digested. You put it in your condenser and it swells up and closes off the leaks."

I began prospecting for a heap of horse manure on Espiritu Santo. While sending out a team to inquire of the French planters, who had horses and who saved their manure. I suddenly thought, if we're simply using the horse as the middle man to eat the oats, why don't we get some Quaker Oats from the galley and do the same thing.

This is exactly what we did and it worked. The Scotchman said, "Laddie, I never thought it would come to this where I go to the cook to get my horse manure."

Q: Of course, the horses on Espiritu Santo might not have eaten oats. They might have eaten something else.

James: Right. He was accustomed with one breed of horses. That was one of my interesting yarns of having to make bricks without straw. While I was in Espiritu Santo I had the privilege of having what we call Rest and Recreation period in Australia where I was given a ten day respite. While I was in Brisbane I stayed one night with Admiral Leggett and suffered further attacks on my alleged piracy on his materials. While there, Leggett received a message that Admiral Cochrane, the Chief of the Bureau of Ships, was making a tour of the area and wanted to go to Sydney. He asked, would I, while in Sydney, serve as his aide? I could think of nothing worse, after almost a year and a half in the South Pacific to suddenly have ten days set for "rest and recreation" and then have to stand by and hold the clubs for the visiting chief of the Bureau. Of course, I had no alternative but to say, "Aye, aye, Sir." I didn't know Admiral Cochrane very well before then, except as a person I respected greatly. I became very well acquainted with him in those four or five days we were together in Sydney.

Q: That, as a matter of fact, didn't do you any harm, did it?

James: No, did me no harm and I found he was as anxious to enjoy the pleasures of the city as was I. So after he had done his business, we enjoyed a very delightful visit together there.

Shortly after my return to Espiritu, the war had moved up toward the Central Pacific, and we had established the base at Manus. I was asked to proceed to Manus to report to ComServRon-10 to serve as his repair officer.

Q: What were the particular merits of Manus as a location for a base?

James: Location principally. It was right on the equator; it was close to the naval base at Ulithi which was the big operating base, but it was remote enough from Ulithi so that it was relatively protected from the onslaught of war. It was a fabulous harbor, twenty-six miles of deep water with coral heads, of course, that had to be blasted out. We didn't use but a small fraction of the harbor. It was completely surrounded by a coral reef. It was just a perfectly beautiful harbor and anchorage. It was right at the crossroads of traffic from Pearl Harbor to Australia and New Guinea, and from the Solomons to the Philippines. Strategically, it was a fabulously situated place. It had been occupied by the Japanese before us. There were many Japanese still there all the time we were. They had run them off during our invasion into the jungle and continued to harass us all the time. While I was there, Jap aircraft bombed our big dry dock, ABSD-3, with little damage.

Q: Had it been prior to that a minor base for the Australian Navy?

James: The Australians had been in Manus and had been driven out by the Japanese after the war started. Then, our forces moved in and there was a rather bloody affair to recapture Manus. The SeaBees got mauled pretty badly because they had been in to build an air base. The Japs knocked them about but finally were driven off themselves. Commodore Boak, who had been at Espiritu Santo, moved up to Manus to become the naval base commander. This became the major supply activity in the Central Pacific. There were all sorts of facilities and it was a lot closer to our basic sources of supply.

I moved in with a number of the ships from Espiritu Santo. We had loaded the maximum we could from our ship repair supplies and proceeded to Manus where we began to repeat the ship repair function. In the meantime, another large floating dry dock had been moved into Manus, one like that which we had in Espiritu Santo. We also had additional smaller floating docks. I've seen Manus harbor when over six hundred ships have been moored or anchored in it, with no congestion problems at all. That'a a fabulous harbor and I think that's probably the answer to your earlier question.

The work there was very much the same as in Espiritu except I had not had the privilege of laying it out. The base was established before I reported. I reported aboard the old ARGONNE which was the headquarters ship for ServRon 10 where I found a repair staff in being, including two naval constructors. One was Cmdr. Tex Moore and one was Cmdr. Jack Fee. Cmdr. Fee has recently been the central figure in a great tragedy. He became an admiral, served in command of two shipyards, and then retired and took over the conversion and modernization of the QUEEN MARY in Long Beach, Calif. In February 1971 he was overwhelmed by the problems and newspaper attacks about costs and committed suicide.

Jack Fee was one of my fine young supporters as was Cmdr. Moore. We had a nice little repair headquarters facility that was on a barge alongside the ARGONNE. We got into some real major battle damage work there. There were all kinds of ships that had been clobbered. I remember in the attacks on the Formosa Straits in November 1944 we had three cruisers badly damaged: USS CANBERRA, USS RENO, and USS HOUSTON. Admiral Carney, Chief of Staff to Adm. Halsey, sent for me to come up to Ulithi where these ships were scheduled to limp in, and to do what we could to make the initial repairs so they could proceed further.

I arrived in Ulithi on board the HECTOR, which I took along to assist in the repairs on these ships, not knowing exactly what the problem was, but knowing that there was severe damage to all three ships.

Q: The problems of the HOUSTON were stupendous, were they not?

James: The HOUSTON was the most severely damaged. The CANBERRA was not much less, and the RENO was not as severe as either. When I arrived aboard the HECTOR, only one of the ships had come in, the CANBERRA. She had suffered two bomb hits that knocked out one full engine room, with many casualties, lots of superficial topside damage, major holes in the hull, and the operable machinery limited to one shaft. Then the HOUSTON came limping in at a very slow speed. I was sent out to board her before she got into the harbor because they were fearful of losing her at any moment because she was settling continuously and was already down to or below her marks. I got aboard her in the open sea and met with the captain. Then I met with one of the most fabulously capable young officers, a Cmdr. George Miller. George Miller was the first lieutenant aboard the ship. In the action at the Formosa Straits, the HOUSTON had taken a torpedo in the after engine room that wrecked the fireroom-engineroom and flooded another fire room. She had taken a direct bomb hit, or maybe it was a torpedo hit in the after hangar space, and she had a third hit elsewhere. The Captain of the ship was Bill Behrens. George Miller, being a very astute young man recognized that survival was the problem of the HOUSTON and that he had to get rid of the maximum amount of topside weight to prevent her rolling over. To do this he had jettisoned everything that was loose, he had even cut loose two five inch guns and jettisoned them. He had cut large pieces of steel plate out of areas that he knew were not strength members of the basic box girder of the ship. He welded these in areas of the cracks in the strength girder of the ship. He had jettisoned an estimated twelve hundred tons from that cruiser with which she probably would have foundered long before I ever saw her.

Q: And two-thirds of the personnel as well.

James: The personnel, lots of the portable stores, and the unnecessary equipment, had been put aboard accompanying ships. They had some very fine officers who were kept aboard to bring her in. We got her inside the nets at Ulithi, where I laid the HECTOR alongside and we started repairs to flooding areas. Suddenly we got warning of a very severe typhoon approaching. It was our judgment that the ship was in such delicate condition that if she went through a typhoon, she'd sink. It was concluded that she shouldn't be left up in the fleet anchorage area of the harbor. I said, "If she's going to sink, let's take her where there's shallow water and if she sinks, she'll go down only a matter of a few feet. Salvage will be that much more simplified." I guess it was Mick Carney who realized the wisdom of that suggestion and before long the HOUSTON was towed to a remote part of the lagoon, however, not before I had landed on board from the HECTOR dozens of welding machines, burning torches, steel plate pumps and all the available shoring that we could spare. I put my people to work trying to patch below water holes to reduce flooding. I put portable gas driven pumps on board because the ship's pumps were out of service. We proceeded down to the lower anchorage arriving there about eight o'clock at night. It was already blowing a gale. There were less than fifty people aboard and about forty of them were my men. About ten were George Miller's ship fitters and comparable ratings to those that I had moved aboard. We had a couple of seamen whom I placed on the bow stern ship draft marks, to give fifteen minute interval reports on the draft of the ship. We labored through the night as we'd been working for a day and a half welding on patches underwater to try and save this ship from sinking. We had shallow water diving gear on board and we had put our pumps to work in compartments having only slow leakage. It was about three or four o'clock in the morning when one of these sailors who had been reporting increase in draft by fractions of inches came and reported "No change." That was a hoped for and helpful sign but we didn't take it literally and continued our frantic work. We got another "no change" on the next report. Then, believe it or not, about five or six o'clock in the morning when we were in the heighth of the storm we began getting a reduction in draft. I can remember that, well, it was just like a reprieve because it had been a hard struggle. George Miller had made all this possible by all the preliminary effort that he had intelligently exerted while the ship was enroute Ulithi.

The work on the RENO in Ulithi and the CANBERRA was principally to assess the damage as they were in no immediate danger of sinking and scheduling them for work to be done back at the base in Manus. I had begun to consider how I could return to Manus when I got a pre-emptory message to report aboard the NEW JERSEY to see Admiral Halsey. When I got aboard I was told to see Admiral Mick Carney. He asked, "You've just come from Manus, haven't you?" I said, "Yes." He said, "Well, I've got a Hospital Evac Plane waiting to take you back." I'd been told to bring my bag so I was ready. He said, "You get in the boat and head for Manus. There's been an ammunition ship that just blew up in the harbor. I understand the ships there are riddled with shells and fragments. The MT. HOOD has disappeared so you get yourself the hell down there and do what you have to do with the objective of getting the least damaged ships back into service in a hurry because we are planning many new operations."

I had already made my arrangements on the HOUSTON that George Miller, with the aid of materials and men that I would give him, would become a member of my repair staff and take charge of work I'd outlined. I was so impressed with his personal ability that I felt I could leave his wounded ship and the other two cruisers khak until they arrived in Manus.

I flew off in the Hospital Evac Plane to Manus and found a shambles. The MT. HOOD had blown up with the loss of everybody on board, including a few people from other ships in the harbor that were alongside in small boats to receive ammunition.

Q: This was the operating harbor?

James: This was right smack in the middle of the operating harbor because the ammo ship was the focal point of ships' resupply. There were only two survivors from the HOOD, as I recall it. They were on the mail run at the time of the explosion and were ashore. She swept an area around her of about fifteen hundred yards radius with major damage to the closer in ships and decreasing damage as the radius increased. There were no fewer than thirty ships that had some form of damage. The worst damage of all was to one of my repair ships -- the converted Liberty ship USS MINDINAO. She had been made into a deisel engine light repair ship but was a very vital unit in our operations there. I just segregated all these badly damaged ships, scheduled them into the dry docks in the harbor and assigned manpower as we could to work aboard. We took care of the least damaged first, putting them back in service as fast as we could. We didn't lose another single ship. We repaired all ships involved in that whole bloody incident putting them back on the line in times ranging from a few days to two or three weeks maximum, including our repair ship. The MINDINAO had suffered some major damage to equipment which we were hard pressed to replace but ultimately we did.

My own repair office got a pretty severe roughing up. I mentioned before it was in a quonset hut on a barge alongside the ARGONNE. The blast knocked this quonset hut flat. In the office were my associates Fee, Moore, and many enlisted men. They had to take refuge under the desks as the roof came down on them.

Later on, as part of the inquiry into this disaster, I was asked to make a bottom survey of the area where MT. HOOD had been to determine, if possible, what was the cause of the explosion. There had been lots of speculation on what had caused it. One notion was that a Jap submarine had lain outside the torpedo nets and when the nets were opened for ships to transit, she just pinged a torpedo down the channel and the MT. HOOD was right in the line of fire. In Ulithi they had a similar incident occur at the same time but damage was much less because the ship hit was a merchantman.

Q: Was it determined that it had been a midget submarine?

James: This I have never learned because the investigation continued long after I left there. In the course of our underwater survey by divers we picked up the original berth that had been assigned to MT. HOOD and began sweeping an area on the coral bottom, progressively examining the area on a hundred yard radius then two hundred, then three hundred and finally four hundred yards. The largest piece of steel we found in that entire area was about the size of a normal household dining table top -- nothing bigger than that. The HOOD had just been pulled to pieces. We did find a hole dredged out of the coral directly under what must have been the shadow of the ship at the time of the explosion, that was over six hundred feet in length and over forty feet in depth where this blast had scoured the coral right out of the bottom. Conceivably, the blast might have driven some of the major machinery units down into the coral but we never did find any and we spent about ten days looking.

Later the RENO, the HOUSTON, and a number of the destroyers that had been in the Formosa straits battle came into Manus and we started the temporary repairs to these ships. By and large, we were able to put the destroyers back into full service. I can recall one skipper who, I think was serious, although he said it in jest, "Gol damn you naval constructors. We thought we were going home for a Navy yard repair and a rest. Now you bastards have put us back on the line and we don't love you for it." Well, my function was to do just that. We've since become very good friends.

We had troubles with some of the captains. One was the skipper of the CANBERRA, who was eager to get his ship back into the war.

I had given her the low repair priority of a badly damaged ship. The Captain kept bugging me, and bugging me, sending for me, sending messages to my boss, and finally sending them to Admiral Halsey saying he was getting lousy treatment from the repair officer at Manus and couldn't they order me to do something for him in a hurry to get him on his way back home so he could get back out in the war. I'm sure everybody applauded his enthusiasm but I can't believe that anybody believed seriously that he was going to make a major contribution to the war for one hell of a long time. He was Captain Alex Early from Seattle.

Q: George Miller told me that one of their great problems that developed at Ulithi and continued at Manus, was the problem with personnel suffering from the strain and the tense situation that existed during this whole episode. Was this a general factor with ships that came in for repair? Did you observe this?

James: If ships had been badly mauled, yes, you could sense it very easily. People were jittery, they were abrupt, and this particularly true of Capt. Alex Early. Capt. Behrens on the HOUSTON on the other hand was a very fine person, very relaxed, and when we finally got his ship on the dry dock. As I said earlier, I made George my direct supervisor on the job. I would go down to the HOUSTON no more often than about once every two or three days. I gave Miller men and material, we outlined what had to be done which in her case was to strip out the damaged machinery, straighten out that which could be put in running order and put it on the line again, and patch the holes in the hull. Then we got her out of Manus and sent her back Stateside for permanent repairs.

Q: He told me that one of the problems that developed in Ulithi was when the engine rooms were entered -- the problem with decomposed bodies was so great that it disrupted things.

James: This was always one of the unpleasant tasks of dealing with battle damaged ships. It started early in my experience. We learned to do what they do now in Viet Nam, just take rubber bags (we didn't have plastic bags then) and pick up the remains. It was always an unpleasant assignment which I tried to avoid but because we were the repair people and we found the bodies, we were asked to handle it. I never will forget in one case, I think it was on the RENO, I came down the ladder into the engine room shortly after they had unwatered it. As I swung off the ladder which was all greasy and slimy with oil, I swung around and I just about stepped into a body. This person was laying face up and it was one of my old Naval Academy friends, Bill Potts. That was a shaker. He had drowned, I guess. Of course, we got the ships opened and pumped down weeks after the battle incident so the bodies were badly decomposed. This is always a very unpleasant, sad and disagreeable task but it had to be done.

The CANBERRA and two destroyers were on the ABSD-3 getting their initial repairs when I got a message directing me to prepare the dry dock for docking of the battleship IOWA. I went to Capt. Early and I told him I had to take him off the dock. Well, I thought he would shoot me on the spot because he had been real cantankerous about his delay. I said, "I have this message from Admiral Halsey to prepare the dry dock for entering of the IOWA on the twenty-fifth of December, Christmas Day. It was the twenty-second when I got the message. I had three days -- first, to make it possible to float these two destroyers and the CANBERRA off the dock so they wouldn't sink; second, to re-pump up the dock and reset blocks for the IOWA; and third, to receive and dock the IOWA, which was having shafting trouble.

It was the worst seventy-two hours I spent in the South Pacific because I was fighting Capt. Early on one hand . . .

Q: He didn't desist with that?

James: Oh, no. He frustrated me in every step of the way. I finally said, "Sir, I must advise Admiral Halsey that I am getting no cooperation, that you will not do this or that, or the other thing." By this time we were at each other's throat -- there was no friendship, no respect from me to him, and he thought I was an insolent young squirt. But we got CANBERRA off dock. It was first necessary to put large steel plates over the holes on the sides, where she had been opened up and cleaned out getting ready to patch the hull permanently. We had to throw in a temporary job to get her off the dock, because this message from Halsey was not a "can you" message, it was a "you will" message, and I never argued with my big boss.

To make a long story short, we got CANBERRA off on the afternoon of Christmas Eve. We then got to work to set the blocks for the IOWA, not knowing at this time what their troubles were. We were observing radio silence and there was very little communication to indicate her troubles. I had gotten the word of shaft troubles so I brought one of my repair ships and laid it alongside the ABSD-1 -- it was my heavy repair ship with greater capability for shafting work -- and we proceeded to make our other preparations. I hadn't left the dock in seventy-two hours, didn't go to bed, and about four o'clock in the morning I get the message from my people that the dock was all set. I piled into my little skimmer and proceeded outside the nets to board the IOWA. She came roaring in just at dawn. I boarded her and went up on the bridge. There was Capt. Jimmy Holloway, the commanding officer, and Admiral Oscar Badget who was the BatDivFour commander. He had been my boss down in Espiritu Santo following Granny Cobb so we had a little conversation and then I proceeded to tell Capt. Holloway the plan for receiving the IOWA. He said, "Where is your dry dock?" I pointed way up the bay and said, "It's about eleven miles straight up this way." He answered, "Okay."

Our instructions to all ships being docked was to bring the ship in fair to enter the dock. Then at a prescribed point, where I would have stationed small boats with lines, the lines would be taken aboard and the ship towed into the drydock. As Navy regulations required, I would then become the conning officer of the ship. We had a prescribed maximum speed for the ship that would be observed at various check points as we proceeded. I kept getting more and more nervous as Jimmy Holloway charged up the harbor with this big battleship, the biggest I'd seen. Ships were rolling all about as he passed through the mooring areas. I finally had to say, "Captain, you've got to slow her down. You're going much too fast." "Oh," he says, "That's your dry dock?" "Yes, Sir." He says, "I'll bring her right in on the line."

We passed the two boats with the lines going about seven or eight knots, which doesn't sound like much but with sixty, seventy thousand tons of ship behind you that's a hell of a lot of momentum. He hadn't stopped or backed engines at all. We got to the point where we were less than a hundred yards to go and I said, "Captain, you've got to back her down -- you're going to wreck my dry dock block set-up." "Oh, no," he says, and with this he eases IOWA into the dock still going four or five knots. He got the ship just about half way into the dry dock when he gave a "full speed astern." The IOWA shook like a damned destroyer and stopped just where she should be. But I'm just absolutely shattered because I know what damage he's done. He's swept the dry dock blocks out from under his ship by reversing his engines full, inside the dock. I had warned him of this and I said, "I cannot dock you now. We've got to sit here until I find out what's happened below."

I called my divers and held an emergency consultation. We put divers into the dock and my instructions were, "Don't try to reset blocks. If you see any block that is out of place which might punch a hole in the IOWA just knock it out, dog it down so it won't float up and we'll dock her on what's left." That's exactly what we did and finally about three hours later than should have been, we sat IOWA down on the blocks. We overlooked one displaced block. It punched a hole right through the ship.

Q: Because Capt. Holloway wanted to demonstrate his prowess.

James: Yes. Then, of course, we attacked the problem of his shafting. It is now Christmas afternoon. Finally we found out what the problem was with the shafting. It was the barrel staves that line the strut-shaft bearing -- a cap on the end had come adrift and staves had worked out. We had all the parts we needed and repairs proceeded. After seventy-two hours of no bath, no shave, no rest, and food off a plate with a pot of coffee always at my elbow, I decided to get in my little skimmer, which I drove myself, and head back at twenty-two knots to the SIERRA, where I was then headquartered. Just as I came alongside the SIERRA, a boat-load of officers from the ship were getting into the officer's motor boat. They spied me and said, "Hey, hurry up and clean up and come over to the Lorengau Officers' Club. There are two hospital ships in; there are women aboard. We're having a Christmas party." I said, "I haven't gone to bed in three days. I'm going up and take a shower and go to bed." "Aw, you're a sissy. This is Christmas Day and when have you last seen a white woman?"

That was too great an inducement. So I went up to my stateroom and started first with a bath. I could smell myself coming in. After I had showered I came out and started rubbing down, then I looked in the mirror at my hair. I had a lot of soap left in it so I went back in and re-showered and came back out again. Then I discovered that I didn't have soap in my hair - I had a gray streak that was born in that seventy-two hour period. I could almost precisely tell you the moment it was born -- when Holloway pulled his high speed throttle jockey stunt on me.

Interview #5 with Rear Admiral Ralph K. James

Annapolis, Md. May 18, 1971

Subject: Biography By John T. Mason, Jr.

Mr. Mason: It's mighty good to see you this morning, Admiral. I was reviewing the tape on the last episode which was your tour of duty in Manus and you had concluded that chapter with the account of the docking of the IOWA, which was very exciting indeed.

Admiral James: I doubt if that episode shall ever be concluded until they lay me away because I wear the gray streak in my hair as a perpetual reminder of that event. It also is a perpetual reminder of my very dear friend, Admiral Jimmy Holloway.

The balance of my tour in the South Pacific was, shall I say, by that time routine. We had many ships having sustained varying degrees of damage that came in for repair and overhaul. I later made a formal record of battle damaged ships which I had tended to in the South Pacific from Noumea, Espiritu Santu to Manus and Ulithi. I'm sure I've overlooked some key ships but the records show in excess of eighty of our naval ships that it was my privilege and perhaps headache to have to deal with. I was so extremely pleased with this experience that I later compiled a detailed record of this work which I presented at an International Conference of Naval Architects held in England but that story is a little further along the chronological order of things.

Q: It's certainly an impressive record. Did Admiral Nimitz take cognizance of this?

James: I was generously decorated for my service in the South Pacific. I received the Bronze Star and the Legion of Merit, which I consider to be two outstanding decorations. I received these from the hands of my respective commanders in the South Pacific and in the Central Pacific.

There were two events that I would like to record. One was the story of the cruiser CHICAGO that had sustained several bomb hits, one in the after turret that penetrated the side and opened up the after end of the ship to flooding. The other was on the forward gun turret which badly damaged the navigating bridge, the communication facilities, radar, ship control equipment up in that vital part of the ship. This occurred just as I was preparing to depart Manus on orders of Admiral Halsey, to proceed back to Tulagi where I was to sweep up all of the remnants of the repair facilities that were present and prepare them for movement into the Philippines. I was already to be relieved by a captain Harry Sims, Class of '25. The CHICAGO arrived just about the time that he arrived, also it arrived shortly after Rear Admiral (then Capt.) George Holderness, another engineer naval constructor, arrived to serve the Seventh Fleet that was headquartered in Manus.

When the CHICAGO came in, the captain, "Germany" Kurtz was eager to get out of the harbor and on to Pearl Harbor where he knew that he had to go to get permanent repairs, if not further on to the mainland, United States. He communicated this concern and desire to me and to Harry Sims, who dogged my footsteps my last few weeks in Manus. I made a very careful inspection of this damage in company with Harry Sims. Having seen literally dozens of damaged ships I was not concerned with the scope of the damage on the CHICAGO as anything that would be hazardous for her to proceed from Manus. Harry Sims, on the other hand, having just arrived from the States, was appalled at what he saw. He also had obviously been clued in with admonitions from headquarters about ships that had been lost due to inadvertencies in handling their repairs. He was determined not to be involved in any such an incident.

When I laid out what I considered essential repairs which were very modest and could have been accomplished in three or four days, that would permit the ship to then proceed on for more permanent repairs, Sims took violent exception of my judgment. Being senior officer to me by some three years, necessarily I had to listen even though I didn't believe in his position whatsoever. We communicated our disagreement to Capt. Kurtz, who of course was inclined to accept my version. At that time George Holderness' role was not to participate in the Third Fleet repairs but as a precautionary measure, and believing that he would bring more light to the problem, I suggested that we solicit his review of my proposals, which Capt. Kurtz did forthwith. The conclusion was reached by Holderness that Sims was right and I was wrong.

I still felt that neither of them knew what they were talking about. Even though they were senior in years they were much less experienced in battle damage repairs than I had become due to the two years I had dealt with such problems as routine. But the conclusion was reached by Sims and Holderness that they should recommend to Capt. Kurtz that he should not proceed with the CHICAGO until certain additional repairs were completed. I stayed with my position -- repeated my position. Ships entering and leaving the port of Manus were required by routine to be cleared by the repair boss in the area before they proceeded to sea. This, in effect, was the placement of the Good Housekeeping seal of approval on the work done and therefore would relieve the captain of any obligation for subsequent damage that might develop from inadequacy of repairs performed.

Capt. Kurtz was advised that it would take at least four more days for him to receive the additional repairs. I can recall the situation rather vividly. He said to me, "You don't believe in these additional repairs, do you?" I said, "No, Sir." He said, "Do you have any qualms about proceeding in this ship yourself to Pearl Harbor the way it is now?" I said, "None whatsoever." He said, "Thank you, gentlemen." And that was the end of that. The next morning we awakened and found no CHICAGO in the harbor. Capt. Kurtz had decided to proceed to Pearl Harbor forthwith. There was some suspicion among my two collaborators that I had engineered this, which truly I had not. However, Capt. Kurtz obviously had concluded that I had advised him properly so he proceeded to Pearl

Harbor, where he arrived without trouble. He took a step to gig my associates in a message that was sent from Pearl Harbor the moment he entered the harbor stating that he had arrived safely with no difficulties whatsoever and was hopefully proceeding to the United States. They got the message loud and clear.

I don't tell this story in criticism of these two men because it was their first exposure to major ship damage and it was, perhaps, my twentieth battle damaged ship that I had processed.

Shortly thereafter I did proceed to Tulagi and executed a rather unique routine on the way. The operations into the Philippines were to include a number of landing ships. There was a whole squadron of landing ships in Manus that were being readied for return to Tulagi to pick up troops, stores, jeeps and whatnot. They were all in a sad mechanical state. Rather than just ride a ship down to Tulagi and probably a comfortable repair ship, I transferred over two hundred sailors from my two accompanying repair ships along with a lot of special equipment and materials, divided them up in the dozen or so ships of this amphibious squadron and proceeded to Tulagi aboard them. I would flit from one to another during the passage from Manus to Tulagi reviewing, inspecting, checking, advising, confirming adequacy of repair work done by the thirty or so artificers that I had placed on board each ship. I can't recall how long it took us to get there -- about ten days. By the time we arrived we had a dozen ships that had had a hell of a fine overhaul. The ships were exceptionally pleased, as was the amphibious force commander who awaited our arrival in Tulagi expecting to get a bunch of old clunkers.

My sweep up days in Tulagi were very short. In about two weeks we had cleared the place. By now it's April of 1945. I had orders to proceed and follow the forces to arrive in the Philippines and to report as officer in charge of ship repair in that area upon my arrival. I packed up the repair ships, packed up my small repair group and packed my own baggage, then I headed over to Guadalcanal to take an aircraft to stage on toward the Philippines. After I had said my farewells to some of my old friends in Tulagi, I got aboard an aircraft at Henderson Field in Guadalcanal. My baggage was all stowed, the plane was just about fully loaded when some sailor on the ground hollered, "Is Cmdr. James in there?" I said, "Yes." He said, "Get your gear and come out." I said, "What's this all about?" He said, "You're going to like it. Get your gear and come out."

So I picked up my bags and tossed them onto the ground, climbed down a little boarding ladder, and I asked, "Who is calling me?" A chap stepped forward and said, "You'll be pleased to read these." So I proceeded to read and it said, "Cmdr. Ralph K. James detached ComServRon 10. Proceed immediately to Commander Naval Forces, Pearl Harbor for return to the United States." I had been out in the Pacific just a scant two years -- about twenty-two months. This was great news.

Q: A pretty strenuous two years.

James: A pretty strenuous two years and then considering the several months I had been in Africa I had accumulated more overseas time than any naval constructor, Engineer Duty Officer, we had in service. So I was ready to go home.

I proceeded to climb out of that plane with enthusiasm and waited a day or two for a plane that later dropped me in Honolulu. Rear Admiral H. Travis Smith was the Fleet Maintenance Officer in Pearl Harbor. He had been out in the Central Pacific where I had just seen him. We had discussed my possible return to the States, he clearly indicated my time was up, and that he would take steps to get my orders. So I arrived in Honolulu expecting to see him immediately and thank him for this courtesy, only to learn he was not on the island, he was out in the Pacific. A Capt. Wesley Haig was acting Fleet Maintenance Officer and was his deputy. Wesley Haig and I were relatively old friends but we, too, had crossed swords during the course of my work in the Pacific. This was in connection with the repairs on the HOUSTON. I had done rather extensive damaged stability calculations on the HOUSTON and thought I knew what her status was only to find that he, too, fancied that he had done equivalent effort to analyse her, following which he considered that the ship was in grave danger of capsizing. We fought this out toe to toe in front of Admiral Smith and, again, I was supported by my senior. As events later proved, the steps that I had taken in connection with her stability to supplement those of George Miller were more than adequate. I'm sure Haig resented the fact that a young squirt had challenged him before his boss and before many others in the audience and had in effect been right. So when I arrived on my way home, I presented myself thinking I would see Admiral Smith and instead I saw Capt. Haig. At that time he made it clear that my transfer to Pearl Harbor was simply to facilitate my reporting to still another force commander in the Pacific. I was to report the next day to Admiral Ainsworth, commander Destroyers Pacific Fleet to become his maintenance officer. I protested to Capt. Haig and told him that I had been assured by Admiral Smith that I was returning Stateside. He challenged this and said, "Not on your life. You report tomorrow to Admiral Ainsworth and he's departing immediately for some far out Pacific destination." Naturally I was shaken. This would have meant at least a six months' extension of my duties in the Pacific. While I enjoyed them, I was prepared to share the pleasure with other EDOs and this development seemed to foreclose on that.

I knew of no course of appeal except Admiral Smith and I had no knowledge of when he was going to return. I took steps to dog his footsteps, or rather his staff's footsteps as much as I dared, to learn when he was returning. In the meantime I delayed reporting to Admiral Ainsworth.

Actually, in less than twenty-four hours after I was to have reported to Admiral Ainsworth, without orders I might add -- just simply a verbal instruction from Haig, Admiral Smith returned to Pearl Harbor. I must have been waiting on the tarmac for him when he came in at the airport. I told him my story. His words were, in effect, "don't get your you-know-what in a flutter." He said, "You go back to the BOQ, pack your bag, book yourself on the first plane you can get out of here for home, and I'll take care of the rest of it." Needless to say, I didn't again present myself in that office so I would not have to face Capt. Haig.

As events developed I left the next day for home where by pre-arranged and a very queer sort of personal code my wife had been anticipating my arrival in San Francisco. Our code was so good as was my timing, in spite of these delays, that she arrived at exactly the same time as I did, and we had our first reunion in two years.

Q: I wonder how general were these private codes?

James: I would say that just about everybody had their private code. I used to base my code on the overseas issue of Time Magazine. I arranged for my wife to receive the same magazine. I would write letters and refer her to certain paragraphs in the Time magazine. With a few very simple little clues that I had left behind me she was able to translate this into such things as, "I am now moving to such and such a place," or "I will be out of here in x number of weeks." Finally the climax of it all was my signal for my return home for which I again used Time magazine. I think it was rather accidental that we were so close on timing because if I had not been delayed one or two days, she would have not been in San Francisco as I arrived.

Q: It was mighty clever to develop that kind of system of communication.

James: Yes. We were, of course, enjoined from such practice by Navy Regs, but I felt that anybody who could figure out my code would have to be a complete star performer. Even if he figured out that I might be home on such and such a date I couldn't think it would hurt the war effort.

Q: So you arrived back in San Francisco.

James: And almost immediately thereafter proceeded to Los Angeles where my wife and family had resided during my absence in the South Pacific. Of course, upon return to San Francisco I communicated immediately with my family, so when a day or so later we arrived in Los Angeles, having taken that beautiful train, The Lark, we were met on the station platform by my two children, my mother-in-law and father-in-law, who were the principal reason for my family being in Los Angeles.

When I stepped off the train and saw our daughter I was so proud of this beauty that greeted me, a young sixteen year old high school girl. She still is a beautiful woman. She then had the extremely youthful freshness of a teenager and was dressed impeccably. I was just busting with pride at both our kids and went home with them scarcely able to contain myself with the enjoyment of seeing them after two years. We arrived home to find that my wife had planned a greeting for me by those friends that she had made while living in Los Angeles. One of them was a very well to do chap who owned a series of super markets. He had done the almost impossible in those days -- he had provided a steamship round of roast beef to honor the occasion.

Another of her new friends had provided gasoline in excess of the standard "A" tickets to permit all the guests to assemble, it was a tremendous affair. I was introduced to virtually all strangers. Our daughter was likewise introduced, and oohed and ahed over by those who hadn't seen her before. A few minutes later I saw this flash coming down from the upper story of our home. I hollered because I recognized this as our daughter, but it was not the same girl I had met at the railroad station. She was wearing an old tattered shirt of mine hanging outside blue jeans that were cut off at the knees in a raggedy pattern. She was a better organized teenager than the current day crop, but the transformation from the gorgeous beauty of an hour earlier to this ragamuffin type was amazing.

The visit in Los Angeles was brief. I had orders to return to the Bureau of Ships in Washington and I had just been promoted to Captain. I was unable, however, to proceed with my family because our two children were in school. It was agreed that we would retain our residence in Los Angeles until after school closed in June. It was now April 1945. So I proceeded by myself, driving the family car across country. I proceeded via Chicago where my father was living and stayed with him for a couple of days, at which point I received telegraphic modification of orders. The modification directed me to continue to the Bureau of Ships but to prepare for duty at the Naval Supply Depot, Mechanicsburg, Pennsylvania. I didn't know much about Mechanicsburg except that I had been a very frequent, long range, critic of its performance.

Q: It had been set up as a base at the beginning of the war, hadn't it?

James: It was a supply depot for routine general stores until by some device which I'm not clearly aware, BuShips arranged to have the so-called supply demand control point for BuShips repair parts centralized at Mechanicsburg and controlled at Mechanicsburg.

Q: Wasn't it also center for diesel . . .

James: This was BuShips repair parts which first were largely diesel engine parts, but later acquired many thousands of other items. I had been fully aware of the difficulties we had in getting materials out of Mechanicsburg and anticipated this would be one hell of an assignment that I wanted no part of, particularly as it was not a BuShips engineer type billet until that moment.

I proceeded into Washington and made inquiries of the personnel officer there, as to how come I was given this stinking assignment. My answers were simply that Admiral Cochrane had ordered it. He was chief of the Bureau. If I wanted to protest I had to go see him -- I had to go see him anyway because he interrogated every returning officer. We had a date within a day or two. I think my opening question after greeting him was, "How come I'm going to Mechanicsburg?" He was then in a rather simple little office over in the T-4 Building in the mall below the Washington Monument -- those buildings are long since gone. He reached into the bottom drawer of his desk and he pulled out a sheaf of papers in a folder and slid them across the desk to me. He said, "Read these."

I turned the cover and I started reading. As I read I felt the back of my neck getting warm. As I read more I'm sure I must have turned crimson. He had a beautiful collection of my acid filled messages from the South Pacific to Mechanicsburg and to the Bureau of Ships bitterly complaining about the inadequacy of repair parts supply for fighting the war.

Q: A perfect example of a boomerang.

James: This went as I read at least a dozen different messages, all couched in vitriolic language, all lamenting the same problem, and all berating those who had anything to do with it. He said, "Well, now you know the problem so well, you're going up there to help Bill Turney solve it." No manner of protest changed his mind and so after a few days in Washington I proceeded to Mechanicsburg.

This is the first time I'd crossed Admiral Rickover's trail. I had known Rickover but never had known the character of his work. With the problems that had been highlighted in my messages and I'm sure those of many other people, BuShips decided what they were getting out of Mechanicsburg was inadequate. In February of 1945 they sent Rickover with a group of civilian collaborators to review the spare parts flow into Mechanicsburg from industry and out of Mechanicsburg for distribution to the ships and to repair centers. Rickover's report, which I have never read in full, but which I read the conclusions of, was another vitriolic condemnation of the Supply Corps in general, and the specific situation at Mechanicsburg. He concluded that BuShips, in order to get what they wanted, would have to create their own operation up there.

Captain Bill Turney was selected to be the commanding officer and I was selected to be his executive officer. Bill Turney had been on the scene about four weeks before I arrived. Between us we proceeded to take what we needed from the Rickover report and to create an organization which we labeled the Ships' Parts Control Center. We assigned people from the Supply Depot into the Control Center. Most of the officers were reserve officers on active duty -- in fact they were almost exclusively reserves. We had over four hundred officers and civilian employees in numbers to match. We started the reorganization and finally in about August we blew the whistle and said we are now in business as the SPCC. Almost immediately the war in Europe came to an end. With that event the reserve officers began to leak out of Mechanicsburg like water out of a sponge. The Japanese war came to an end after the European cease fire, and suddenly all the wars were over.

By this time our officer forces were leaving for home at the rate of ten or twelve a day. Before long the organization that we had postulated on the strength we had seen when we arrived was no longer feasible. We had to start all over again.

Q: Before this exodus began, however, were you able to set up as an outfit more in accordance with your own ideas?

James: We had moved in that direction. We had even begun to receive a few bits of applause for the accelerated delivery of repair parts. I remember the operation to land our forces in Japan was then being staged. We had a tremendous shopping list of repair parts to support the Amphibious Forces which it was expected were going to be very roughly handled during the landing. We concentrated on that effort, even while we were reorganizing the activity. I think we put practically everybody that could be assigned to the job of insuring receipt in Mechanicsburg of repair parts from manufacturers and then reshipping them. Where there were possible delivery delays, we sent people to manufacturer's plants to re-direct repair parts directly from the manufacturing point to the overseas shipment point. We must have had six full train loads that pulled out of Mechanicsburg late in June and early in July headed for West Coast trans-shipment points. This material was enroute across country when the war ended in Europe. It wasn't long thereafter until the war in Japan came to an end and, of course, the landing on Japan proper was never consummated. Much of this material, not just these six train loads but much of that which had come directly from manufacturer's plants to the West Coast shipping points then lay fallow for awhile and finally was returned to Mechanicsburg, but that was a relatively minor problem.

Your question, however, was had we begun to make some changes that were effective at Mechanicsburg even before the end of the war and the answer is very definitely yes.

Q: How useful was Rickover other than the initial study?

James: Rickover never entered the picture again except as his written report was a reference document which I used only when necessary. I didn't consider it the greatest example of brevity that I'd ever seen. Furthermore, I was highly critical of Rickover and his own supply techniques when I later found that there were literally warehouses full of armored cable that he had purchased and stored in Mechanicsburg anticipating a war that had to go on for twenty more years in order for it to be consumed. When I learned this I didn't think that he was a particularly qualified expert to judge the Supply Corps performance at Mechanicsburg. Most of his material later went on to the salvage scrap sales. Not only Rickover's material, of course, but that of many others who bought deeply and way beyond requirements. Many of us were not privvy to the nuclear bomb and its arrival on the weapons scene. We, therefore, gave little credence to some beliefs that the war could end in a short time. I think we were all prepared for a longer term operation and stocked accordingly.

Q: When this material at Mechanicsburg was ultimately dumped on the market in one form or another, did it cause any cry from the manufacturers? Was this considered competition to their current effort?

James: Not too much of it was dumped on the market in the sense that we unloaded it then and there. The biggest single thing we had to do at Mechanicsburg was to discover what we had in stock, to collate it, catalogue it, and make it available for use in the service. In about six months after my arrival I became commander up there -- Turney left and I was promoted. I virtually had the job of reorganizing for the third time and proceeded with the effort of identifying and cataloging our materials. If I'm not mistaken, we had in excess of a quarter of a million stock numbers on our records at the time we began to dig into this problem. We knew that there were less than seventy-five thousand active parts that were needed to support the basic equipments of the Navy. Not all of these stock numbers represented different items of hardware but they were different means of identifying similar hardware, or even identical hardware.

I proposed that we get on with a cataloging job of great proportions. I also stated that I was unable to recruit the kind of people to do this from the local labor market and suggested the employment of an outside contractor. I got approval for this and canvassed the market. I found a group named the H. L. Yoh Co. in Philadelphia. They were hired, moved in people who had been doing this sort of work and before long we had a couple of hundred of their men on board to start the BuShips repair parts catalogue program -- a project that took several years. Long after I left they were still working on the catalogue. It was, I believe, the genesis of the effort to catalogue military stores which became standardized within the Navy and subsequently became standard within the Department of Defense.

Q: What happened to Mechanicsburg as a supply depot? Does it continue today?

James: Yes, Mechanicsburg continues to perform that function. They've simplified the operation and the command has passed from an Engineer Duty Officer back to a Supply Corps officer after about three subsequent commanders. The Bureau of Ships decided in 1953 that they would relinquish responsibility and return the control of this center to the Supply Corps. It remains in Mechanicsburg in the site in which we opened for business. They continue to provide repair parts support for not just NavShips parts but for NavOrd and other bureaus. There are several similar supply demand control points -- one for aeronautical material. One of my efforts was to consolidate the one for submarines parts into the SPCC at Mechanicsburg. I did not succeed at the time I was directly involved but it has subsequently occurred. This SPCC function now has been very streamlined. Its catalogue is virtually finished although I guess no catalogue is ever finished - as they bring new components into ships and require new repair parts for them, so cataloguing is a continuous effort.

Q: Have some of the war time facilities been used for other governmental activities? Does not archives have something up there now?

James: I'm sure there are other naval activities that are making use of the storage facilities at the Supply Depot. In my day this was a separate command headed up part of the time by one of my dearest friends, Vice Admiral Charles W. Fox, retired. The activity in Mechanicsburg, however, is essentially a naval activity and I have been out of touch for so long that I'm not really sure what other agencies might be in there.

I had gone to Mechanicsburg anticipating a six months tour of duty. With the end of the war it obviously became necessary to extend that to a year if there was to be any continuity to the establishment of SPCC. After I had gotten command . . .

Q: It did permit you to have your family there, didn't it?

James: Oh yes. We lived in a private residence for a year -- a residence we rented. The end of the year came and I was tenatively slated to go to the Naval War College. At that point, however, to the surprise of Admiral Cochrane, I recommended that I be retained for another year, the reason I gave was that I was in the middle of the program of reorganizing and getting it operating in a manner that I thought was essential. He enthusiastically agreed.

Q: This really underscored the wisdom of his original decision, didn't it?

James: Yes. Then I approached the end of my second year and to the utter amazement of the then Chief of the Bureau of Ships, Admiral Earl Mills, I asked for still another extension. He thought I had lost my buttons, but again he was pleased to agree. He said however, if this was my attempt to avoid going to the Naval War College to forget it -- I was going there come hell or high water.

It truly was not the reason although I must say that at the time I had made a cursory review of what I could get out of the Naval War College and didn't come up with any great enthusiasm for the assignment.

I continued on at Mechanicsburg then for a total of three years and had the great pleasure of seeing it reach a status of prominence and certainly of greatly improved performance. Of course, we were not then in a war time situation but we built for the possibility of a war and I think that we built well. We were the second of the more fully developed supply demand control points. Aviation's supply center was the first and was a pattern for much of what we did. Later it was copying some of the things that we had instituted.

I had a rather delightful personal experience about this time. Sears-Roebuck had their headquarters in Philadelphia and had learned of our efforts at Mechanicsburg. They sent a team of experts to visit and have a look-see. Shortly after that I was again approached by Sears to see if they might send down some of their more senior executives who went through the operations and saw what we were doing. In about two months time, I was made a very generous offer by Sears-Roebuck Co. to retire from the Navy and come and run their supply control system at their headquarters -- an offer that was treble my Navy pay. I'm sure that if I had gone on and succeeded with them it would have done that several times more. I was tempted but I reckoned without the depth of enthusiasm for the Naval service which my wife had acquired in the years of our marriage. She was the one who virtually said, "If you go, you leave me." Not quite that brutally but her message was loud and clear. She liked what she was doing and wanted more of it and none of this bras and buckets routine that I would have been involved with had I gone with Sears-Roebuck.

We completed three delightful years in Mechanicsburg area, actually living all the while in Harrisburg which is only a dozen miles away. Our last year and a half was in government quarters which we had managed to create from some enlisted WAVES barracks. We made many friends and many enduring friends amongst the wonderful people of the Navy Supply Corps. I became almost as a supply officer because I had served longer with them than any other known outsider. In fact often times I got my mail addressed to me then as Capt. R. K. James, Supply Corps, U. S. Navy.

Charlie Fox jokingly once said, "I'll make you an admiral in the Supply Corps if you will transfer." I was still hopeful that I would get back in the ship repair and shipbuilding business.

Q: Why did the Bureau want you to go to the Naval War College?

James: I guess just career development.

Q: You were tapped for higher things.

James: I suppose this was in the minds of some people early in my career. BuShips always had an officer or two at the Naval War

College. I followed Bobbie Snyder and Floyd Shultz, presently two retired EDO admirals. I must say that I went there protesting but I came away realizing that I had the greatest one year experience in my life time.

Q: Why did you protest? What was it predicated on?

James: Principally my three years at Mechanicsburg where I was out of touch with the technical side of my profession. I was not required to use technical background and knowledge very extensively at Mechanicsburg and I saw another year of the same situation at the War College. I was, therefore, anxious to get back into a shipyard. However, wiser people than I concluded to the contrary and I went to the War College. I couldn't have been happier having done so, than I was. The exposure to many up and coming line officers and Marines, particularly as I took the senior then called Senior Strategy and Tactics course generally reserved for line officers. I was plunged into operational situations which I knew nothing about and had to scramble like mad to learn about. While learning the problems of the operators I also learned to know many operators themselves and generated friendships which have long endured.

When I finished my year at the War College, I was extended a great courtesy of an invitation from the president to remain on the staff. Rear Admiral Cat Brown, chief of staff, urged me to become a member of the staff. By this time I was really getting nervous because I had been off the main stem of my technical specialty for four years, and this would have meant at least five and possibly six. So I protested and this time my protests were respected by the deputy chief of the Bureau of Ships, Rear Admiral Charles Wheelock.

Q: Would you tell me what you focused on particularly while you were there? What sort of papers did you prepare?

James: We all prepared the same papers, the same reports, and the same operations projects. One war game, I was made commander of the "opposing forces." I was the Russian commander of forces in one of these maneuvers. I thought that was a tremendous tribute to the EDO adaptibility that I would be picked. I concentrated on being a good line officer. However, I used to always throw in to the very serious debates about how you would organize for an operation, a reminder that ships didn't just steam because you turned the wheel and generated the steam -- you had to logistically support operations throughout. I found little or no attention being given to the logistic side of our studies so I used to always harp on that point, only to become known as "One note Charlie" amongst my contemporaries at the school.

Q: It was another dimension.

James: It was an important dimension. One that the junior logistics course in what was nicknamed Aggies Hall were given in great depth. Our high flying flag and fleet commanders were more or less loath to get involved with logistics so they needed a "One note Charlie." Maybe that's the reason why an EDO was always a member of the senior course. Henry Eccles, who later became a retired rear admiral, was the big logistician at the War College. He was located down in the so-called Aggies school, and his influence extended into the Strategy and Tactics course. It was not the same however as having a constant reminder from some character such as I.

That was one of the more delightful years of naval service. I treasured the experience and found it invaluable in later years as I proceeded into higher echelons myself.

Q: Particularly the contacts, I suppose.

James: Yes. I was not tongue-tied when exposed to the line verbiage that described their kinds of interests and so found it extremely valuable.

From Newport, which my family and I thoroughly enjoyed . . .

Q: Incidentally, did you get an adequate house to live in during that year?

James: We did the usual. We rented one of the old estates which had been converted into apartments for students at the War College, and paid usurous rates for a very inconveniently located but an adequate apartment. We lived on Catherine Street in the house that Fifi Stillman, of some notoriety when I was a boy, had lived. Fifi was the socialite that disappeared into the north woods with an Indian guide for a week or more and it came out to the consternation of her parents, to later bear a child for the Indian that she had shacked up with. This home that we were in had been the family estate. We were one of seven apartment dwellers in that one single house, so you can get an idea of how large it was.

My next tour of duty was at the Mare Island Naval Shipyard where my duties initially were as estimating superintendent. We lived in quarters in the shipyard, very sumptuous quarters. My family had shrunk. Our daughter was off to college. She had entered Stevens College in 1949, so she was not in continuous residence although she was at home from time to time. Our young son, Dick, was a high school student at that point. Dick, being a fisherman and a hunter was delighted with what he found in Mare Island. Both were easy to do. We had some very wonderful excursions up in the High Sierras for both fishing and hunting. Duck hunting could be done right in the back yard of the Navy Yard. It was on the Pacific ducky flyway. Duck blinds were built right out in back of the Mare Island Ship Yard. Some of us used to make decoys regularly in the hobby shop. We built ladders and walkways over mud flats to our blind and had a tremendous time which Dick just loved. We also filled up our freezer with ducks and fish that we never ever got around to eating entirely. We had to give many away.

The duties at Mare Island were essentially those of a routine shipyard tour of duty. After a while, I was transferred from the planning department to the repair department as repair superintendent which put me on the waterfront in direct charge of all the work on the ships that came in for overhaul. This I enjoyed more than I did the planning job.

Q: Had anything momentous happened in the interim between Manus and now in terms of repair of ships that you could latch on to?

James: No, nothing significantly different. In fact, out in the forward areas during the war we had to invent many new approaches to ship repair that were beginning to find their way back into the shipyard practices -- removing propellers without docking ships, for example; the use of dynamite caps in blasting propellers loose from line shafting; things which our friends were aghast at when first suggested because they thought it would jar loose the shaft bearings and create havoc. It took the first example to demonstrate that this was not so.

Q: Had some of these innovative things been written up or was it simply that you imparted this knowledge to the people?

James: They had all been written up. They were recorded and passed around but like all documents of that sort they didn't get the attention that personal exposure to the techniques would provide.

Q: The people can't read.

James: People won't read. There are too many of them disinclined to read large volumes and thick tomes so as to benefit by past experience. The same timidity was true of pressurizing compartments to remove shaft bearings, and packing and other fittings that penetrated the hull. These were considered hazardous practices till trial made them routine.

I don't think I had any experience at Mare Island that was particularly impressive and unique -- the program of overhauls on many cruisers, many destroyers, and many submarines became routine.

Q: But it would seem that you contributed something.

James: Oh yes. I'm sure I did. Heavens to Betsy -- that was our regular responsibility. Shortly after I arrived I was chosen to be the Navy's representative to go to an International Conference of Naval Architects and Marine Engineers in England. Needless to say, I was delighted. I had anticipated a possible assignment to be the naval architect with the British Navy on our London Naval staff. This hope was frustrated by the fact that the incumbent, Capt. Vic Cole, wanted an extension of a year on this assignment so the job didn't open up for me. I guess it was as a sort of a second prize that I was asked to attend the conference in England, represent our Navy and deliver a paper. I began to ponder a suitable paper and concluded that my experience with the Pacific Fleet maintenance was a paper in itself. With the help of Lt. Cmdr. Wayne Hoof, who was then on duty in Mare Island, to collect and organize material for me, we produced a very interesting paper. I had it published and prepared and in due time and with my wife proceeded to England aboard the SS AMERICA to attend the conference. On board were some thirty-five other representatives of the American Society of Naval Architects and Marine Engineers, all going to the conference. We became very dear friends with a number of them on that trip.

We went to England and spent roughly three weeks in London where a number of papers were presented. Then we toured the ship yard facilities in England and Scotland, principally on the Clyde. Then we proceeded to Newcastle-on-Tyne where I presented my paper as the next to the last paper to be presented to this august group which included representatives from at least fourteen different nations. The sponsor of the meetings in Newcastle was the East Coast Institution of Engineers and Ship Builders.

Interview #6 with Rear Admiral Ralph K. James

Annapolis, Maryland   June 15, 1971

Subject: Biography   by John T. Mason, Jr.

Mr. Mason: It's good to see you again this morning, Admiral. Last time you concluded a most interesting chapter by telling me about your trip to London as naval architect and representing the U. S. Navy at this international conference. I think you want to add something more to that story today.

Admiral James: The conference in England, was a very impressive assemblage of naval architects and marine engineers from around the world. I believe there were fourteen countries that were represented by one or more persons. The U. S. Navy had two -- myself and Admiral Charles Wheelock, who was then Deputy Chief of the Bureau of Ships. Our Coast Guard also had a representative, Vice Admiral Kenneth Cowart, who was then the chief engineer of the Coast Guard.

Q: Admiral Cochrane was there too. Was he in the capacity of an observer?

James: Admiral Cochrane was president of our Society of Naval Architects and Marine Engineers and as such he was the principal American representative at the meeting. No, he was not then the Chief of the Bureau of Ships. He had retired and was head of the school of naval architecture at M.I.T. But he was there in his other capacity and, of course, Admiral Cochrane was a well known American figure in England. He had been decorated as a Knight of the British Empire and so was entitled to be called Sir Edward. This he loathed but we twitted him about it from time to time.

The meeting was divided into three major locations -- the opening sessions were held in London, it was a very festive, gala affair. We were wined and dined by the Lord mayor of the city of London amongst others and reciprocated with an American sponsored banquet that we gave to our fellow attendees at the Dorchester House hosted by Admiral Cochrane.

After a series of papers were presented there, we proceeded by a special train layed on by the British government that took us up to Glasgow, later to Newcastle-on-Tyne and back to London. It could have been a real delightful trip but the equipment that the British railways laid on was simply ghastly -- dirty, coal burning. It seemed the train stopped at every crossroad for a tea break. The crew of the engine would get out, sit on the bank, get out their tea caddies and have their snack. When finished, the crew would board the train and we would proceed. It was tremendously disappointing to the British who were our hosts. They made a big issue of the matter with the government after our return. The newspapers in London were filled with stories of this shabby treatment of this distinguished group by the British railways. Quite a political row ensued later from this experience.

Q: They were state owned railways?

James: Yes. However, the Americans had been forearmed by equipping ourselves with sufficient liquor and were able to make the trip generally enjoyable until the water supply ran out. I'm touching on this in a light vein because taken in retrospect it was really funny.

We went to Glasgow as the second stop where we held other sessions and other banquets. The biggest thrill was a beautiful boat tour of the Clyde aboard the earliest of all steam turbine driven ships. We boarded the fifty year old KING EDWARD that was the first passenger turbine driven steamer built in the world. This in itself was an interesting marine museum piece and was part of the reason why it was brought into service for this occasion. The tour of the Clyde permitted one to see the fantastic array of shipbuilding yards that lined the river. They ranged from little yards to the more magnificent Fairfield shipyard. We saw Denny Brown that built the original Queens. I see in the morning paper today that the upper Clyde shipyard, which is a consortium of several yards combined by British government direction about ten years ago, is about to go bankrupt.

Q: They make a demand of fifteen million or so on the government, don't they?

James: Right. A shipbuilding subsidy.

Q: By the end of the month, or else.

James: Is it quite that pre-emptory?

Q: Yes.

James: This was one of the spectacular yards and now it's sad to see the passing of such a famous old yard.

Our next stop was Newcastle-on-Tyne, which was the headquarters of the Northeast Coast Institution of Engineers and Ship Builders. This is where I delivered a paper in behalf of our Navy. As I said earlier my subject was the battle damage activities and repair work that was conducted in the Pacific during World War II.

Q: And a copy of that we shall add to the appendix of the entire recollections.

James: That will give you whatever record is needed of the specifics of that paper. The paper was based on my experiences while serving in the South Pacific. I was very ably assisted by (then) Lt. Cmdr. Wayne Hoof, who later became Capt. Wayne Hoof of the Department of Engineering at the Naval Academy. Wayne did a great deal of research for me to dig out photographs, statistics, and battle damage reports for some of the ships that I had worked on.

From the comments on the paper's content, it apparently was an eye-opening revelation to the British particularly. They were most outspoken in their amazement as to the tremendous size and capability of the repair regime our Navy established in the Pacific during World War II.

Q: So many thousands of miles from home base.

James: Right. I am reminded of an article that I had read and commented on in my paper, reporting Admiral King's observation that over a half a million men were employed in the logistics part of the fleet during World War II. Not all of these, of course, were in the ship repair business, but a sufficient number were to permit us to do the type of repairs that returned a high percentage of damaged ships directly into the war instead of returning them Stateside for service. Those that were badly damaged such as the CANBERRA, the HOUSTON, the RENO, the FRANKLIN and others that I have forgotten had to come back home. But I think the overall repair capability of our Navy as presented in this paper for the Pacific area, at least, was one of the major reasons why we kept a very strong force of fighting ships in the Pacific that might not have otherwise been there.

For my effort in Britain I was honored some six months to a year later by being awarded by the Northeast Coast Institution of Marine Engineers and Ship Builders, their annual award for the outstanding paper that they had had presented to their society during the year. Curiously the medal was named the James medal and some of my more intimate friends have suggested that it was only because of the similarity of names that I won the prize. I insisted it was because I had told this august and dedicated technical group a cute story about the first American admiral ever to get to heaven as the reason for my receiving the award.

Altogether, this was a delightful experience that substituted for my earlier ambition to go and serve in London as the American technical officer on the staff of the naval attache, in which hope I had been thwarted.

Q: You in turn probably thwarted somebody else by staying at Mechanicsburg three years.

James: At that time I don't think Mechanicsburg was as popular as London was and I'm sure that I have not heard anybody ever complain that I prevented their achieving that post.

However, in the light of subsequent developments -- I guess it was the most fortuitous development that I didn't go to London for a two year period. My duties subsequently were such that catapulted me into the spotlight, which would not have been the case if I had been in London. I think that in a measure the events I shall soon cover and duty assignments I received in the aggregate led to my being nominated to be Chief of the

Bureau of Ships. This, of course, is a role that all naval architects and marine engineers held as our principal goal.

On my return from England I was ordered to set up a brand new naval facility. This occurred just about the time that the Korean War was hotting up. The Navy, taking very proper precautions, began anticipating the start of another major naval shipbuilding program. The lessons learned in World War II about how we had put together the magnificent fleet that finally was delivered made it clear to the Bureau of Ships that there had to be a more positive control of materials going into ship construction than had characterized World War II construction efforts. The lesson perhaps had its origin in the experience in building the landing craft program for the Navy when Gibbs and Cox, naval architects from New York City, were brought into the act to institute a material programming and material control over all of the bits and pieces, auxiliary equipment, and weaponry that went into these landing ships. In doing so they minimized the conflict between different shipyards in each trying to acquire the same piece of equipment at the earliest moment for their own purposes. This was sometimes carried to ludicrous extremes. There are some stories, perhaps apocryphal, but stories that nonetheless, that expediters from different shipyards took up residence in the cities where various important major naval ship components were being manufactured. As these components would move through inspection in the builder's plant to the shipping platform, the shipyard expediters with their own set of stencils, would surreptitiously get to the boxes and crates and re-stencil the destination so that they would end up in their own shipyard to the detriment of the shipyard for which they were originally intended.

I don't doubt that there was some of this going on. As a result of many difficulties in moving material, Admiral Homer Wallen, then Chief of the Bureau of Ships, and his deputy for shipbuilding, Admiral Wallace Sylvester, concluded they needed to have a shipbuilding scheduling control center. I was nominated to create such a center and to pick the site. I was given the limited direction that it had to be in a triangle from Boston to Cleveland to Washington, to get cracking and be ready by the time the shipbuilding authorizations for new ships to fight the Korean War were approved. The purpose of the activity was not just to control material but to schedule the erection of the ships in specific detail so as to be able to identify when the components, the turbines, the propellers, the shafting, the ventilating sets, the electric generators, all the myriad of items that go in the ship were needed to arrive at the individual shipyards for a specific ship to allow its erection in the orderly fashion.

Q: What was the rational that limited the location of this new establishment to the eastern seaboard area?

James: This triangle embraced the major manufacturing centers of our country where the great majority of the component parts of ships were manufactured. It also embraced to a major degree the shipbuilding yards, and certainly did embrace the naval architectural offices that were primarily located in Philadelphia and New York. Because of this we had easy access to these different plants, to the different naval architects who were developing detail working drawings of the different ship classes, to the Bureau of Ships, and, of course, to the ship yards where much of what we were scheduling ultimately would move.

The site selection was actually left up to me although Booz-Allen-Hamilton were brought in to do an initial survey. It was their contribution that this triangle should constitute the area in which we located our facilities. The decision as to where within this triangle we located was mine, mine to recommend and the Bureau of Ships to accept.

As I started into this task there was a little uncertainty as to whom I would be responsible to. At one moment it was believed that I should be under the supervisor of shipbuilding in New York City, A Capt. Ells Roth. He was located in the offices of Gibbs and Cox and because they had contributed significantly to scheduling of materials during part of World War II shipbuilding program, it was thought this might be a good location for our function. I opted otherwise, however, for reasons that aren't too clear at this late date.

Q: Perhaps greater freedom.

James: Undoubtedly that was a consideration but I also didn't think that being in New York was the most suitable starting place for our over the road traveling to get to many of the places we were going to have to visit, such as Mechanicsburg, the industrial centers in the Cleveland-Pittsburgh area and the like.

Q: At that point did you envision the complement of people involved in this project?

James: I was given a general indication of the probable size as being around six hundred people. These would be engineer types predominantly -- people who had been in shipyards in material control, in the actual waterfront production of ships, naval architects, marine engineers, designers, the whole gamut of a shipyard organization. The heavy emphasis needed to be on the sequence of building ships, the scheduling of the construction events, the scheduling of material requirements, and, of course, the physical ship erection including the problems of putting these parts and pieces into position.

So we started off -- initially it was myself and no other. I insisted that I needed some help to get started and was offered the services of Capt. Frank Jones, later Rear Admiral Jones, and now the Inspector General of the Naval Ships Systems Command. Together we divided up the location triangle and did our research into available properties. We had to do this rapidly as it was about the end of February that I was given this task and I was told to produce the first schedule by the first of July of the same year. The first schedule, as I recall it, was to be for the destroyer class ship.

Q: Were there any funds in sight at that point for this increased program?

James: I never did bother to inquire whether there were funds or not. I had to assume there were for whenever we needed a budget, we got one. Obviously in the accelerated effort to prepare for possible war in Korea there were funds that the Bureau of Ships could allocate to this function.

Frank Jones and I concluded that the area for our offices that gave the greatest promise was Philadelphia. We found a suitable piece of property at 1409 North Broad Street. It had an old automobile sales and service building -- about a six story building which had about 75,000 square feet in it, and except for the ground floor, which had been a display area, it was very adequately subdivided. So we leased the property and the two of us moved in. In the meantime, I acquired a third person, a Capt. Chris Engleman. As we knew we were going to be heavily in the electronics area, I brought him on board to serve in that capacity. By virtue of his seniority he became my deputy and initially I put him on the road around the country recruiting employees. He toured the East and West Coast shipyards, both private and naval, and gave such glowing accounts of the prospects that in nothing flat we were overwhelmed with applicants. We started our recruiting in March and by July first we had a cadre of a hundred and fifty people and had produced our first schedule. Our biggest problem was the need to invent the system of scheduling which we did from earlier knowledge some of us had gained in prior shipyard experience, using less than fully organized control efforts to put ships together.

Q: Did you first have to determine the scope of this?

James: The scope of it was announced. We were told how many ships and what classes the Navy was in prospect of building. There were very few of these finally authorized because the scope of the Korean War did not develop as first expected.

Q: This is rather unique, is it not? This anticipatory program?

James: I think it was extremely unique and I think it was in recollection of the need for this in the World War II programs that prompted Admiral Sylvester to stand very rigidly in his insistence of this kind of an operation. He was my direct military superior as Assistant Chief of the Bureau for shipbuilding. To a large extent, however, he left me to my own devices which precipitated a lot of anguish, and a lot of tedious hours. By the time I came onto the scene to acquire military personnel for my function, the other activities had already gone through IBM personnel records with a fine tooth comb, had discovered all the jewels that were then available, and ordered officers to their particular function. I spent much time pouring over records of available individuals, retired or reserve officers, to select my staff. I did get about three regulars assigned. Finally we put together a group of about twenty-one or two officers, largely engineer types and a few Supply Corps types. Our maximum population before the Korean effort began to taper off, was around three hundred and fifty people.

By the time we reached that plateau where I was instructed to remain until the direction of the Korean War became more clear, we had generated manuals on scheduling techniques, we had set up procedures for controlling materials within plants, we had established our preemptory right over all mate rials going through those plants, had organized the inspection service to respect and respond to our requirements, and had acquainted shipyards with the technique of building the ships to a prescribed class type of schedule that made it possible to insure them of the receipt of material as required to meet those schedules.

Q: What percentage of these techniques was derived entirely from World War II experiences -- the wisdom that you collectively had accumulated there?

James: I think that the wisdom gained from the experiences of World War II ~~were~~ *was* limited to awareness of the lack of this sort of program and the acknowledgement of the fact that it was a vital consideration. It was a negative contribution. The composite wisdom of those of us who had been in shipyards and had been in charge of shipbuilding, plus, of course, many contributions from others that were not in our immediate cadre of personnel, led to the techniques that we evolved which we first tried on shipyards, both private and naval, on Bureau of Ships people and tested in that sense before we gave them the Good Housekeeping seal of approval.

Q: How did you test them?

James: Simply by presenting the technique, describing it, discussing it, and getting people with shipbuilding background and experience to review it for defects, minor or critical, and adjusting it, accordingly. Our techniques were largely a reflection of the personal experiences of many of knowledgeable persons who had worked to produce ships in this country.

Q: Did you use prototypes in approaching a shipbuilding yard like the one at Newport News?

James: Schedules were always based on the first ship of a class which was the prototype of that class, but it was not a prototype in the sense of build it now, look at it, change it, and then start building the others. These were simply the first ships on the production line of perhaps as many as fifty, sixty, ships of a type that were projected as possibly being required.

I always looked upon that period as one of the sadder times in our Navy's history. We had a magnificent and tremendously large shipbuilding program in World War II that provided us a large number of very fine ships. But because of the urgency of getting bottoms to sea, they did not fully reflect the evolution of certain weapons and control systems that evolved in the seven or eight years from the end of World War II to the Korean War. We cut off the shipbuilding effort promptly at the end of World War II, delivering only those ships thereafter that were in an unfinished state when the war ended. Nothing in the way of new ship construction was started again for a number of years. If we had gone into the large shipbuilding effort contemplated as being necessary to fight an extended Korean War, we would have a much better posture than our Navy has today. We would have brought on modern ships that would have been delivered to the fleet in the period roughly 1956 to 1958. This would have been a major step to upgrade our Navy ships. For many reasons, and I'm sure most of them were financial, our government decid-d that we would not go into this major shipbuilding effort because of the Korean war. The Korean War tapered off rather quickly after MacArthur started leap frogging up the peninsula and using amphibious forces in the manner which the Navy had proved so effective during World War II.

Q: Admiral, is it possible that our idealism as a people gets in the way of the concepts of the continuing program?

James: To a degree. I'm sure that our general revulsion to military conflict is a factor that has to be taken into account by the political animals of our nation and I'm sure that there was a period of revulsion to continuing to build our military machine after World War II. But how short-sighted these actions were in contrast to military and security needs of this nation. We now witness the potential conflict between a giant with a brand new fleet including all of the modern improvements that could be cranked into them, while ours has aged to the point where we are having to retire ships in great numbers because of their antiquity and their unsuitability for service as opponents to the giant, the Russian Navy.

Whatever the reasons, we didn't build the new fleet. The Ship Building Scheduling Activity continued to exist, however. I left it after a two year period.

Q: How much was turned out in that time?

James: Schedules for virtually the entire program of ships that had been contemplated, from mine sweepers to aircraft carriers. I would say this covered perhaps twenty major shipbuilding schedules. These don't come easy. You have to take the ship apart into its smallest component pieces, the welding rod, the steel plate, as well as the turbines and gears, and know when to schedule them for erection. It had taken months to bring industry into accepting these schedules as the gospel lesson of the Navy. All of this finally was considered superfluous to Navy requirements because the few new ships being built were not in multiple quantities, rather were only one or two ships at a time.

Q: I suppose your task was made more difficult and especially in terms of industry, in that it was considered just a minor kind of war and not one that was declared.

James: I don't believe that was a consideration. I think as much as anything our difficulty with industry stemmed from the fact that the Army and the Air Force were out doing something of the same sort for their materials and we found ourselves in conflict with them. This, of course, led to the need for some super coordinating agency which was contemplated when the Navy set up the Office of Chief of Naval Materials some years ago. We advocated the resumption of some sort of that control. There were certain areas in industry where we were preeminent contractor and we had little or no difficulty with these.

Q: What I meant is the psychology of business as usual more-or-less prevailed during that whole period.

James: Certainly. That is always a consideration. It's a reflection of the general attitude of the public, the unwillingness to foresee the prospect of need for the engines of war in the near time frame.

Q: What sort of focus did you give to landing craft in this overall scheme?

James: At that time I don't believe we had concentrated too much attnetion on landing craft because they were relatively small consumers of material. While the volume of these craft would undoubtedly have been high, the total requirements in contrast to a destroyer building program or carrier building program were relatively small.

Q: Your picture wasn't complicated as it was in World War II by the fact that we were producing for Allied nations as well.

James: At that particular moment we were not complicated by that aspect -- no. There were other major nations than ourselves involved in the Korean conflict but we didn't have to worry about it as you point out. Not like the things we did for the British, for example, in building large numbers of certain types of ships for them.

The assignment to NSSA was a very delightful period that came abruptly to an end about March of 1953, when I was invited to Washington to see the then Chief of the Bureau of Ships, Admiral Durawrd Leggett. He announced to me that I was to become the Comptroller of the Bureau of Ships. To me that was a name given to the old finance officer of the Bureau of Ships which was considered one of the most God awful dead ends that any technical officer could wallow into. Weirdly enough, a number of those who had been finance officer reached flag rank but more recently this had not been the case. I was really set back on my heels by this announcement.

Q: In retrospect, there was wisdom in this, wasn't there?

James: I'll lead into that. It shows that too often the judgment of the officer looking up is not as good as the judgment of the officer who is up looking down. I literally came into the Bureau of Ships on my shield, which I think was the second time I had been ordered into an assignment I didn't want -- the Mechanicsburg post and this one.

After I arrived back in the Bureau, we went through the formal rigamarole of dissolving the Fiscal Office and creating the Comptroller's Office. I thought this was all just sop to my injured feelings. Then as I began the program of reviewing the Bureau's requirements for funds for the various programs, the operation of our ship yards, our laboratories, and our supervisors of shipbuilding, and the Bureau headquarters, itself, I began to realize what a tremendous new experience was opening up before me. I had superficially known of the SupShips, the Bureau's laboratories, the shipyard commands, and all the rest of it without really knowing what made them run -- I learned the fuel is money.

After a while and perhaps because I was fairly articulate, I was used by the Chief of the Bureau to present many of the Bureau's programs before the different subcommittees of the Congress. I began to find a completely new field of interest. I then had the fascinating task of putting together the budgets, defending them in turn within the Bureau, within the Navy Department, within the Department of Defense, and finally defending them, single-handedly in some instances, before the curious, critical, and seemingly unfriendly members of Congress on the Appropriations Committees, and the Naval Affairs Committees.

Q: Would you recall some of these experiences with the Congress?

James: I served both during the periods when we had a Democratic Congress and the brief two year period when we had a Republican Congress. I was the Comptroller of the Bureau, Admiral Leggett was the principal witness at most of the hearings. As I said earlier, many times I had to go up alone to the Hill and defend separate issues, generally not the overall Bureau programs.

I remember the first time I appeared before Congressman Harry Shepherd from San Bernadino, during the time when the Democrats had organized the House. Harry Shepherd was a tippler who came barging into the hearing rooms and with great ostentation and a pontifical manner asked questions, then sat back to listen to the responses. I observed that his attention would wander, to find out that he was asleep in his chair. This gave somewhat of a comforting feeling to know that you need not be precise in your answers in view of the fact that the chairman seemed to be enjoying the somnolence of the discussion rather than the content of the responses.

Q: Where there not some other members who counted?

James: Yes, there were, but generally he ruled the committee rather sternly and it was possible to let down your guard just a wee bit. By contrast, when the Republicans organized the Congress, the previous senior minority member became the chairman, Congressman Wigglesworth from Massachusetts. He was a detailist of the greatest order. He knew his Navy budget better than the assorted Navy comptrollers did and was able to trip us up on all sorts of details. It was a mentally exhausting experience to be before Congressman Wigglesworth, believe me, because you had to be alert to all the nuances of his questions. You had to be prepared to answer everything from the construction costs of the original CONSTITUTION up to the present FORRESTAL type carrier, because he knew all the answers before he asked the questions, or at least he had a very sound grasp of the problems.

Q: He was a Boston nautical type.

James: That experience with him was one of my most educational ones. It taught me the need to be complete and precise and know my subject from A to Z.

It took a lot of candle burning to achieve that degree of preparedness but I think the education served magnificently in future appearances before the Armed Services Committee chaired by Chairman Carl Vinson. He, too, was a gentleman who knew his Navy inside and out. He had the advantage of the over view of all systems of the Navy, not just the ship system which was my particular specialty, and subsequently added considerably to my personal education as to what it takes to put together the total Navy war machine. I have always considered him one of the grandest gentlemen of the Congress. He was a very arbitrary individual. He ruled his committee with an iron hand. If any young Congressman member of the committee ventured a question out of turn he was more often likely to be slapped down than he was to be accorded the privilege of continuing.

When you got through with the hearings before Carl Vinson, you knew that the whole of the Navy soul had been bared, the requirements had been rationalized and justified. There wasn't too much input from the Defense Department during this period that I am speaking of and so you had the fragmented and sometimes competing presentations (and I say fragmented advisedly) of the Air Force, the Army, and the Navy. The services were often competing for the same project, or same money in what I considered to be many duplications. This situation disappeared under MacNamara at a time a little further down the road.

When I had completed two years in this assignment I really understood the financial workings of the Navy. I had also become intimately associated and acquainted with the Defense Department comptroller, Wilfred McNeil. I had come to regard him as a man of tremendous capability. I was privileged later as Chief of BuShips to work with him in the development of a system which we thought would make possible the funding of ship construction in a much more knowledgeable way. Up to this date, when you got authorization for ships to be built -- I don't say it was deliberate but it certainly was the practice to minimize the options of cost by always presenting the lesser options in order to reduce the budget requirement. Then as the program proceeded, year after year, after year, you went before the Congress for deficiency appropriations to make up the growing costs. This went on almost indefinitely until the contract to build was completed.

Q: Which in the end made it cost more than it would have.

James: I guess that's a fair statement in spite of the effort to keep down costs which was continuous throughout construction, but it certainly didn't reveal at the outset what the total commitment the Congress was making when they authorized the start of a program. I thought that was a serious defect in the system.

Q: Was it always possible to know what the total commitment might be?

James: As we later developed it, the answer was yes. But it took a lot more extra effort and it took a lot of projecting, things like inflation rates and the evolution of new systems. After years of building ships the records of the Bureau of Ships were replete with this kind of historical data that you could almost plot on a curve, then extrapolate into the future.

Q: This is the sort of thing you and McNeil accomplished?

James: Later we sold to the members of Congress the idea of full funding of the ship at the time it was initially presented for authorization. It took a lot of doing because it meant the appropriating of money at the outset for what used to be aggregate of yearly increments. These became fantastically large suns.

Q: This was upsetting the traditional practice of the Congress and it must have been difficult to change it.

James: It was extremely difficult. But for McNeil's determination and our mutual belief in this system for which I developed the details from his original concept. I don't think we would have been given the full funding system. However, he was able to convince the Congress that we should have it and we proceeded under that program. Both of us recognized one serious pitfall down the road.

As you begin to accumulate the money for the total cost of building a number of ships, the size of this pot that is held in reserve for year by year allocation (our practice in paying off our bills) becomes great and a target for people with other interests. They believed it wouldn't hurt to dip into it and take out a hundred million dollars or so and apply it to their program to get that program started, then pay the money back later. We were extremely worried about this. As long as McNeil and I were in office we thought we could control it and we thought others might have the same ability also, but --

Q: Part of your difficulty was that there were two systems in operation simultaneously.

James: That we overcame by getting appropriations to cover the end funding of those ships that were in process.

Q: But the people who saw this money allocated and thought they could borrow some of it for the time being were operating on the old system, were they not?

James: They weren't necessarily of such a class, they were just a bunch of vultures flying about that spotted large pot and wanted to dig into it. As long as we had good strong secretarial support it didn't happen. Years later, however, it did happen just as we had predicted it would. The control of the reserve ship building account became more a matter of lack of control and the monies began to disappear. It wasn't too long before the Navy was back to the practice of having to request yearly deficiencies, which we truly believed resulted in greater total cost because you couldn't lock up the entire program at the outset with prevailing prices. We also thought the new system of control eliminated the need to go through many of the aberrations that characterize the appropriation of money. We wouldn't have had to worry about what we are going to do when Congress was slow in authorizing appropriations. They would pass continuing resolutions in the Congress but you were always required to do something like slowing down the expenditure rate and in doing so you weren't necessarily doing the job in the most efficient way.

These are the sort of things that we thought the total funding concept would eliminate and for several years we were gratified to see just exactly that result.

Q: Admiral, the concept of the total funding -- was this a part of the original idea back of a unified Department of Defense?

James: I don't believe I am knowledgeable enough to make a comment. I really don't know whether any such an idea was considered then, but as far as I know this total funding concept didn't come along until the middle '50s, the Defense Department was organized in '47.

Q: You spoke earlier of the duplication which was discovered among the three services. This, it was hoped, would be eliminated.

James: That's another subject. When I became completely conscious of this situation, I had been made Chief of the Bureau of Ships. I can recall many meetings of the CNO's advisory board, of which I was a member (I don't know if that was its proper name), when someone present would report the fact that the Air Force had started a program to do thus and so, or the Army, for example, had just conceived a new approach to amphibious landing. When these matters were presented the Navy's almost routine reaction was, "let us create a team to investigate and if we find it appropriate to do so we'll come up with our own program to accomplish the same basic objective." The intent of this was to minimize the intrusion of the other services into the prerogatives of the Navy.

As a Navy enthusaist, I guess I am a throw-back. It used to revolt me to listen to these discussions because of the experience I had gained before the Congress earlier. There I witnessed for myself the raw attempts of the military services to perpetuate themselves through their proposed programs irrespective of which service was the best qualified to produce some new weapon system, some new approach to using old weapons, and the likes. This is what I meant by the service duplication that I witnessed. In all fairness to Secretary McNamara's administration which I consider to have been very poor, he evolved the system of review of programs of all branches using the "cost effective" approach. This system selected one of the three services to develop the new function at the least possible cost. I believe this effectively did reduce unnecessary service inspired jealousy to protect its own prerogatives by duplicating in a somewhat different manner what the other services were doing. Although I can't give McNamara's administration high marks as to the cost effectiveness of the over-all defense effort, certainly there are many areas where this system was extremely useful. There are also areas where it proved to be extremely stupid -- the TFX or the F-111 is a classic example of how by consolidating under a single program the fighter aircraft procurement for the Air Force and the Navy he did one of the most fantastic jobs of buggering up our present military readiness, and added greatly to total cost.

But the concept of the cost effective approach, which came into being in 1961, undoubtedly was a useful tool which I am sure the Navy and the Defense Department must continue to use in spite of its shortcomings and some less than brilliant applications.

Q: In the earlier period when you were there as comptroller, did Secretary Wilson show any inclinations in this direction?

James: Not to my knowledge. There was no indication of this sort of effort. The Comptroller of the Defense Department I believe was then the sole instrument for sorting out military programs and trying to minimize duplication. To this end I believe Wilfred

McNeil was an extremely effective one. He was continued in office under an assortment of Presidents and Secretaries of Defense. I think he served Louie Johnson, Wilson and McElroy and part time for Tom Gates. He did a great deal but there were many subtle ways by which the various services could push repetitive programs. You could observe this in the various top level service meetings. I'm not critical of CNOs who practiced this. They were out to ensure that the Navy had the maximum utilization of every potential new concept that came down the pike. However, I don't believe that the thought, "Is this a better task for the Army or the Air Force to perform?" ever entered the mind of a single CNO that I served, to the point where he would relinquish Navy's interests to another service. I may be doing them a grave injustice but I say it wasn't apparent to me.

Q: Empire building is something inherent in men.

James: My tour of duty as comptroller ended with a complete feeling of satisfaction.

Q: Your point of view had changed.

James: My point of view had redically changed. It started to change early in the game. I was not the Fiscal Officer or the bean counter as I like to twit myself and others who served in this capacity. In fact a little joke that I think first brought the attention of Tom Gates to R. K. James, was when he was the Assistant Secretary of the Navy for financial management. I told him this definition of a comptroller: "A comptroller is a man with a heart of feldspar, ice water in his veins, cold blue piercing eyes, no warm human feeling, no sympathy for his fellow man, generally a most unsatisfactory and undesirable individual. The only saving grace is that no comptroller ever reproduces and ultimately they all go to Hell." Tom Gates thought that was funny and I'm sure he's used it many times since. That's perhaps one of the earlier occasions where he had reason to acknowledge the existence of a Captain Ralph K. James.

Q: I take it you established real rapport with Gates.

James: He was the man who ultimately made the decision that I would become Chief of the Bureau of Ships, so I guess I should say yes.

I have almost overlooked a very important event that occurred during the period of time I served at the Shipbuilding Scheduling Activity. This was the wedding of our daughter. Pat was enamored with a young West Point graduate who was a captain in the Air Force. How she became enamored is another story. She was his blind date that was arranged through a friend who had pursued her with great vigor. She considered him to be somewhat of a jerk and reasoned that any friend of this chap had to be the same type. She therefore resisted the invitation to a blind date. Finally, out of boredom as much as anything, she accepted and to make a long story short, this Air Force captain, who was a B-52 pilot at the time, married the daughter of a Navy captain in the Naval Academy chapel in February 1953. His groomsmen included Army officers, Air Force officers, and midshipmen. I think Mrs. James and I gave more to service unification on that one occasion than perhaps most individuals in any of the services have given.

It was a delightful affair from which we have acquired two wonderful grandchildren and a fine son-in-law -- a very competent young man who left the Air Force, however, after their first child was born. He saw no future in flying B-52s under General Curtis

LeMay, who was head of SAC at that time and a hard task master. OUr son-in-law would report to his plane early in the morning in a U. S. airbase, thinking he might be back for dinner, only to find he then spent the next three weeks over in Africa. This was repeated so frequently that he decided it wasn't worth it so he resigned from the Air Force and is now in the real estate business in Santa Rosa, California.

Interview #7

Rear Admiral Ralph K. James, USN, Ret.

Annapolis, Maryland

by John T. Mason, Jr.

July 13, 1971

Mr. Mason: Admiral, this morning I believe you begin chapter seven with an account of your tour of duty as Commander of the Long Beach Naval Shipyard and as Industrial Manager of the Eleventh Naval District. This assignment was taken up on the 15th of August 1955.

Admiral James: I think the circumstances that led up to my rather precipitous assignment to the Long Beach Naval Shipyard are of some interest.

The Chief of the Bureau of Ships in the spring of 1955 was Rear Admiral Durwood Leggett, who was relieved in April by Rear Admiral Al Mumma. Prior to his departure to the retired list Admiral Leggett assured me that I was leaving the Bureau some time in the summertime, and it was his intent to send me to the San Francisco Naval Shipyard.

The Shipyard was one that I thought very much of, as well as being a delightful location. Just before he retired, he reported that he'd check out his plan with the soon to be new Chief and got the confirmation of this intent.

So I was proceeding happily in anticipation of moving into the San Francisco Shipyard as its Commander. I had also been asked by the then Deputy Chief of the Bureau of Ships, Rear Admiral Benny Monseau, to let Captain Bill Turney, who was then commanding the yard, be aware of the fact that I was reporting out there some time in September. This was to be done during a pending visit I had planned to the West Coast.

I arrived in San Francisco, and to my amazement Turney was completely unaware of any intent to relieve him. Although he'd been up to bat before the selection board and failed the selection, he should have been aware of the prospect of early transfer. Seemingly he thought he had it locked in that he would remain at the Yard until the time he retired. This action to relive apparently provoked him, and weirdly enough it provoked him at me.

We had served together on two prior occasions. I never had such fine fitness reports as I'd gotten from Bill Turney, but all of a sudden everything was turned around because he was quite determined to stay in San Francisco.

I came back without full awareness of this. One bright morning in July of that same year I was suddenly and pre-emptory called into the Chief's office, where I was told to wait because Mumma had people with him. While I was sitting there finally Admiral Bob Swart stormed out of the Chief's office. His face was as dark as a thundercloud.

I tried to be casual and pass a friendly greeting, and I got nothing but a grunt as he slammed out through the door. I was next, so to witness this preliminary did not give me any degree of enthusiasm. I didn't know whether I was related to Swart's problem or not, but soon discovered that indeed I was.

Admiral Mumma was a long term friend. He told me that I was going to have to go to the Long Beach Naval Shipyard instead of San Francisco. I was terribly provoked by this, because I'd done all my planning; my arrangements for the summer had been completed. He said not only was I going to have to go to Long Beach, but I was going to have to leave by the end of the week.

So I said, "Give me a clue as to what this is all about." He said, "Rickover has popped out again."

Rickover had been up before a Congressional committee which asked him how things were going with he being an Assistant Chief of the Bureau of Ships, and an officer of later vintage being his boss as Chief of the Bureau of Ships, and how was it going.

Apparently, and I have not read the Congressional Record, he stated that it was going all right as far as Mumma was concerned but there were other problems in the Bureau. Under questioning he was asked what or who were the other problems and he said,

"Admiral Swart," who hated Rickover's guts, who organizationally was an indirect senior to Rickover.

I don't believe the Congressional committee session was over more than half an hour when Charlie Thomas buzzed for Mumma. The word was, "Move Swart out of any responsibility over Rickover." Swart had one of the very important ASsistant Chief's jobs.

So to fill this vacancy Mumma concluded that the then Commander of the Long Beach Yard, who'd only been there about a year and a half, Admiral Mike Honsinger, was to be brought in, to succeed Swart. And this was all to happen virtually overnight, because Mumma had to report to the Congressional committee (Carl Vinson was Chairman then) and advise that he had taken steps to remove the burr from under Rickover's saddle.

There were those, and I surely number myself amongst them, who thought Rickover needed intelligent burrs periodically under his saddle to keep him from becoming too much of a demagogue.

The whole thing was shaken up, so instead of going to San Francisco, which I had anticipated I would do in September, I had to be in Long Beach in July, a week after this message.

Mr. Mason: Why did your plans have to be changed?

Admira. James: Because I was apparently the only potentially available new shipyard commander, and therefore I had to step into the breach because I was rounding out my tour in the Bureau. I was also appraised on this occasion of something else, but first let me conclude my own immediate reaction.

When Mumma told me of his plan, it was a distinct blow personally. Not that I thought that San Francisco was the greatest shipyard, but it was the shipyard that I thought very much of and I was fully aware of all of the problems then confronting Long Beach - the Subsidence problem where the shipyard was gradually and gracefully sinking into the sea as the surrounding community pumped out all the oil from under it.

Mumma and I had a very heated discussion, Mumma was not only my Chief but he was a long term friend. A man a few months younger than I, that I'd known for years.

In fact, at one stage our daughter was engaged to his son, much to their delight and much to our distress because he was still a collegian at the time.

I told him I wouldn't go to Long Beach. I said, "I'll resign first. I'll have my resignation on your desk by the morning." He said he thought I was nuts and said, "You go home and sleep on it, and come back and tell me that again in the morning before I believe you."

He was smarter than I was because at this time I was proposing to blow about twenty-seven years worth of active military service.

By the next morning I'd cooled down, and had made rather extreme arrangements to continue our son in prep school where he was prepping to reenter the Naval Academy.

Mr. Mason: Welshmen are sometimes explosive, aren't they?

Admiral James: I guess I am certainly. I'm a second generation Welshman. I do have that problem from time to time.

Mr. Mason: May I ask you one question - in your estimation did Rickover deserve that sort of consideration? Are his abilities commensurate with the kid glove treatment?

Admiral James: We didn't think so, those of us who had to serve with him. Later I became his boss when I became Chief of the Bureau. I certainly didn't think so then, but he had quite a coterie of Senators and Congressmen with whom he was the absolute word.

He would take on the establishment repeatedly. You recall his blast at the Naval Academy curricula, and many other matters where he was anything but knowledgeable to talk about, but nonetheless he had gained a large following on the Hill.

Mr. Mason: What is the secret of this?

Admiral James: A guy by the name of Clay Blair I think is the secret of it all. Clay Blair was a reporter for the SATURDAY EVENING POST.

Rickover was passed over for Admiral when his normal turn came up, and in my opinion with complete and full justification. I was not a member of the Selection Board. Of course there are many things that you have to be aware of that only the Board knows about, to reach such a positive judgment as I have just expressed. However, he was passed over.

This guy Clay Blair for reasons that I do not know knew Rickover and believed that he had a story in that here was the first Jewish EDO candidate for Admiral who was rejected. He tried to make out that this was because of his religious and ethnic background. I really shouldn't say 'religious' because Rickover was and I believe still is a practicing Episcopalian. Nonetheless in the eyes of the Jewish people he was a full-fledged Jew, even though he was a turn-coat Jew.

Clay Blair wrote a series of articles that got Homer Wallen, who was then Chief of the Bureau of Ships, into very hot water.

A couple of years later Rickover finally was selected, I believe, by edict of the Secretary of the Navy. It was two years later I believe. So he had garnered a large audience of people who thought there was an oppressed minority race member being given a rough time by the Navy brass. He evoked a great deal more sympathy than he deserved.

That was the background of Rickover. That was why he was receiving more attention from people outside the military than he deserved.

With the event of his selection to Rear Admiral he became almost impossible for the senior line types to handle. He didn't stay within his last, within the technical environment of the Bureau of Ships; he was all over the Navy acting as an expert if not soothsayer.

He still has throttle control on the input of all younger officers to the nuclear program. All have to meet his standards, which are sometimes weird and wonderful, in order to break into the program in any capacity.

However, I don't think I could go on about Rickover and maintain a reasonable attitude toward the rest of my biography here. I get too thoroughly worked up when I start dreaming about him.

Then because of this Rickover inspired incident I was destined to go to Long Beach, but the next morning . . .

Mr. Mason: And Turney remained in San Francisco?

Admiral James: I'll tell you about that briefly later.

The next morning I went in to see Admiral Mumma, reported that I had cooled down and that I was prepared to take off for Long Beach.

Then he said, "Let me tell you one other thing - there was something that I didn't tell you yesterday."

He said, that Admiral Jack Redman, who was the Twelfth Naval District Commander, had called him about a month earlier and said that James was not an acceptable relief for Turney. Mumma asked him why. He apparently didn't give a bunch of sensible reasons.

The gist of it was that Turney, who was a close friend of Jack Redman, had gotten him to go to bat. Redman actually told Mumma that if I came out there, If Mumma persisted in sending me out there, that I would regret it.

When Mumma told me this I was flabbergasted. To my knowledge I had never seen, and certainly never met, Jack Redman in my life. And why he had notions about me that were so strong as to prevent me from coming to take command of one of his several commands I couldn't understand until I realized that he must have been fed a lot of 'who struck John' by Bill Turney, whom I said earlier had given me some of the greatest fitness reports that I've ever had from anybody. He obviously had convinced Redman that he should stay, and Redman was determined that nobody would relieve Bill Turney until Turney's retirement date came up the following year.

Al Mumma was not the kind of a guy to be pushed around but he did say, and I think very logically, that if he persisted in sending me to San Francisco (which was my ambition), that I would probably fall by the wayside as a result of rough handling by Jack Redman. This is pure speculation, but it could have happened.

With this knowledge I was more placated with my assignment to Long Beach, although it meant quite an upheaval personally and family-wise. Our son, as I say, was in prep school, and wouldn't have been out until weeks after I had to be in Long Beach. I had to proceed alone in one of the family automobiles to Long Beach, hightailing every inch of the way.

One of the nicer things that Mike HOnsinger did in advance of my arrival was to mail me a little booklet where he had fifty or sixty individual photographs of key personnel, both military and civilian, in the shipyard, He listed their duties, and provided a little biographical sketch of each of the persons. It arrived about a day before I took off for Long Beach.

As I was driving myself down thru Texas, where I went to visit our daughter and her husband - he was then on duty at the Randolph Air Force Base in San Antonio - I would flip the pages of this book, look at the photograph, and scan the biographical sketch.

By the time I arrived at Long Beach I could call by sight over fifty key personnel. When I started to do this, after arrival, halting people on the street and calling them by name and introducing myself they thought I was an absolute genius. It was all because of the thoughtfulness of Mike Honsinger.

You can be assured that I did the same thing for my successor. I thought this was one of the finest ways of breaking in the new man at the top of an organization - to be able to identify and speak about the people in the new command.

One chap in the book I saw riding a bicycle as I was driving around the shipyard on the second or third day after my arrival. I stopped the car and I hollered out, "Hey, Webb." He stopped his bicycle and he said, "I don't know you." I said, "No, but you're Webb Ay, and you're this, that, and the other thing." He responded, "I'll be God-damned."

He became one of my closer friends and has always marveled at our first meeting, even though I told him how easily it had been done.

To get back to the shipyard - when I arrived, Honsinger had limited time to turn over the command. After giving me a quick tour of the area and having condensed social contacts with the key people, he devoted the rest of his time to describing a cataclysmic problem facing Long Beach - the withdrawal of oil from under the city of Long Beach that was causing sinkage of the yard and city to an alarming degree.

Across the street from the shipyard entrance was the Edison Power and Light Company whose main building had dropped in the period from 1941 to 1955 twenty-six feet from its original ground elevation. This phenomena radiated out from that point. The shipyard was experiencing sinkage at its entrance amounting to twenty-two feet below its 1941 benchmarks. It then faded out to three or four feet sinkage in extremities of the shipyard, remote from this power plant, which was known as the 'epicenter' of the subsidence phenomena.

Mr. Mason: Is this a unique experience?

Admiral James: This is a story in itself, but I believe it's the reason I later became the head man in my specialty, so I think it's worth devoting a little time describing it.

Honsinger told of having devoted considerable time to trying to alert the populace of the city to this problem and how he had not succeeded too well. He felt that this was the number one problem because it threatened the very existence of the shipyard, which was what I had heard before I was ordered out there and one of the reasons for my reluctance to go to Long Beach.

Mr. Mason: How long had this been going on?

Admiral James: The shipyard was first authorized in 1941, and the construction was started on Terminal Island that year. This included digging deep graving dock about forty-five or fifty feet in depth and about 1000 to 1100 feet in length. This hole in the ground was dug right near the Edison Pacific Power and Light Company plant.

People in Long Beach charged that the sinkage in the area started with the construction of this drydock. So the Navy, in a desultory sort of way, had done some examination of the problem and made some determinations that this was not a fact.

In about 1946 with this phenomena of sinking of the surface continuing . . .

Mr. Mason: At the rate of how much per year?

Admiral James: At the rate of twelve to fifteen inches a year in some places, tapering off to two inches in others. In the epicenter it was as much as eighteen inches a year.

However what was overlooked at that time was that concurrently with the construction of this drydock the discovery wells in the Wilmington Oil Field started to be pumped.

The Wilmington oil field extends from the city of Wilmington, a little north and west of the shipyard, on a southwesterly line that took it right through this power plant, cut a corner off of the naval shipyard and extended out into the Bay. New wells were being drilled every day thus adding to the number of wells being pumped. I don't know the rate, but let me guess at no fewer than four or five new wells a month.

Mr. Mason: And how deep was the oil lake below the surface?

Admiral James: There were several zones. There wer five different zones, the deepest of which was around 6,000 feet and the shallowest of which was producing at around 2,300 feet.

These wells were part of the perimeter of the shipyard. When the city deeded the land that made the Naval Base and the Shipyard they reserved the right to conduct offset drilling from the northern boundary. Offset drilling means to drill straight down and then angle your drill bit out into the area which you wish to pump oil from. You can go as far as a mile horizontally from the position where you start your drill. From a wide band around the outer edge of the shipyard and the naval base, they were pumping away merrily and filling the coffers of the city of Long Beach with the returns of this oil production.

It wasn't until some time later on, I don't recall just when, when someone came front and ceter with the belief that the subsidence problem was not the drydock but that it was the extraction of oil from underneath the area. The affected area extended all the way up into the city of Wilmington and into downtown Long Beach. While the epicenter was where the worst of the subsidence was occurring there was in the order of three to five feet sinkage right in the city center of Long Beach.

The city stores were losing windows, curbings were breaking, power cables were popping, the shipyard and drydock was sinking, water was lapping over the edge of the land into the Yard. We finally were at a point where there had to be a dike built or we'd been inundated.

I remember one day when I was sitting in my office and I heard this loud report. I got on the phone to find out what it was. It was a railroad rail that had popped, because of the vertical shear stress that developed in this rail due to the uneven settling of the ground around it.

The problem was one of getting the city alerted to the extreme hazard that was represented there. Honsinger had started this. He'd gone to meetings and he'd made speeches. He talked to the people on the City Council, but no one was prepared to admit responsibility for this phenomena who were benefiting by the intake of oil money, the city least of all.

The state was the owner, but the city was the controller of the oil operations, and until the years later the city skimmed off all the profits. They had organized a consortium of oil companies to do the drilling in the majority of the area affected, and they were banking seventy-five, to one hundred million dollars a year.

So when I was educated to the problem, and this took several months, I found there were several people that were laboring in the vineyard to try and alert the locality to the imminence of catastrophe. We joined forces.

We created the 'Hard Core Committee,' meaning the hard core of determined laborers that were going to see this problem eliminated or else. We consisted of the President of the employees' association, a chap named Don Sutherland; the business man with the largest single business in town, Harry Buffum, a Mr. Darrel Neighbors who was a real estate agent and trust officer for a large real estate holding family, the Bixby clan, and one or two others, including a member of the local newspaper staff.

We used to meet periodically and plot strategy. We then would go around and make speeches and belabor people, with all sorts of propaganda telling them that unless something was done to curb this wanton removal of oil the city would sink out of sight.

The reason this situation developed in the particular locality, and it had only happened one other place in the world, Goose Creek, Texas, was that the discovery of oil in this underlying terrain was in an area that in the glacial days was an alluvial desert. The soil was anything but competent structure. It was the difference between a mud formation and a rock foundation that underlay most of the city of Long Beach. All of the shipyard area and much of the surrounding area was the Los Angeles River, as we now know it. In the glacial days the river deposited silt that did not compact, did not create a competent rock type structure below the surface. So as the oil was removed the interstices in the soil left by removing the oil allowed the surface to close in the gap and sink below original ground level.

This effort of ours finally resulted in the city employing competent geological and petroleum experts to do a study.

The producers, of which the city was the largest, were all fearful of having any judgment rendered that this was indeed the cause of the problem of subsidence and the sinking of the surface, because it would open them up to literally hundreds of million dollars worth of damage suits.

Mr. Mason: Did they foster the idea that it was the result of the graving dock?

Admiral James: Oh yes, this was always popping up. And there were nineteen other reasons that were advanced, none of them with any rational support.

The oil producers went merrily on their way, even though the petroleum experts said, "Now if you start pumping water under ground as you take the oil out you eliminate the problem of leaving cavities below the surface. You drive what residual oil you've left behind to the well head, you produce more oil, and you have no subsidence problems thereafter."

To get water injection started was a seemingly impossible task. It had to be salt water, because the quantities of fresh water needed were not available in Southern California. There was salt water seepage into some of the oil zones, but not at the rate of the oil removal or enough to prevent subsidence.

I'm seemingly devoting a great deal of time to this subject, but I think it's a matter that ought to become a permanent record because it involved the saving of the shipyard and ultimately the city of Long Beach.

I have a cousin who at the time was Vice Chairman of the board of the Hartford Insurance Company. He remembered that I was on duty in Long Beach and he wrote me to get what information he could about this phenoma, because he said his company was withholding loans for construction in the Long Beach city area because they thought it was a losing game. He wanted to know what the prospects were of this situation ever being resolved.

Hartford wasn't the only insurance company that withdrew financial support. The city began to die right in front of our eyes. The people refused to move in the direction of saving themselves because the oil companies were pooh-poohing the whole matter.

I was so thoroughly convinced in my own mind and had devoted so much time and effort that might otherwise have been devoted to running an otherwise beautiful shipyard that I felt ready to suggest to the Navy that we sue all oil producers in the Wilmington Field. Also to get an injunction that would stop all oil production until water injection was instituted, to sue them for damages to the shipyard where we'd had to build up dikes to keep the sea out.

I used to have to fight for Congressional funds to build our dikes higher and higher, to put lips around the shipyard to keep the sea out of the shipyard until finally we had them twelve to fifteen feet high around the water front.

The city's approach was to start filling in their harbor area, which had sunk so that their piers and their warehouses were at or below sea level. They just raised their warehouses, and brought in millions of truckloads of fill or pumped it out of the ocean and rebuilt the harbor, which might have been a good thing for the shipyard too. However, the cost of it would have been fantastic to raise that industrial plant twelve to fifteen feet higher than it then was.

Finally after getting the support of this Hard Core Committee, and by this time having recruited some significant support from the one newspaper owned by the Ridder Publishing interests. We began getting all sorts of editorials in support of the need for water injection, water repressurization.

I then came back to the Bureau of Ships and convinced Al Mumma that he should sponsor this effort to sue. He was able to get an appointment for me to meet with the Secretary of the Navy's Advisory Board, which consisted of all the Assistant Secretaries and a number of the key military officers. They met informally on specific problems confronting the Secretary to render advice.

So one day I was alerted to come to Washington and present the case for instituting suit in federal courts against all of the producers in the oil field. There were 122 people producing oil out of the Wilmington Field. Long Beach city was perhaps producing sixty percent of it, and companies like Union and Richfield and Standard of California and many smaller companies were producing the balance, also a few independent one-well operators.

I spent a whole day before this Advisory Committee with charts and material. After giving them about a forty-five minute presentation of what the problem was and what my recommendations were, I stood there and took my lumps for four or five hours from all these people, including Arleigh Burke, Secretary Tom Gates, Under Secretary Bill Franke, and the rest on why the Navy should sponsor a suit by the Justice Department.

About two-thirty or three o'clock I was dismissed, while the Advisory Board went into action on their own.

About five o'clock I was called and told that I had convinced them, and that the Navy was going to request the Justice Department to file suit, and would I initiate all the necessary steps, including the seeking of a proper attorney to handle the case on behalf of the Federal Government.

I was delighted, and went back to the city with this news. Of course, those who were opposed to this action thought I was a Judas and should be shot at sunrise. Those that thought there was some logic in believing that this would solve the problem were delighted.

The case was assigned by the Justice Department to the Federal District Court in Los Angeles. We shopped about and found a very highly intelligent young attorney named Bill Gray, an aspiring attorney, who was employed by the District Attorney to carry on this case.

Bill Gray devoted better than a year and a half of his personal effort, I would say almost half time, to building the case and getting close to being ready to put it before the court, when I got ordered back to Washington.

We'd expended a great deal of effort. We'd hired our own petroleum consultant, the Navy that is. We had built up the case very carefully, as we were experiencing an estimated thirty million dollars worth of total damage at the shipyard.

Mr. Mason: Were the oil companies at the same time building up their case with lawyers?

Admiral James: I'm sure they were. Even before I left the preliminary hearings were conducted, and we saw then what the opposition was advancing. They went back to this drydock concept, among other things.

So I got ordered back to Washington, and suddenly discovered in my new capacity as Assistant Chief of the Bureau that the Justice Department had called off their dogs.

I went over to see an Assistant Attorney General, I can't recall his name, only to learn that he felt there was too much public opposition. There had been a case that the Justice Department had taken to court down at the big Marine base, Camp Pendleton. They had a problem involving fresh water rights that had been taken to court. The public howl was so tremendous that Justice Department had been frightened off. The Long Beach case seemed to be headed towards a similar situation so they just dropped the bricks and weren't pursuing the case at all.

When I got word of this I went over and just raised cain. This guy Ramsey Clark was an Assistant Attorney General. He was more or less the director of the case, but had turned it over to this other chap whose name I can't recall.

The gist of it was that if they were to continue with the case they needed clear cut evidence that the suit met with the support of the responsible people in the city.

I charged out to Long Beach again and met with my Hard Core Committee, who were five or six of the key civilians in the city, including one chap as I said from the newspaper, named Sam Cameron, who was the publisher of the newspaper. Together we sat down and we plotted a campaign to convince Justice that the city was prepared to support them one hundred percent.

These people came back to Washington. They had prepared a series of news articles, editorials, that they were prepared to run in the paper, all demonstrating support for the urgent need of doing something now about the subsidence problem, because the city was dying inch by inch before your eyes.

The shipyard was having trouble getting necessary appropriations, and it took time to build these dikes higher and higher.

There's a phenomena out in the far Western Pacific - when earthquakes occur tidal waves that are known as 'tsunamis' are generated. They come traveling across the Pacific. They would roll up on the coast of California right out of the blue, with waves eight, ten, twelve feet in height.

As I used to drive in the shipyard entrance in the morning from my quarters, which was on relatively higher ground, I used to just say a word of prayer to the man upstairs that we wouldn't have a tsunami or an earthquake that would break the dikes in the shipyard that day. I felt that if either did occur there weren't enough coffins in the city of Long Beach to carry out the dead that would have drowned in the shipyard.

Mr. Mason: Is Long Beach near that Fault that runs down . . .

Admiral James: No, it's not on the San Adreas Fault, but it is near enough to be affected.

If the dikes were broken, and they were real spindly little things at that time, we would have had casualties that I estimated would run to two or three thousand. That's pure speculation of course, but it was the nature of concern that I had.

So with the support that was evidenced by the city, the Justice Department put the suit back on full speed.

Bill Gray got a scheduled date for the appearance in court. Of course, there were all the customary delays in the filing of whatever they file, and the responses, and all this hoky-poky that took months.

Finally the case was to be heard in its full scope. By this time I'm Chief of the Bureau of Ships.

The general counsel for the Navy, Merritt Steigler was the Navy's man now actively following the problem. He went out to Los Angeles when the case was due to be called up. I think it was due to be called up before the judge about nine-thirty on a given morning.

About eight-thirty that morning the attorneys for the defendants met with Bill Gray and made an offer of a settlement. This was the first indication of willingness to accept responsibility for subsidence. Between Bill Gray and the Navy's general counsel we made a settlement. The court hearing was then cancelled.

This was a unique and clever little stunt on the part of the defendants. I guess they had concluded that we had them dead to rights. Rather than risk getting a judgment in court as to the cause of subsidence, which would have opened it up for suit by every little piddling guy that had a broken window, they decided they'd better settle on the best terms they could without ever having a declaratory judgment as to the cause of subsidence recorded in the law books.

This is the way it went - the Navy settled for 'title in fee simple,' as the lawyers call it, unrestricted title, to many hundreds of acres of filled land that was in part of the area in which the shipyard was built. The Navy had put in fill there without anybody's prior approval, and this the city claimed was its own even though it was an adjunct to the shipyard property which they had given us. We also received half of a very large new pier area, known as Pier E, that had been built up by the city to original ground level. (It is where the shipyard will now build its new engineering building, where the major aircraft carriers that come into Long Beach are berthed. It's a fantastically important addition to the shipyard, which otherwise was restricted in ability to expand, and six million dollars cash.)

This settlement was considered very adequate from the Navy's point of view. Of course all the other affected individuals were no closer to getting a settlement for themselves than they were at the start of court proceedings.

The oil companies then proceeded with the most vigorous program of water repressurization that you have ever seen.

With my collaborators we had estimated that they would need a million barrels of water a day to retain the surface at its then depressed elevation, and that this would generate a hundred percent increase in oil production in the Field.

The city and the other operators are now putting in slightly over a million barrels of water a day into the field. Subsidence has stopped as of today. The ground level actually, and this we did not anticipate, bounced back a few inches in some places. And the oil companies have produced about ninety percent more oil than they otherwise anticipated they'd get out of this Field.

Mr. Mason: What is the potential of the Field?

Admiral James: The Field extends out into an area along the waterfront of Long Beach city. Part of our injunction was that there be no production in new areas until water injection was initiated concurrently with initial production.
With the settlement of the suit the city started erecting islands of rock and fill right in the harbor of Long Beach just offshore of the main drive, Ocean Boulevard. It began to drill oil wells from these islands concurrently injecting water.
There are still untold resources of oil in this Wilmington Field that will be tapped, but the city is requiring concurrent water injections with oil production. The subsidence problem has been virtually eliminated.

Mr. Mason: You must be something of a hero in Long Beach.

Admiral James: I went from an absolute bum who was threatened with a million dollar suit by one of the oil companies to a hero, I guess you could call it, a saviour of the city, and all sorts of other nice terms.

In a more concrete way the city has elected to make me a contract employee of theirs to represent them in naval matters here in Washington.

So indirectly I have benefited through my labors in behalf of the Navy by becoming a friend of the city and a laborer in the vineyard for continuous health and success of the city of Long Beach.

Mr. Mason: A very interesting episode.

May I ask a question or two about it? Somewhere along the way did you enlist the interest and support of the potent Sierra Club?

Admiral James: No, they were not involved in our effort. In fact, I don't believe I even knew of the Sierra Club at that time.

Mr. Mason: Did conservationists in the Congress become interested, because of the necessity of the Navy to go for additional funds?

Admiral James: No, the interest of the Congress was curiously the absolute opposite. The Congress sent out a special commission, headed up by Congressman Clyde Doyle, now deceased, including the Congressman Bob Wilson from San Diego who is still an active Republican member of Congress, to inquire into the wisdom of continuing the shipyard at all.

Mr. Mason: Step aside and let the oil companies take over.

Admiral James: Yes. Close down the shipyard, move the facilities out, and let nature take its course.

Mr. Mason: If the episode arose today, I think the reaction would be somewhat different.

Admiral James: I wouldn't want to speculate about what it might be today, because we had to fight this attitude - when I'd come front and center with money requests for building dikes and repairs to subsidence, there was an understandable reaction, "Why bother? We've got as many shipyards as we need, let's close this one down, and get the hell out. It's a sad venture."

Mr. Mason: One other question that occurs to me - why the weak-kneed attitude of the Department of Justice?

Admiral James: Principally because of their concern with the public reaction, which at that point was being expressed as being very unfavorable to a federal suit - big Uncle Sam coming in and assaulting this far city of Long Beach and taking away its millions in oil production money. That was this general reaction. Also I'm sure, although I couldn't document this, the oil companies were lobbying like mad in the Department of Justice.

The determination in court of the liability of these 122 oil producers for subsidence would have probably wiped out a large portion of profits, if the case had been settled in favor of the government. Their trick of avoiding a full and complete judicial determination eliminated that possibility, and the increase of their profits through water drive that followed the water injection placated them. They apparently got to the Department of Justice, I don't know who. Justice didn't turn it off, but they sure slowed it down to the point where it would have simmered and then gone out.

Mr. Mason: Did the State of California get involved or interested at any time?

Admiral James: The State of California got very considerably interested. I spent a great deal of time up in Sacramento on this matter. Goody Knight was then the Governor. This Alan Cranston, now a U. S. Senator, was the controller. Both of them, on different occasions, came to see the problem. We were seeking State support for our effort.

I don't think we did much more than alert the State to the tremendous income that was being deposited in the banks to the account of Long Beach city. So as a side issue - they legislated against Long Beach taking most of the oil revenues. Legislation cut down gradually Long Beach's share from one hundred percent to what is now around twenty-five percent with the State's taking the rest.

The State owns the oil fields, there's no question about that, but Long Beach was the one that had the wisdom and foresight to produce the oil.

So that was a side issue - the State's role in settling this was one that was of great concern to the city, more than was the determination of responsibility for the subsidence phenomena.

Mr. Mason: I'm very glad that you included that episode.

Admiral James: It's a fabulous story. It is recorded piecemeal in various places. I haven't given you the whole of the story - the agony, the insults, the problems that one had to bear while fighting for a seemingly unfavorable cause even though it meant the very existence of the shipyard.

There was no question within the Shipyard as to what had to be done. Eight thousand employees were dedicated to continuing their jobs in that location. So we had complete support of the shipyard, and they were heartily in support of what I was doing.

Of course with Mike Honsinger back in Washington I had another ally, who knew the case very well, even though it had just really started to be fought when he was there.

It was a very interesting period of my lifetime. And one I'm sure that was responsible to a major degree for some of the notoriety that I acquired within the Navy and certainly with Tom Gates. He was the one who made the ultimate selection that I would succeed Al Mumma as Chief of the Bureau in 1959. You never can tell in advance what's going to happen when you start a battle.

Admiral James: In all this re-telling the yarn of the subsidence battle, I've given little comment on my service as the Commander of the Naval Shipyard itself.

Long Beach, as I say, was a wartime creation inspired by the need for a major shipyard in Southern California with the main focus of the Pacific Fleet being in the San Diego - Long Beach area.

It was closed in 1951 by then Secretary of Defense

Louie Johnson as an economy move, because it was the newest of shipyards.

It was sort of a jerry built shipyard. The people that had been sent out there originally were recruited from shipyards by allocating numbers to be transferred to the Long Beach area from the other naval shipyards. As a result of which I don't think the greatest people were ordered into the Long Beach from the other yards. They did recruit some very fine people, but it was perhaps less than the most efficient yard prior to its closing in 1951.

So with his inspiration to reduce cost of military establishments, Louie Johnson closed down the shipyard.

Then within months, less than a year, the Korean War came along and the requirements for a naval shipyard capacity were greater than before, so it was reopened.

When it was reopened some of the original key personnel were returned to Long Beach to reactivate the yard under the leadership of Captain Emmett Sprung, who was to be the shipyard commander.

Personnel previously employed were recalled to the shipyard, but a very careful selection of persons to receive the recall notices was made. The bums were eliminated, and the cream of the crop were called back in. The yard started up in 1952 with one of the finest cadres of civilian personnel that any shipyard possessed.

Mr. Mason: Were there problems with the labor unions as a result of this calling up?

Admiral James: I don't believe so. The labor unions were not recognized in the shipyards in these days, although most of our shipyard employees were members of one union or another, but there were no recognized labor groups in the shipyards. We have them now as a result of Jack Kennedy's brief presidency.

The recruitment of people was the significant thing. Around this nucleus Captain Sprung built up a shipyard that grew to be in excess of 8500 people. I think the population was around 82 or 83 thousand when I went out in 1955. They were a group of people who could almost run the shipyard with one hand tied behind their backs.

The shipyard commander there had a great deal to do, but he could also do as little as he wanted and the shipyard would still run very efficiently.

I was not one to do very little, although it was comforting in my efforts in fighting the subsidence battle to know that things were going to go on even though I was diverted more perhaps than is normal for a shipyard commander.

Mr. Mason: How many jobs on the average were performed? How much business were you doing?

Admiral James: I can't recall the numbers now, but we seldom had less than thirty ships at any given time along the waterfront undergoing ship repairs. We had everything from aircraft carriers down to small mine sweepers. The mine sweepers and similar small craft made up the bulk of the population, but there were always several cruisers, tankers, and logistic support ships, and occasionally an aircraft carrier. It was a very active yard as you can well imagine when you remember that the Pacific Fleet was based in the Long Beach and San Diego area.

It was also a Supply Center, a move that the Bureau of Supplies and Accounts made just as I came to command. I opposed the move but was unable to reverse because it was too far gone. It has since been reversed by their own action. It never should have happened in the first place, but that is neither here nor there.

The yard did no shipbuilding. It was concentrating on ship repair work, and major alterations to ships. We got heavily into the missile business.

In a limited way, we got into the Polaris missile program early in its development by building missile test vehicles that were used in San Clemente Island. It was part of the effort to prove out the ability to fire the missiles from under water.

Mr. Mason: You were intensely interested in that.

Admiral James: Oh yes. By this time my good friend and classmate, Red Rabor, was in charge of the Polaris program. He and I made very sweet music together. I had little really to contribute to the total effort, but what we did we did with great enthusiasm, and with great success, I might add.

We also did a few ship conversions, destroyer escorts. Generally we received the high approbation of the Force Commanders of the various Pacific Fleet units that we overhauled. I think our biggest contribution was in the destroyer repair area.

I can think of no really outstanding event or circumstance that took place out there, except that while serving that command I was selected to the rank of Rear Admiral.

It happened when I was in Long Beach, but I actually received word that I had made my number while I was visiting in the San Francisco Naval Shipyard. They broke my flag in the San Francisco Naval Shipyard ahead of Long Beach, which has always bothered my Long Beach advocates somewhat - that my flag was first flown over the San Francisco Naval Shipyard. This bears a rather curious relationship to my determined effort to go to San Francisco initially to command the shipyard.

Mr. Mason: Had Redman gone by that time?

Admiral James: Redman had gone by that time.

I was there for only a one day conference when I got the message that I had made my number and to don the stripes forthwith. They promptly broke out a flag and flew it at the flagstaff in the San Francisco Naval Shipyard to honor my presence.

Mr. Mason: Tell me about your obligations, your other hat, your job as industrial manager for the Eleventh Naval District. What did that entail?

Admiral James: That entailed the assignment of naval ships to private shipyards for repair work. This was part of the Navy's commitment some years back made by Charley Thomas when he was Secretary of the Navy, that private shipyards would overhaul ships of the logistics types - the tankers, the store ships, the repair ships, ships of that type - in private yards to the extent that the Navy yards could do without that sort of work.

It laid the foundation for a fight that I am still fighting today, which became known as the '65-35 fight when I was Chief of the Bureau of Ships, the private shipyards lobbyed hard to get a Congressional statement of requirement that the Navy put thirty-five percent of its work in repair of naval ships in private yards while sixty-five percent was permitted to go into the Navy yards.

That's a separate story. I fought it in 1961, '62, and '63, and lived with it for two years, and finally got it washed out., as such an arbitrary division of work was completely unjustifiable and fouled up work assignments completely.

Now I find that today the same idea has raised its ugly head again and by the same people, the Shipbuilder's Council and the Western Shipbuilders Association. Private yards are slowly starving to death today due to the reduction of fleet strength and the diminished U. S. Merchant Marine. They have little or no work needed to keep alive the private sector in shipbuilding and ship repair. They are screaming to Congress to get not 65-35 division declared but a 50-50 division of work.

Mr. Mason: Will you tell me that story in detail when you reach it chronologically? Your experience in Philadelphia with ship scheduling must have made this a breeze for you.

Admiral James: Yes, this was all adding very significantly to my background and capability. The work, as the Industrial Manager, was largely administered by a separate office with a Captain in charge. It consisted essentially of allocating work to the shipyards after the bids were solicited and received, and the low bidder for a given specification of work was selected. Then it included the review of the nature of the work, and determining whether it was done satisfactorily and accepting it for the Navy, and approving payment to the shipyard.

Mr. Mason: Did you have to fend off political overtures?

Admiral James: Not to any significant degree, except in this ever present determined effort on the part of the private yards and their General Managers to get more and more Navy work.

The General Managers for Bethlehem Steel yard, named Bill Harrington, lived and operated right near the Naval Shipyard. One time at a luncheon affair where he was introducing me for some reason or other he said, "I want to introduce to you my friend Jimmy James, who is my biggest customer, my biggest competitor, and my landlord. How in the hell can I survive in that situation?"

By being his biggest competitor he meant I was running the Navy Shipyard. By being his biggest customer I was giving him the repair work on auxiliary type ships. And by being his landlord, most of the plant that he occupied had been built by the Navy during the war and leased to Bethlehem. So he had a multiplicity of problems as his humorous introduction suggested.

One other function I fulfilled was also to be the Supervisor of Shipbuilding in the Eleventh Naval District. However, during my tour of duty this consisted of supervising the shipbuilding principally of a few mine sweepers, one rather large store ship at the Todd Yard in San Pedro, and several small ships building at National Steel yard in San Diego.

I also had a separate Supervisor of Shipbuilding office with officers in charge in each for these different locations. Mine was the overall responsibility for those ships being built in the 11th Naval District.

I had a pleasurable occasion when the builder of one of the little mine sweepers, the Harbor Boat Company, came to me one day and said they'd like my wife to sponsor a mine sweeper being built under the military assistance program for Denmark.

My wife had christened a Navy ship earlier so she was ineligible, but our daughter was visiting at the time so she was accepted as the sponsor of this Danish mine sweeper.

Years later when my wife and I were visiting in Copenhagen, I'd all but forgotten this incident, but the Chief of the Navy Staff of the Danish Navy had obviously done his homework. He remembered that I had been shipbuilding supervisor and that my daughter had christened that ship. So he said, "The ship is in the harbor and the captain is on board. We'd like you to come aboard for a little reception this afternoon."

I went down there and saw the King and Queen of Denmark's photos hanging high on the wardroom bulkhead, with my daughter's hanging immediately below theirs. That was a rather interesting little experience.

I don't believe that there were any other major events

that occurred in the shipyard that are worthy of recording. It was a high grade shipyard capable of doing exceptional work at an extremely competitive price - a condition that I attribute to the great care and selection of the people that were to be returned to the shipyard after the brief nine month closing.

Mr. Mason: What sort of liaison was maintained between your shipyard and other Navy shipyards on the West Coast? Was there an actual physical liaison?

Admiral James: There was a day to day contact on material problems, exchanging items of material, rescheduling of work. Then of course the Chief of the Bureau would periodically, generally every six months, have conferences of all shipyard commanders where mutual problems were aired and discussed and reviewed. This was just routine. The entire shipyard complex is a pretty cohesive organization and does what has to be done to insure the completion of work on time to get ships back into service.

I think our biggest bulge in work came at the time of the Suez crisis, when the need for restoring a lot of ships to active fleet duty and for hauling of Mid-East oil that now had to come around Cape of Good Hope instead of through the Suez Canal. We had a bulge in work that occurred at that time, which required support from about everybody around.

I think I would be deficient if I failed to note one very pleasant experience that I enjoyed in Long Beach. It was the custom of the Service clubs there to invite commanders of various naval commands to take an honorary membership.

I was privileged to be asked to become a honorary member of the Rotary Club of Long Beach. It was a very active club with in excess of 250 members. I could not hold office, but I certainly found that it was extremely worthwhile to Navy yard relations with the city, and to my ability to get to know people who later I used to great advantage on the subsidence fight, by becoming a regular attendee at the Rotary Club meetings.

I think I was respected and regarded as one of the truly contributing members of the Club during the three years I served in Long Beach. Relationships that grew out of that association have continued, and they're still continuing. I have enjoyed thoroughly all of my exposure to Rotary.

When I returned to Washington I thought I might join the Washington Club, and was invited to do so. However, in checking my calendar in Washington I found that I would be unable to take in more than twenty-five or thirty-five percent of the regular Wednesday meetings. So I decided that I'd be a very poor member, and did not join.

Some day here in Annapolis maybe I'll find an opportunity to join again.

I thoroughly enjoy their purposes and their work, especially that of the Long Beach group. They used to invite me back for an annual speech for two or three or four years after I left Long Beach, and it was always a delightful experience.

The city of Long Beach itself was one of the most dedicated cities in the country to its naval relations. They really have a red hot love match with the Navy for obvious reasons. The Navy is a major economic factor in the city's well being. The Navy people that come and go achieve prominence elsewhere. And the people in Long Beach are delighted to provide facilities for YMCAs, for special boat landings, locker clubs and they use their oil income to great advantage in providing the maximum facilities they could for the Navy in the community. The City Council makes a point of maintaining what they call an Armed Services Commission. This group of prominent citizens makes it their special business of seeing that all Navy affairs are duly sponsored, attended, and supported.

Long Beach, I think, of all the Navy cities that I've been in, or cities with major naval establishments, is more determined, more dedicated, more skillful in making the Navy feel wanted and at home in their community.

This is part of the reason why they have a naval liaison representative here in Washington, and is part of the chore that I happily perform. The major job is done by the citizens in Long Beach where they meet the Navy on a face to face basis.

One little sidelight - one of the principals in the Chamber of Commerce's Navy Military Affairs Committee is a chap named Clint Furrer. He conducted monthly a program of meeting with all the commanders of all the military establishments - (Army, Navy, and Air Force - in that community) for breakfast in various military establishments. There we talked about our mutual interests, and established effective contacts in the business community. This has been going on for years. Annually Clint Furrer comes back to Washington and throws what he calls an Alumni Dinner, of former station commanders.

This fine gentleman has been in rather bad health lately, so at the time of the annual dinner for this year we turned the tables on him. The ninety to one hundred former commanders of naval ships or bases or establishments in the Long Beach area that are in the Washington area threw a party where he was the honored guest. Illness prevented his presence. We put on a simulated affair as he would have run it, recorded it all, and kept him on the telephone to enjoy most of it, and showered him with little mementoes and a lot of love and affection.

It's typical of what Long Beach thinks of and does for the Navy personnel that are stationed in that community.

Interview #8

Rear Admiral Ralph K. James, USN, Ret.
Annapolis, Maryland

by John T. Mason, Jr.
August 10, 1971

Mr. Mason: As usual it's good to see you this morning, Admiral. Last time you gave me the Long Beach story of your career. I think you have one or two items that you want to add to that, one that pertains to Rear Admiral George McMillan.

Admiral James: You had mentioned George McMillan as being someone you knew. He was involved in a funny little incident while I was a resident in Long Beach.

George, as you know, had been appointed the Postmaster for the city after his return from incarceration in Japanese prisoner camps. He was captured on Guam early in the war.

I have a very dear friend, who was a sportsman of sorts. He sent me a telegram one day from North Dakota stating that he had been up shooting pheasant, had great success, and was sending me a brace of these by air express in dry ice, and to be on the alert for them. I estimated the time of arrival, but when the birds didn't show up I thought it necessary to call the Postmaster and alert him to my problem.

I got George McMillan on the telephone and told him what I was expecting and asked him would he kindly see if there was any holdup in the delivery because of the perishable nature of the merchandise.

About twenty minutes later I got a telephone call back from George. He said, "As I left to go to find the superintendent of mails in the office I found him carrying a package headed for me. The package could be smelled from the length and breadth of the Post Office. The Superintendent said, "You know Admiral James. You'd better call him and tell him that his birds have died enroute, and they're giving off a terrible stench here in the Post Office. Would he get them out of our hair?"

George called immediately to describe the situation. I said, "George, obviously they were delayed too long getting here. Can you dump them somewhere? Let's forget about them." "Oh no," he said, "the regulations require us to deliver the mail. We have no authority whatsoever to deposit these in the garbage can where they belong, so I'm sending a special messenger out to your home with these birds."

I wasn't able to reach Mrs. James in advance, I guess she was out. When she received the birds after returning home, and without any warning from me, she was equally distressed as were the postal authorities.

So I was commanded to return forthwith from my office and get rid of these smelly pheasant which my former Navy roommate had tried to make as a pleasant gift.

I'll always remember George in that context, and he and I relive the incident whenever we meet. I'm sure that he can still smell it in his nose, even though it was many years ago.

My return from Long Beach was to the position as Assistant Chief of the Bureau of Ships for Field Activities. This meant responsibility to the Chief of the Bureau for the administration of our eleven naval shipyards, the scheduling of work to the yards to maintain the proper work balance, and the granting of authority to the shipyard commanders to hire or fire personnel within the ceiling limits set by budgetary considerations and generally fixed at budget time by the Congress, or if not then by the Comptroller of the Navy.

Mr. Mason: Was it also a kind of a grooming process?

Admiral James: Any position, as you move up the ladder, is obviously grooming you for higher and greater responsibility. I don't think it was pointedly selected that I go into this spot with any intention that I might succeed the Chief of the Bureau, even though that is what happened.

I also had been responsible for the supervisors of shipbuilding in the various private yards, and so had a very interesting job.

However, I didn't find it too time consuming, having come from command of a shipyard where the problems were relatively the same and easier to handle than if I'd come in fresh from some other post. The budget problems, which are always severe, were not part of the job that I had to administer. I merely had to operate within the budget allocation.

So I found myself with some time on my hands, and began to interest myself in the fact that the cost of doing business in our shipyards particularly seemed to be inordinately high for the production we received. I started piddling around with efforts to reduce costs by various means.

I outlined my intentions to Admiral Mumma, who was Chief of the Bureau at the time. He was very much intrigued with the idea, and concluded that what we were doing should be done in a more formal and perhaps more effective way than just the individual effort that I was attempting in conjunction with my other duties.

Mr. Mason: By what percent did you think they were off target?

Admiral James: I had no idea. I just had an intuitive feel that we could eliminate some of the things we were doing, modify others, and achieve cost reductions through this effort.

Discussing this with the Chief we agreed that I should head up a very formally constituted panel to examine costs of shipbuilding and ship repair, not only in the Navy yards but in the private yards where most of our new ships were built.

I asked for and was at first rebuffed in assigning associates that I wanted to help me on this task. I'd gone right to the star-studded cast of Captains and picked off three of the better ones that I could find even though they weren't then available.

Mr. Mason: Rebuffed by whom?

Admiral James: By the Chief of the Bureau, who thought I was just overdoing my enthusiasm for this project.

However after some debate it was agreed that I would have as my associates three Captains - Captain Frank Jones, who is now the Inspector General of the Bureau and a Rear Admiral; Captain Jack Fee, whom I believe we talked about the last time when I described the unfortunate incident of the suicide of Admiral Fee after he had retired; and Captain Moose Brown.

We determined on a course of action, and started an examination of the problem with additional part-time assistants that we recruited from different areas of interest within the Bureau and Shipyards. We visited private shipyards, naval shipyards, laboratories, all of the Bureau of Ships facilities and activities, endeavoring to examine their methods of doing business and suggesting means by which these could be simplified and done at a lesser cost.

Our work carried on for over six months. We spent perhaps thirty percent of my time and a hundred percent of the time of the three chaps I named making these visits, analyzing the information we obtained and reaching conclusions as to what improvements might be made.

Finally in about March of 1959, we concluded what is known as 'the Ship Cost Analysis Panel's report.' The acronym for our group was SCAP, for Ship Cost Analysis Panel.

It contained in excess of 50 specific recommendations for various types of operations, including internal operations of the Bureau itself, which we estimated would result in significant cost reductions. We very gingerly estimated the potential cost savings in excess of several hundred millions of dollars, I've forgotten the exact number, and reported perhaps two hundred millions as projected savings in order to be very conservative in our estimates.

We were very pessimistic about the application of our recommendations with the same vigor that we'd made the study of the suggested changes.

Mr. Mason: Was it thought of any value, Admiral, to have a concept of what went on in foreign shipbuilding yards?

Admiral James: We made no effort to examine any foreign shipyards, because the scope of the undertaking would have been significantly greater than we would have been able to handle. We were not organized to get into the foreign costs, although we had foreign shipbuilding costs available from domestic sources, particularly the Maritime Administration.

We knew that we were operating in a much higher wage rate in the U. S., and we knew intuitively that it was a basic difference in the cost of living in the United States and that which you'd find in foreign countries, particularly in low cost shipbuilding centers such as in West Germany and Japan. This was not an element of our study.

Our study was received with great enthusiasm. I can remember rather humorously when it was delivered to all of the Assistant Chiefs of the Bureau in session with the Chief the question was asked, "What son-of-a-bitch will be able to execute this program now that Al Mumma is leaving office, and before we know who his successor will be?"

We all laughed. People made their estimate of some of the tougher characters in our organization, and I was generously identified as being one of the SOBs in our organization.

It wasn't until about six weeks later that I was appointed Chief. It became obvious then that it was going to be my baby to execute this program.

In the meantime the Secretariat got wind of it, and were extremely interested, particularly the Assistant Secretary Cecil Milne. He was so pleased with what had been done that he carried it over to McNamara as a project that needed to be known. I'm sure he took some credit for stimulating it, which to a very limited degree he had. He had formerly been in the office of the Secretary of Defense, so he knew what their concerns were.

About six months to a year after this, McNamara came out with the identical program Defense Department wide. I considered this a high compliment, but I was also distressed that McNamara chose to identify it as his program without giving any credit to the Bureau of Ships from whence it had come, for our having prepared and shown the way by doing it in one segment of the Defense Department.

Never one word of credit was given to either the Bureau of Ships or to the individuals involved, it was identified strictly as Mr. McNamara's big cost reduction effort.

If you were ever to compare the reports of the SCAP panel with those techniques ordered for the subsequent study - you can see that it was lifted verbatim from the SCAP effort.

Mr. Mason: Do you have a copy of the SCAP panel?

Admiral James: Yes, I do. It's a very interesting summary. I will make this available to you.

That was just one major interest that I had, but perhaps chronologically speaking we ought to talk about how I moved up to be the Chief SOB of the Bureau of Ships.

Mr. Mason: And also if there are any interesting experiences as you traveled around to the various shipyards in your position as overall inspector.

Admiral James: I didn't have the title of inspector. We had an Inspector General. I was simply a specialist and I had no problems in entering the private yards. By simply telling them what our purpose was, the Navy of course being the shipyard's biggest single customer, they were disposed to be responsive even though some times they thought we were idiotic in the things that we were trying to do. However, this was received with great acceptance, and I don't recall any particularly amusing incident.

Actually the travel was done to a greater extent by my three associates than it was by myself. I guess I participated in roughly a third of the trips out, and these were primarily in places of some importance where the presence of a couple of stars was important.

Mr. Mason: I wonder if it would be worthwhile to outline the areas wherein you thought the savings could be achieved as you studied the whole picture?

Admiral James: This has been over ten years ago, and I'm going to have to beg off on that. Maybe we can insert something on that later when I've had chance to run over the material that we submitted.

However, in generalities we thought, for example, that too much effort was being devoted to detailed drawings that were nice to have but not essential to construction or modification of ships, things could be done with a lot fewer engineering drawings, and these are very expensive.

We also felt that there was too damn much red tape involved from direction to start and to actual accomplishment of the work. We outlined different approaches to what was known as Planning Department functions in Navy yards. We simplified their procedures.

There are many more, as I said we had over 50 different specific recommendations in this document. In our next session I'll have some additional material. This story goes on for several years, and is still going on.

The departure of Al Mumma to the retired list at the end of his four year term as Chief of the Bureau was approaching. There was great speculation as to who would succeed him. I think all of us who were senior EDO Rear Admirals in the Bureau of Ships had aspirations, perhaps none so great as Admiral Mike Honsinger, who had been Deputy Chief of the Bureau to Admiral Mumma.

Finally while all this speculation was rife and rumors were running about, Mumma called three of us in turn to his office to advise us that we were the three front-running candidates. One was Admiral Mike Honsinger, the other was Admiral Jimmy Farrin, and myself.

Each of us thought the other was a more likely candidate and each of us kind of hoped that it might be our turn next, although it was hard to see how the other two could be set aside in your favor.

Finally one day I was called into the front office and asked to accompany the Chief to see the then Secretary of the Navy, Tom Gates. I went over and sat and talked generalities for a bit, and finally specifics, and finally got to the question - how did I get along with Admiral Rickover?

I thought this was a rather curious question, but obviously it was pointed. So I said that I really knew him so little that I had no knowledge of how well I got along with him. I said that if I couldn't get along with Rickover he'd be the first man in the world that I didn't find some means of working out a rapport for conduct of business irrespective of personal feelings.

At the conclusion of about a three-quarters of an hour conversation that seemed meandering, but obviously was pointed, Secretary Gates said that he had concluded that I was to be the successor to Admiral Mumma. That he was prepared as of that moment to make such a recommendation to President Eisenhower, and that hopefully I would be nominated and confirmed by the Senate.

In very short order the White House nomination was forwarded to the Congress, and very quickly the confirmation was given. On the 29th of April 1959, which was the anniversary date of Mumma's appointment, I was sworn in as his successor at a very heartwarming affair which was held in Secretary Gates' office. For this event my son came on from college to join us. My wife and I were later the luncheon guests of Secretary Gates.

One of the more unpleasant tasks that I had to perform at the very outset of my term was to discharge the lady who had been secretary to the Chiefs of the Bureau of Ships from the beginning Bureau days in 1940. In my first tour of duty in the Bureau of C&R in 1939 she had been my secretary. She was an extremely competent and lovely woman, Gladys Train, one of the yeomanettes of World War I.

She served all the Chiefs from the creation of the Bureau until my day with great distinction. Al Mumma had told me after my nomination was confirmed that she was getting impossible because of her insistence upon her prerogatives and her recollections of all the ways that it used to be done. He felt that she should be retired because of her advanced age. I believe she was then in her mid-sixties.

I felt this was his job, to move her out or move her on, and told him so. He agreed, but I arrived in the office, after gigging him from time to time, to find her still unaware of the fact that she had been marked for removal from her position.

And so I had the unpleasant task to do. Almost the very first thing I did on taking over was to discharge this fine lady by offering her an equal position in a much less active area of the Bureau, but with all the perquisites that attended her present position. She was a very smart individual and realized this was the kiss of death, so she retired instead of moving on.

Mr. Mason: She was under Civil Service, wasn't she?

Admiral James: Oh yes, but she had long passed the age of retirement.

I always felt that that was a rather nasty little bit of business that Al Mumma should have disposed of but did not. I resented it because I didn't like to start out on that basis in a new position, even though it was customary for people to change their secretaries. She'd been a fixture f for so long that it just didn't seem right.

I got myself a very delightful successor who had been the Assistant Chief's girl, and one I'd known for years, who was considerably younger, one who served the Bureau until just last year, Miss Dorothy Otten.

Mr. Mason: What about the Assistant Chief himself, did he continue - Honsinger?

Admiral James: No. I kept him on for a matter of a few days of course, and then asked him where he would like to go, because he could not remain on as my Deputy. He was a senior to me in graduation from the Academy by a year. I knew he was terribly disappointed by having failed to be appointed chief. It just didn't seem right. So I offered him his full and free choice. He elected to become the shipyard commander at Mare Island, where I sent him in a matter of a month or so.

In the meantime, having been a naval constructor by educational background, I concluded that I needed a marine engineer as my Deputy. I looked over the list very carefully. I knew all of the officers, all of the EDO Admirals, of course, in varying degrees of intimacy. One whom I didn't know too well, but had rather high regard for, was Bob Moore. Robert L. Moore, who was then commanding the shipyard at Portsmouth, New Hampshire.

I concluded that he would be the best man for my job and I called him to offer him the position. I think he was a little non-plussed because he was so very comfortably situated in Portsmouth. He enjoyed it and was his own independent boss - all the things that you aren't when you become the Deputy Chief of a Bureau in Washington. But being a loyal sailor man he responded affirmatively. After negotiating a few little situations he was ordered in as Deputy Chief.

A more dedicated, intelligent, knowledgeable, and loyal Deputy Chief of the Bureau I don't think any Chief ever had. I came to admire and respect this man with a passion that continues.

He's a resident here in Annapolis, by the way, in the Amberly section. That was one of the negotiated items - he wanted to live in Annapolis while being Deputy.

At first I thought this might be okay, but on second thought I realized how much of the activity occurred at the spur of the moment, and it was hardly appropriate to be down here in Annapolis with the action taking place in Washington. So I required him to move into a home up there, but after about three years I relented and he came down here. By that time things were tapering off anyhow. He has lived here since.

The administration of the Bureau under Al Mumma had been a very effective one. Al is an extremely competent guy. He retired from the Navy, and went as Vice President of Worthington Corporation, and later became President, and finally became Chairman of the Board.

At the moment I relieved him, even though he had served four years in the office of Chief, I was still his senior by several months in age. He was an extremely young person when he was appointed chief. The appointment was for a period of four years.

He presently is Chariman of the President's panel on shipbuilding requirements of the United States, a very interesting assignment. I don't believe he's very active with Worthington any longer, but he is carrying on this job for President Nixon at the moment.

There weren't many serious problems that affected the Bureau of Ships' administration. There were extremely serious problems that affected the Navy, primarily the aging fleet and secondarily the failure of the Congress to appropriate sufficient monies to replace the aging fleet. This was not directly the concern of the Bureau of Ships, except of course that we built and maintained them. It was an overall Navy problem, but the Bureau of Ships Chief was a major element in convincing the Congress that we actually knew how to manage our money, and how we could build our ships without expecting them to be too expensive.

It was at this point that I embraced the program that I think I mentioned earlier, which Wilfred McNeil had advanced - the full and final pricing of the ships at the time of initial authority to build them, rather than going in for yearly increments to cover escalation and increases due to ship and material changes. So when Congress authorized a ship, they would know what the total cost was likely to be at the outset.

I mentioned the one concern I had with this approach being the creation of an extremely large pot of money that would lie fallow to be applied year after year as the program proceeded, and how people would try to dip into it. I was able to forestall any such action while I was Chief, but it happened shortly after I left office four years later.

Mr. Mason: Admiral, the principal deterrent to a modern fleet was a question of expenses. Congress was economy-minded. But also was there not a kind of euphoria which may have existed? President Eisenhower states in his final state of the union message that the U. S. was far and away the leader in sea warfare. Here we were on a pinnacle in our own estimation of our Navy. Was this not a kind of euphoria?

Admiral James: Oh, I'm sure it was. Not perhaps to the extent to which we witness it in the Congress today, but certainly there was a belief that we were almost invincible. There was no real serious Russian shipbuilding effort going on, and what were we building ships to fight against? There didn't seem to be much. However, it was an inescapable fact that our fleet was largely a World War II built fleet in the early 1960s.

By the time I took office the war had been over for fourteen years, and the number of new ships that had been authorized and built was rather insignificant. I mentioned in an earlier interview how Korea might have sparked a major shipbuilding program, but then it petered out. Had it taken place we could have avoided the rapid approach to block obsolescence of virtually three-quarters of our fleet in the early sixties, which today has become universal. The shipbuilding surge didn't happen, so we were then faced with the problem of finding the means to upgrade our existing fleet at the least possible cost.

About that time after discussions with the Chief of Naval Operations (Admiral Burke), we concluded that we could modernize many of our destroyers by what became known as the FRAM program (Fleet Rehabilitation and Maintenance Program).

In Buships, we started the engineering for such an effort. We divided the ships into two separate groups. Those that were reasonably modern, which by upgrading their installed equipments and giving them an extremely extensive repair job, could be put back in service for six to ten additional years of uninterrupted effective service. We determined that some of the older ships could be treated similarly, have changes made to armament and other onboard installations and so extend their life and also improve their fighting capability. The ships were divided into these two categories. We were able to sell this program to Congress.

I think we spent in the order of four to five million dollars a copy on the lesser job and upwards to ten or eleven million dollars on the second group.

We put quite a number of our destroyer fleet primarily through the FRAM program while I was still active. I don't recall the exact number, but it was in the order of sixty or seventy ships.

Mr. Mason: And by how many years did this program update the life of them?

Admiral James: I said earlier that it updated them roughly six to ten years, depending on the nature of the program applied. And that was a pretty cheap price to get that many more years of service out of these older warships.

I think the FRAM program was extremely fine from the materiel point of view of the Navy, but it also added to the euphoria that you spoke of.

We had taken older ships - we had improved their fighting capabilities and their lifetime expectancy. This simply postponed the evil day when replacement of the total fleet would have been undertaken. Consequently we saw little brand new ship construction authorized.

I believe when I came into office I had about a nine hundred million dollar shipbuilding program. Our requirements were more in the order of about a three billion dollar yearly program. Working as hard as I could throughout my four years of tenure I was able to finally have the shipbuilding program authorized at a two point eight billion dollar level for my third year in office and slightly less than that for my fourth year. These were significant increases and they permitted the building of a larger number of ships, mostly the nuclear powered submarines and several attack carriers.

Mr. Mason: Admiral, may I ask a foolish question - when the FRAM program was applied to a given destroyer and the program completed, its life then was extended by ten years, but wherein was it still deficient and still obsolescent?

Admiral James: The ships were not increased in speed, the power plants were not changed. Our destroyers could always use higher speeds than they've gotten. They didn't have the size to carry the more modern of anti-submarine weapons. There was the general deterioration of the ship's structure, although in many cases we would rip out large areas of questionable hull to restore them and minimize the concern with the ship's structure.

An old automobile can be upgraded by putting on nice nickel plated exhaust pipes, new twin-barrel carburetors and very fine wide-tread tires and all this, but these are superficial things that do not really upgrade that automobile. Neither did the FRAM program upgrade the warships to the modernity that we felt was essential for our fleet.

I say the tragic thing was that it discouraged people from seeing the critical nature of the need for new ship construction, because of the belief that we had in fact improved ourselves so greatly, and at that moment the Russians were still not a major shipbuilding nation nor did they have a competitive navy in being.

So all in all I don't think that the FRAM program served our Navy in the manner that we hoped it would. I think it gave us an extension of time that we paid dearly for by not getting a replacement ship program underway years ago.

Mr. Mason: I take it the real impetus for new ships came with the nuclear powered program.

Admiral James: Let me restate that statement. I think that the impetus for nuclear powered ships gave us that area of new shipbuilding to the exclusion of almost everything else, and consequently it was limited at that time and in my time at least, to the submarine fleet, to the ENTERPRISE and to the first nuclear frigate, the BAINBRIDGE. These latter ships were delivered during my tenure of office.

Rickover is, of course, credited with the concept. I don't think this is a fair assessment. On the day I took office, Rickover came to the little reception that we had, stood in line with hundreds of others in the Bureau who just walked through to shake hands. His comment to me was, "Just remember one thing - I am not your shipbuilder assistant, I am your boiler maker assistant. It's a nuclear boiler to be sure, but I make your nuclear boilers."

If we had continued our association on those terms, I would have come out of the Bureau job holding him in extremely high regard. This was just part of his customary smoke screen. He no more intended to be just the Bureau of Ships nuclear boiler maker than I intended to become an elf in fairy tales.

The relationship with Rickover is another subject that I guess I should touch upon, but at the moment I believe I can pass it by, well, perhaps not.

I recall now one of the comments of Secretary of the Navy GAtes, when he was asking me about my ability to get along with Rickover. He made it clear, though I don't recall his words, that he considered Rickover was a serious problem, if not a menace, in his present Navy position.

He said - we have tried to find the ways and means of removing this man from office and have not found a successful means yet. So he admonished me to keep my eyes and ears open, to work for the good of the Navy irrespective of personalities, but if ever an event ever should arise that in my judgment could make it possible for the removal of Rickover from his office, to bring the matter front and center immediately and he would take over from there.

Mr. Mason: The deterrent being the political backing?

Admiral James: Yes, of course it was. Rickover's position was more of a folk hero than it was anything else up on the Hill, and they felt that anything Rickover said or did was just absolutely the last word.

I don't think that position has changed much. He has a unique manner of handling the members of Congress that seems to generate affection. With others I would think it would generate the desire to see the man scalped.

I remember one time I was at a hearing where he was presenting the nuclear side of our submarine shipbuilding program to a group of Senators. Present was Senator Flanders, I believe he was from New Hampshire.

Senator Flanders said, "I would like to ask a stupid question," and proceeded to ask a question which wasn't stupid at all. Perhaps the question of an uninformed person, but certainly that of one seeking to be enlightened.

Rickover turned on him and said, "Indeed that was a stupid question." The gist of his remarks were - how can you waste my time forcing me to answer people's questions who have no more sense of the technical subjects, and why do you waste your time asking the questions. He went on at some length.

I thought I would see this man scalped right then and there. Instead Senator Flanders apologized all over the place, and his colleagues in the hearing began to twit Flanders instead of taking off after Rickover.

This was typical of the treatment of these men. He was boorish, he was impatient, and they seemed to lap it up and love it. I've never understood why.

Mr. Mason: But was he impatient and boorish with the ones who really counted?

Admiral James: He did more of his business in their private

offices than he did in hearings. Although of late I think he's taken to using committee hearings for purposes of maintaining the aura about him. He was extremely successful. He succeeded where others in his job might have succeeded, but not as rapidly as he did. I credit him with being the Navy's greatest expediter.

He has acquired his technical knowledge along the way, but he didn't start out as a nuclear expert. He had nuclear experts assisting him. When they would achieve a degree of prominence on their own, he'd promptly remove them from the public view. One of these was Bob Moore.

Bob Moore had been supervisor of shipbuilding up at Groton, Connecticut when the first of our nuclear submarines was being built, the NAUTILUS. Bob Moore, more than any other single man, put that ship together. Rickover, of course, provided the nuclear power plant. Bob Moore's feelings for Rickover are not fit to print. It even broke out one day in my office when I had all the Assistant Chiefs, Rickover was one, in my office for discussion of shipbuilding efforts. The discussion got acrimonious. Admiral Farrin is a rather short-fused officer. He took on Rickover and challenged some of his statements; Bob Moore joined in with him.

Rickover, in a moment of distress, which is seldom characteristic of his attitude, turned on Bob Moore and said something to the effect, "Don't you ever come to my office. Ever since you chased me around New London with a knife in your hand I've got a thirty-eight caliber revolver in my desk, and I'll use it if you ever set foot in my office."

That shows you the degree to which this man was distressed by his associates and in turn distressed those associates.

I didn't have any overt break with Rickover in my four years. I managed to get along with him. The only time I thought he was thoroughly dishonest was at the time of the loss of the THRESHER, which occurred in the closing days of my tenure. He called to remind me on that occasion that he was not the submarine shipbuilder, he was simply the nuclear power plant producer.

I don't know that the Navy Board of Investigation has ever identified the real cause of the loss of the THRESHER. I have my own opinion, because, of course, in the ultimate analysis I was the person responsible for building that ship.

I feel from what I know of the inquiry in which I participated, what I know of the ship itself, and events that occurred up to that time, that a failure of a silver soldered pipe fitting somewhere in the boat caused a discharge of a stream of water on the nuclear control board and "scrammed" the power plant. Because of the inadequate design of the nuclear controls for the power plant, power on the boat was lost at a time where the depth of the water in which the submarine was operating forced enough water into the hull that prevented her from rising again because they couldn't get the power back on the boat. That's a very incomplete, semi-technical intuitive, evaluation on the situation.

Rickover went to great extremes to disassociate any likelihood of failure of the nuclear plant from the THRESHER incident. I consider this thoroughly dishonest.

Mr. Mason: Doesn't this, in a sense, point to the real secret of his power? Not only his agility with the Congress, but also the fact that he has become an expert in an area of awesome power which sort of makes people stand?

Admiral James: Stand in awe, yes, I'm sure this is one of the elements of his stature today. Plus the fact, as I started to say, that anyone who began to challenge him in the preeeminence in this field wasn't long for the program.

He's arranged for the transfer out of the program, never to be reentered into it, any number of senior engineering duty officers, who had tremendous technical capability, greater by many measures than Rickover ever possessed. Among these were Lou Roddis, Eli Roth, Ralph Kissinger and others.

I say again, I thought Rickover was an expediter, a person who knew how to twist people's tails and get the maximum out of them by threatening more than by leading.

I don't recall the names of many of these younger officers, but one by one if they would reach the point of being considered as a possible successor to Rickover, that was the beginning of the end of their affiliation with the program. I have in mind at least four such senior officers who might have carried on the program with equal, if not greater, success because they wouldn't have been so brutal and wouldn't have achieved their pinnacle of success by stepping over the recumbent bodies of their associates, which was typical of the Rickover approach.

Enough on that subject. It's a distasteful association for me, a man I have never trusted. His accomplishments can not be denied him, but I say again others could have made them and with less personal distress along the route, to his associates.

Mr. Mason: Just one question - one man told me who was in a position of power in the Navy Department that when he came into his office where there were conferences that had to do with nuclear power Rickover was not invited. He was not a part of it, and it was simply because of his personality. This fellow saw to it that he was included in spite of his personality, and he felt that something was added.

Admiral James: The line officers of the Navy acted very childish in this whole Rickover affair. It kind of sickened me towards these so-called naval leaders.

I went to a conference of all senior officers out in Monterey within the first year that I was in office. Present were all the fleet commanders, Atlantic and Pacific, CNO, all the heads of the OPs, the fleet type commanders, two technical bureau chiefs, myself, and the weapons boss, P. D. Stroop.

Throughout this very wonderful meeting of the senior officers, who reviewed Navy problem areas and discussed them, one problem that kept recurring for which there was no solution was Rickover - how he not only dominated the technical aspects of the nuclear program, but thad then started to infiltrate himself into the personnel and training aspects of it to the exclusion of those people in the Navy Department who felt that was their prerogative.

Page Smith was then Chief of Personnel. He got up and made the most pusillanimous review of the Rickover problem that concluded by saying essentially, "There isn't a damn thing we can do to him or about him, because he's got the Congress on his side, and we'd just better live with it."

And that was the attitude throughout. The Line took some rather stupid actions and silly little slights to show Rickover in what low regard they held him.

For example, his wife was never invited to christen a submarine until this fact became so obviously insulting that through my own efforts and those of Admiral Smedberg we got Mrs. Rickover invited to christen a new submarine.

This was in the days before the politicians took over sponsorship of new Navy ships as part of their fun and games. Christenings used to be divided up between wives of senior naval officers and some few political types. The Chief of the Bureau along with the shipbuilder had a great deal to do with selection of the sponsor.

That's all gone now; it's all regulated out by the White House. Kennedy was the one that brought that practice into being. He started the procession of Congress and Cabinet officers wives and the likes into this delightful channel.

Mrs. Rickover was entitled to such a distinction because after all he had been a major element in the construction of these ships. Finally when the invitation was extended, Rickover refused it, and I'm not sure that I wouldn't have done the same thing myself.

You mentioned not inviting him to meetings reviewing nuclear matters - I remember such meeting which was held at the NAS Jacksonville, Florida. I went down to the meeting of very senior naval officers. I got down there and found that Rickover wasn't on board, although I should have known this beforehand.

I found to my amazement - here we were sitting there

talking about nuclear powered ships, which I was fully competent to talk about, but when it got down to the nitty-gritties I felt Rickover's presence was vital and I felt that it was a great discourtesy not to have him present.

The group debated whether to extend him a delayed invitation or not. Finally the Vice CNO Jim Russell, who was the Chairman of the meeting, concluded that, "Yes, Rickover ought to be invited." He arrived the next morning by air.

Those silly little slights were typical of the reactions that the Line exerted in an attempt to control Rickover. I thought that forceful action by the Secretary or the CNO at the beginning could have done a great deal to channel his efforts in a way that would keep the Navy from having to bear the cross that Rickover has become.

I said a bit ago I was going to knock off talking about Rickover, and I think I should. It's a subject worthy of a full and exhuastive study and a book by an objective person. If such a study or book were ever published, I don't think Rickover would come out the folk hero he is today.

Part of my responsibility as Chief was to build ships offshore for NATO countries including Japan. They were built to Bureau of Ships specifications who awarded contracts for their construction and supervised their construction. To this end we had naval ship supervisors in Spain, Italy, Holland, and in Japan.

It was a curious part of the government Foreign Aid program, this offshore shipbuilding. It was designed primarily to build anti-submarine and minesweeper ship types. In Japan we built destroyer escort types to reconstruct the fleets that had been destroyed in part during World War II. The Foreign Aid Program was in full bloom in those days.

This was a new facet of my responsibilities. So very quickly I toured European shipbuilding centers and the headquarters of naval forces in Spain, Portugal, Italy, France, Holland, Norway, and Germany looking into our programs determining the nature of them, and also generating notions that might be applied to their administration.

I had some very interesting trips and was always of course a well-received guest because I was again the representative of the 'great white father,' Santa Claus in fact, who was allowing all this shipbuilding to be started again.

Mr. Mason: Were these respective countries financing this?

Admiral James: No, they were financed in their entirety by the United States. Built in the several countries, using their materials and manpower, but supervised by my people. The ships were designed in the Bureau of Ships.

Mr. Mason: Were these the very latest designs that we possessed?

Admiral James: In those categories, yes. They were largely the smaller ships - mine sweepers in Belgium and Holland, submarines in Norway and West Germany. The ships built in West Germany actually were for Norway. There were no submarines built in Italy. In Spain it was primarily the rehabilitation of their own aging fleet, sort of a FRAM of the Spanish navy. In France it was more of a technical data exchange than anything else, as it was in Sweden.

I was tremendously enthused with my visits. I remember one time being permitted to do something that no American military officer had done before. That was to visit the Swedish offshore islands where they had an almost impregnable fortress dug into the mountains on these islands in the Baltic Sea. We proceed in through a hole in the side of a mountain in deep draft ships, and suddenly entered a cavern where there was a full-blown navyyard with drydocks, shops, ammunition storage, and all connected to the mainland by tunnel that went under the Baltic. It was an amazing experience for me.

Mr. Mason: What was the rationale for this from a neutral country?

Admiral James: Sweden is right on the edge of the Russian complex. They then considered Russia a potential enemy, and had their navy in these protective complexes to keep them from being wiped off the face of the earth in nothing flat in the event of war.

They had made tremendous set of facilities available. I was in some that were finished, and others that were still being constructed. I'd never quite seen anything like it in my life before.

I was the guest of the Chief Engineer of the Swedish Navy with the full concurrence of the Chief of the naval staff and accorded a privilege I don't believe was extended to many foreigners before me.

Our work with Sweden was largely in assisting them in the design of ships. We helped them in the design of their naval submarines. For this and other contributions the King of Sweden awarded me the highest decoration they give to foreigners, their so-called Order of the Royal Sword. This was a fine gift.

I was also decorated by Queen Juliana of the Netherlands with the Royal Order of Orange-Nassau with crossed swords for the work that we did in conjunction with their Navy shipbuilding program.

We had very close intimacy with the Dutch Navy. The two different Chiefs of Staff were close personal friends.

I found these trips abroad to be extremely interesting. I was able to take Mrs. James, when I visited in Europe, although she had to proceed via surface transportation because of the problem that she has with her ears. We managed to get together at various point as I flew around. We both enjoyed the experience.

I think I did a great deal to sell the importance of the Bureau's technical functions abroad to such an extent in fact that the Royal British Navy sent over a team to study the Bureau of Ships organizational structure which they copies in part in the reorganization of the Naval Dockyards.

It is tragic to think that after the McNamara administration got in they saw fit to dismember the Bureau of Ships and destroy what other nations though well enough of to copy.

We went to the screw ball system that we have now of the various system commands like electronics, ordnance, ships and all these other things. This is a subject that I could rant and rave about for hours, but won't say much more about here.

A year later I made a similar trip to Japan and the Philippines. We had major Bureau of Ships activities in the Philippines. To my surprise and amazement I was also the financial angel for the Naval Hospital at Subic Bay.

I only learned this when I was greeted on arrival at the Naval Air Station there by the various senior officers of the station. I found the senior medical officer present who when I asked him why he was there said that I paid for all of his operations, and the thought he'd better come and butter up the financial angel. That's the first time I knew the Bureau of Ships had a hospital under its budgetary control

Mr. Mason: That is rather strange. Why wasn't it under the Bureau of Medicine and Surgery?

Admiral James: I couldn't tell you how this happened.

I took steps later to divest myself of it, because obviously the Bureau of Ships was technically incapable of doing anything for a hospital. Later the Bureau of Medicine and Surgery assumed it.

James #9 - 299

Interview No. 9 with Rear Admiral R. K. James, U.S. Navy (Retired)

Place: His residence in Annapolis, Maryland

Date: Tuesday morning, 21 September 1971

Subject: Biography

By: John T. Mason, Jr.

Q: Admiral, we'll postpone any further discussion of the SCAP report which is a very important one and which I hope you will attach as a copy to the oral history eventually.

Last time you told me about your appointment as chief of the Bureau and I think we stopped at that point in a chronological sense.

Adm. J.: The responsibilities of the chief of the Bureau of Ships had been beautifully handled by my predecessor, Rear Admiral Al Mumma, so it seemed rather strange to step into the front office and still find much left to be done. I believe this showed a bit of my naivete because I had no more than gotten into office than I realized there was a tremendous amount to be done. One of the major programs current in the Bureau was, of course, the start of the Polaris program. It had been Mumma's responsibility to deliver submarines capable of carrying the Polaris missile and in an absolute minimum of time to make possible an early commissioning of a limited number of these submarines. He conceived the idea of taking the standard nuclear attack submarine, cutting it in half, pulling it apart about 110 feet, inserting a middle body, which became the missile battery and later was known amongst the crews of the Polaris submarines as Sherwood Forest. The ability to take ships on ways that were well along in construction and make these major modifications was tremendously important militarily as well as being unique naval architectural development for which full credit must go to Admiral Mumma and his administration.

However, the pressure was still on to get more Polaris submarines. I believe the total number postulated at that time was 41. We had major problems to accelerate the program of the ship, while Admiral "Red" Raborn was producing the missile. He had overall responsibility for the entire system, of course, but part of it, the ship, was still the responsibility of the Bureau of Ships. It was a very high priority program that was carried forward at top speed. I might as well continue on this particular project to the end of my affiliation - rather than start off with a chronological review of other programs.

The change of National administration which occurred in January of 1961, of course, brought new personnel from top to bottom, in appointive positions and also the requirement to accelerate the Polaris program way beyond that which initially had been planned.

Q: Admiral, was this a political move predicated on the claim that there was a gap?

Adm. J.: I hesitate to say what motivated the President Kennedy to require this acceleration. I would say it was as much the U. S. military incapability to control the world situation as anything and the need to have a fleet of these boats and missiles in being, as a national defense shield was considered vital. From a program of about four boats a year, I was called into McNamara's office early in 1961 and asked to deliver one a month at the earliest possible moment. This was quite a challenge because of the complexity of those ships, the importance of buying the major components in advance, not just the propulsion machinery, but all the electronics and control equipment and the likes. Normally this required long-term planning and purchasing, but we were given our instructions and, after examination of the program, I believed we could accelerate to start delivering them, one a month, beginning about January 1962.

Q: Less than a year from the time of the order!

Adm. J.: Yes. We actually anticipated receiving formal instructions to proceed. I made all the preliminary preparations, called in the shipyards that would be involved, called in the major suppliers, and proceeded to give orders for the materials and for the ships. Very quickly - in fact, I believe it was late in February of 1961 - I was able to report to the Acting Secretary of the Navy, at that moment, "Red" Fay, that I had successfully placed orders for the increased number of boats and on the accelerated production schedule. He was high in his praise, and thought it was really wonderful that we were able to do such a fast job of getting the project under way. I was to learn that Red Fay, even less than I, knew little about Secretary McNamara and his determination to personally control such things. Although he issued the instructions to accelerate the program, when he found it had been done without clearing all major steps with him in advance, he really chewed out Red Fay who, in turn, chewed me out for my exuberance. I was stunned, because obviously THE MAN wanted the program accelerated. To do so we had to use every available moment of time, and I had organized it only to find that his methods of doing business were considerably different from his predecessor. It was made clear I should have walked each phase of this acceleration effort by his front door in order to have his full blessing.

I should have learned at that time the true nature of the man. However, I just put it down to a desire to learn his job quickly and not let anything as important as the Polaris program get out of hand.

Well, the program, as you undoubtedly will recollect, was tremendously successful and it was my great privilege to contribute significantly to the effort. I do not in any sense minimize the work of Admiral Red Raborn who, as the program and project manager, was completely and fully responsible for the entire effort.

Q: How did you resolve your differences with McNamara?

Adm. J.: I made no such attempt. I just had a sharp lesson in his methods of doing business. I was gratified about my own position of having accomplished the assigned task or, at least, arranged for its accomplishment. I didn't take the lecture too seriously although, as I mentioned briefly, I should have learned about the man from that experience because I had more of the same with him later on that I might have avoided.

Q: This is something in the nature of a footnote, but, inasmuch as Mr. Fay was a close personal friend of President Kennedy, how did he fit into the picture?

Adm. J.: He was just the middle man, I guess. He was the messenger boy, so to speak, on this particular occasion. He was acting Secretary of the Navy on the particular day when I elected to call and report on progress. I don't know whether he ever went directly to the President with the problem or not. I never heard from him critically about it again. I don't believe that he was personally responsible for my being admonished for being too eager. I think he was simply relaying the views of Mr. McNamara who did not directly confront me about this matter at all.

Q: Admiral, one other question at this point. Inasmuch as the Kennedy administration, at its inception, speeded up this program, how did this jibe with President Eisenhower's final state of the Union message in 1961, when he said the U. S. was far and away the leader in sea warfare?

Adm. J.: I think the very existence of the Polaris submarine and the Polaris missile system gave us a superiority at that time that was unequalled. The judgment to increase the number of ships in the program and to accelerate their readiness for sea was a matter of importance to the new administration and it could be related to the alleged missile gap that existed, although at the time, I had not related the two. Certainly there was a lot of political hoop-de-do about the fact that we had a missile gap and this might just have been an effort to fill it in, although later we've learned that, indeed, there was no missile gap. The whole acceleration effort if it were premised on that situation, would have been an out-and-out phony. I haven't analyzed it myself and I'm not prepared to say that it was. You raise the issue that we unnecessarily accelerated the program and, of course, by accelerating we increased the ship costs and that the situation might have been handled in a more orderly manner. But now we have a Polaris fleet and a very effective one, and it has been the major shield of our nation ever since it's been at sea. Today, of course, developments are overtaking us and we've now got the Poseidon missile. Except for first group of five ships that were the lengthened nuclear attack submarines, all others are capable of carrying the Poseidon missile and they're being back-fitted rapidly with this new missile that will extend their effectiveness and, to a degree, will extend the ship's life. But I'm no longer a student of military strategy, so I'm not sure I can offer this as the sole weapon to protect this nation. We hear talk about ULMS and other undersea missile systems coming down the pike. I would imagine that, like any other system that is now entering its second decade, the Polaris submarine has become obsolescent as all ships virtually are from the day they're launched, and the degree of obsolescence is increasing as they get older. These ships are halfway through their nominal lifetime, therefore there must be something on the horizon to replace them, and ULMS just might be it.

Q: At that point of time, the beginning of the Kennedy administration, was there any thought given to putting missiles on merchant vessels?

Adm. J.: Actually, one of my recommendations as Chief was to take a number of Liberty ships that were then out of service, recommission them modestly, fit each one of them with a battery of no less than four and no more than eight missiles in their cargo holds - place 20 or 30 of these around the periphery of the world, and we would have the Russians guessing from then to kingdom come as to what were our intentions. The cost would have been very low. The ships could have steamed about at 5 to 10 knots. We would have had to have some sort of crew rotation system. But all we needed for that job was a missile tube, a few air compressors, navigational and fire-control equipment, and we could have made an overt presence for our Polaris missile rather than the covert presence which characterizes the Polaris submarine.

Q: What reception did this proposal receive from the submarine contingent?

Adm. J.: I wouldn't limit it to the submarine contingent. I would say that it was listened to politely and rejected because it was not a proper warship, and the idea wasn't seriously pursued by anybody. Even in the Bureau of Ships we didn't go to the extent of doing what I call a preliminary design or study of this concept. We just drew up a few very simple little sketches showing how this might be done.

Q: But it was a bona fide conviction of yours?

Adm. J.: Well, I wouldn't say a conviction because I wasn't that smart about the Polaris missile. It was a bona fide notion that this might have merit and, therefore, should be considered. It was in this vein that it was presented. I don't believe anybody very seriously considered it, though I'm sure that Red Raborn and Company must have had this or other schemes of the same general type proposed to them almost every day of the week. So, let's say it was just a brave idea that was offered and, I'm sure, considered, and then set aside.

There were many other programs that were going on in the field of nuclear-ship construction. It was my great privilege to be the chief when the first three nuclear surface ships were delivered in the Navy, the USS Long Beach, the USS Enterprise, and the USS Bainbridge. None of these, however, had been contracted for in my tenure as Chief. They'd all been laid down under contracts placed by my predecessor. At least I had the privilege of seeing the Navy with its first coordinated nuclear fleet elements, and they were very wonderful new ships, particularly the "Big E," or the Enterprise. It was a ship that got out of hand costwise. We thought it was out of hand in those days but, as subsequent developments have indicated, maybe we were real parsimonious in the way we doled out the money to build the Enterprise. Here, Rickover again had a major hand in the project, because he was again supplying the nuclear boilers. He preempted much of the responsibility for the ship, although the basic ship and most of its features were not his responsibility. Nonetheless he parlayed his position into one where he even dictated who would be the first commanding officer. He wanted desperately to have a submariner with nuclear-ship-propulsion experience as the CO, but the aviators won that one.

I think it was one of the very few that the Line people won from Rickover. They had to yield the USS Long Beach to "Rick," I guess as a quid pro quo, and Dennis Wilkinson who commanded the first nuclear-powered submarine was made the captain of the USS Long Beach. Dennis is a hell of a fine submariner, but the black-shoe boys were fairly shook up when he was ordered to command the Long Beach. But that again is an indication of the power which Rickover was able to exert over not just the nuclear boiler activities but every aspect of the vehicle into which it was placed, including personnel and even the contributions of private industry.

One of the mementoes that I've carried away from my last military assignment is a composite drawing in which photographs of Enterprise, the Long Beach, and the Bainbridge are placed in formation. I cherish this because I went through the agonies of seeing the ships finally completed and delivered.

I remember one little humorous experience. I went to Newport News in the course of the construction of the Enterprise on several occasions. One particular time, in the interest of cost reduction which was being imposed on my very forcefully by Arleigh Burke, CNO, my boys had been instructed to eliminate everything that was nonessential in the interest of cost reduction. One of the cost reduction items offered which I approved, was to eliminate the personnel elevator in the island structure. On this particular visit, I was greeted by the powers that be at Newport News and a chap by the name of Tilly Smith - Tilford Smith - was my guide. I believe he was general manager at the time. He asked me where I would like to start the inspection of the ship, up at the top or down at the keel. I elected to start at the keel and work up. We did. We went through the ship and it took us several hours. By the time I got to the flight deck I was bushed but we still had another five or six levels to go before we got to the top of the island structure. We started trudging up ladders from one level to another. By the time we got to the extreme upper level, which was the objective of my inspection, I was so pooped I could hardly lift one foot or the other. Whereupon, Tilly Smith pulled out of his pocket a piece of paper and he said, "I've got your signature on something that you ought to read," and shoved under my nose the letter which gave the change order to eliminate the elevator in the island structure! He said, "What do you think the guys who are going to run this ship are going to think about you when they know that you personally knocked the goldarned elevator off of the ship?" Well, I had to laugh like hell and said, "If I've got any strength, I'll go back and revise that order and put the elevator back in."

This matter of the cost of the ship, however, is one that became politically embarrassing to the Navy.

Q: How much did she cost?

Adm. J.: By the time I took over as chief, she was committed for over $425 million. The original estimate, I think, was on the order of $350 million. What with changes, with escalation, and the likes, the cost had risen to a figure that began to embarrass the Navy Department. I was called in and asked what the final cost to complete was. I think I estimated somewhere in the order of $525 million.

I remember that Arleigh Burke said "this ship will not cost one cent more than $464.8 million" one of the numbers I had in my presentation. I said, "That would mean cutting out a lot of things." For example, we had a phase-shifting radar, I think it was the SPS-26 - I could be wrong on the identity. It was a completely developmental radar. Instead of a rotating "mattress," it functioned with an electronic phase shifting of a whole series of grids that enclosed the island structure. The rotation of the radar beam was done electronically. The cost was going up by leaps and bounds. Many other new features of the ship were likewise in difficulty costwise. I remember having to struggle madly to keep within that arbitrary figure of Admiral Burke. I hate to admit it now, but I'm sure the ship cost more than $464.8 million, but the accounting data showed no more than $464.8 million. I think Arleigh Burke's basic concern was that if it got over half a billion dollars it might be the last of the nuclear carriers, and well it might, for even then we were estimating a follow-on ship which was well over half a billion dollars.

There is a conventional-powered carrier that was built after the Enterprise - the Kennedy. My memory is horrible, but at any rate because of the cost of the Enterprise, we couldn't get authority to build another nuke. We were required by SecDef to make our next carrier a conventional-powered ship. There was a great deal of internal Navy stress over this, particularly from

Rickover and Company and from some members of Congress who thought the Navy was stepping backwards.

Q: How much did that reduce the bill?

Adm. J.: Oh, it reduced it from something in excess of half a billion dollars for the next new ship to something on the order of $325 million. The differential in cost was applied to construction of other ships for the Navy which was, by many people's judgment, more urgently needed than were big carriers at that time. We were beginning to see the schism between the aviators on the one hand, and the surface tacticians on the other hand who thought the CVAs were becoming less and less important to naval tactics. Finally the Congress did authorize and we built this conventionally powered carrier. It was part of the trauma that then existed because of rising shipbuilding costs which were beginning to plague us in every aspect of our shipbuilding program.

Shipbuilding costs are not precise. Bids for ships are never precise. They represent the builder's best figure to recapture his costs and his best judgment as to how much the market would bear in terms of additional return on his investment. In days of large order backlogs in shipyards, prices are high. In days when their order boards are low, the bids are generally much lower. So price charged and costs of ships bear little direct relationship.

Q: There is also the time factor, is there not? It takes years to build a ship of this nature.

Adm. J.: We used to include in our contracts what was known as escalation clauses, which allowed for direct labor cost escalation. We made a routine of estimating what would be required. As I recall, we estimated at around five and a half percent *a year*. In other words, in a four-year building program of a carrier, of course on the diminishing amount of value still to be put in place, we would pay as much as 21 or 22 percent over the original estimate to cover that particular aspect of the ship construction costs by the time the final bill was paid.

Q: And that would hardly be adequate in this day with inflation being what it is?

Adm. J.: Well, in my era, we averaged around 5 1/2% per year. It got a little higher than that and occasionally it was somewhat lower. But that was an accepted figure we went to the Congress with our requirements for annual increments of funds.

Of course, it was about this time that Admiral McNeil and I were able finally to sell the total ship cost package to the Congress. I've mentioned this before. This was the approach to estimate the total cost to build the entire ship, including all escalation, design changes, new developments, and the like, and then to ask for that total amount of money. Congress, when they approved the ship, then knew what they were committing themselves for in its entirety. Here the problem, as I've also mentioned, was the generation of large appropriated fund reserves that would be held awaiting expenditure based on the progress of the ship construction. Ultimately these reserves got to be the size where everybody was aware of them, that's when they began to be chiseled upon. It didn't happen in my watch, but my successor was subject to the pressure and had to yield to let this total cost approach go down the river. I still think total cost estimating is a smarter way to do business. If you didn't spend all your money, it reverted to the Treasury. At least when you start out, you know that Congress has approved building this ship and they know what obligation they have undertaken in making that commitment. Otherwise, when you come in on a year-to-year basis for handouts, they would have to be as smart as you are to know what the ultimate cost would be, so why not tell them in the beginning? However, that's now gone by the boards and other approaches are being used.

One of the Bureau's major efforts in this connection was the program which I labeled "Dollar Stretch." It was a direct outcome of our SCAP investigation, how to get more bang per buck, A slogan that we applied to part of the SCAP program. We planned to apply SCAP across the board in all facets of the Bureau of Ships establishment. I'm sure that we achieved much in the way of cost reduction, a fact we modestly reported, and I truly say "modestly" and "conservatively." We reported in excess of 300 million dollars savings from our SCAP operation in a period which I think was the year 1961-62. It was here that this program caught the eye and fancy of our new Secretary of Defense who preempted the project, the program and the approach, as though it were his own. I'm sure you've seen or heard of his many presentations on the Hill of how he was stretching the dollar. His projected savings escalated into the billions. I'm sure there were a lot of phonys in his program. Those we presented were actually supported by a physical reduction of force of personnel or a significant reduction in contract prices we negotiated before we took any credit for savings. He went to the extreme of trying to convince people he was a great savior of the Treasury by disapproving programs that had no likelihood of being approved under any circumstances, and then taking full credit for the amount saved.

This SCAP program went on during my entire tenure as Chief. It gained significant recognition, at least among our own people. Every place I went to visit, I was always titillated by the boasting of what they had done in this shipyard or that shipyard carrying out the cost reduction effort of the Dollar Stretch program.

Another one of the things that I quickly found after succeeding Mumma was the depressing state of affairs in the physical plant of our naval shipyards. I had been in several and was aware that a number of them were literally falling down. I was aware that a number of our technologies had advanced to the point where machinery and equipment in the shipyards were incapable of carrying out the new approaches to machine-shop operations, the computer programming of different machine tools, and the like. So I started an effort aimed at shipyard modernization. I was given a tremendous stimulus in this effort when I visited abroad and witnessed the beautiful new shipyards that were financed to a large extent under the Marshall Plan that were going up in Holland, West Germany, in Italy and France and to a lesser extent in Norway which, of course, had lost much of its wartime capability, as did all the other nations involved. As these countries rebuilt their shipyards, they made them the most modern that the equipment and technology permitted. They had photo-lofting of ship lines, automatic burning, automatic steel plate treatment, the creation of unitized flow of material and modules through shipyards - simply a revolution in the type and equipment of shipyards all of which we had failed to accomplish in our U. S. yards because we needed and used all of our facilities throughout the war. None were damaged by direct war effort. The anomaly was that here was our country virtually financing shipyard modernization around the world, including defeated Japan, while we made do with aging if not antiquated set of shipyards of our own.

Q: And suffering from the competition that we had set up?

Adm. J.: Right. In the private yards, this was indeed true. In the Navy yards, of course, competition was nonexistent.

I came back from the trip to Europe, particularly dedicated to the effort of modernizing our naval shipyards and hoping through outspoken but constructive criticism - to get private yards to do the same. At first, the private yards were horrified that I would degregate their facilities. They claimed I knew little or nothing about their capabilities and stated how they were putting in a $20,000 new brake here or $50,000 new burning equipment there, or even photo-lofting which was then in its embryo state and that new machine tools were beginning to appear in most of our private yards. But I must have jolted the industry. Almost immediately after my outspoken presentation of this subject while I was president of the Society of Naval Architects and Marine Engineers, a number of the shipyards sent teams of their own abroad from those yards. . .

Q: To see for themselves?

Adm. J.: To see for themselves. Included amongst those that I know to have gone were people from Newport News Shipbuilding and Dry Dock Company, Todd sent a group, and others that I've since forgotten. Some came back and began even further developments within their yards beyond those which they paraded in front of me when I charged them with being backward and failing to keep up with the developments. A great deal has been done since in private yards to upgrade their facilities. Not as much as would be apparent in those yards that were demolished abroad during the war and rebuilt from scratch, but a major improvement in private shipyard facilities has taken place. It has taken a long time and it's been done not so much by my initial criticism, which goes back for at least ten years, but rather to the fact that some of the newcomers into the shipbuilding field have constructed complete new shipyard layouts in the manner of the European yards and have frightened some of the old traditional yards into following suit.

Q: Wasn't money a real factor, however, in bringing about renovations?

Adm. J.: Oh, of course, it was. It was a major factor and shipyards were not exactly making handsome profits. In fact, while we're on this topic I might say that it was always distressing to me that our system of taking contracts for naval ships required that the shipyards prostitute their best interests in the interest of getting contracts. Some yards were "buying contracts" at bargain-basement prices for a number of years while I was in office until the acceleration of shipbuilding generally caught up with events and yards began to bid more sensibly. But shipyards in that era were scarcely making adequate profits and hence were not in a position to do much about upgrading their facilities to the extent that I thought was appropriate. I recognized this but nonetheless I continued to twit them. I'm sure, in the long run, the recognition of the need to upgrade the yard facilities has been achieved. As I say, perhaps the entry of newcomers into the shipbuilding field gave more of a stimulus than anything.

As an example, Litton Industries acquired the old Ingalls shipyard in Pascagoula, Mississippi. When they did, they began planning for a brand-new shipyard. Very smartly they got the citizens of the state of Mississippi to underwrite a bond issue to finance the construction cost of what is perhaps one of the more up-to-date shipyards ever built in this country. It is known as their West Bank Yard, and is in Pascagoula, Mississippi.

Q: Was there any talk of the need for subsidies in order to get the yards to modernize?

Adm. J.: Not subsidy of the private shipyards. More business would have been the most appropriate type of subsidy and, of course, we've seen the shipyard complex shrink because in the early part of my term in office there were more shipyards in this country striving for major ship business than there was any need or justification for. I used to really worry about this problem. It caused this cutthroat bidding on ships, and it caused good established yards to teeter on the brink of bankruptcy. It wasn't gratifying to receive bids from a group of shipyards that you knew were not the kind that should be building our ships. One of the large yards, New York Shipbuilding and Drydock Company, owned principally by this guy, Louis Wolfson, who was an opportunist not a shipbuilder, later went out of business and it was no great loss. They never should have been in business with that administration, but it was one of the companies that was always bidding and always pushing other yards to bid improvidently. I hope I'm not conveying the impression that all shipyards were bidding below cost. They weren't, but they weren't bidding in a manner that would give them an adequate return and permit yard modernization.

Not only in the private sector, but in the naval shipyards this program was vitally required. In the naval shipyards, we had done a minimum of machine tool replacement continuously over the years, but there were new ship equipments coming into being, there was much more electronics equipment much more fire control gear, and weapon sensors, and the likes. All this ultimately needed overhaul, and our shipyards needed updating to achieve the capability of handling these kinds of new equipments. Not the least of which was the need to overhaul nuclear ships, both submarines and surface ships. This takes very special training of personnel and a limited amount of additional facilities to handle the nuclear equipments to cope with the radiation problem. So there was a major deficiency here so I undertook personally to try and find the solution.

I assigned one chap by the name of Commander Bill Harrison, as my principal shipyard modernization specialist. I took him with me on one trip to Europe where we visited shipyards, mostly private, to witness what had been done. After we came back he went to work and reported regularly to me on proposals for naval shipyard modernization.

We brought this to full flower in a program which came to a head just a couple of months - before I was due to be relieved. I recall bringing the Secretary of the Navy, Fred Korth, and a number of key military personnel together in the Bureau of Ships and sitting them down for a protracted review of our shipyard situation and our modernization program. I estimated it would take 20 million dollars a year for a ten-year period to achieve the desired improvement of our naval shipyard facilities. I was gratified to get complete endorsement from Fred Korth and others in support of the program beginning with the next budget.

I believe the program was carried forward for one year under my successor, but then, like all things that are not screamingly immediate, it began to get short-changed as it proceeded, and I think finally it was cut back to 5 million a year. I wouldn't know what the total figure is now of what has been spent to upgrade our naval shipyards but certainly nothing approaching $200 million.

Q: Hasn't there been something of a revitalization right now?

Adm. J.: Well, a sub-committee of the Armed Services Committee headed up by Representative Charlie Bennett of Florida, two years ago began looking into the entire problem of shipbuilding in this country, both for merchant shipping and for naval ships. He has come out with the very positive statement that the naval shipyards might not be capable of performing their assigned mission of supporting the fleet in wartime unless the modernization effort is revived. The program is all there. It's simply a question of funding it and getting on with the job. I would say that the Naval Ships Systems Command has diligently pursued the effort and has put as much money into it as it could, but nothing on the order of magnitude which I suggested and was needed in 1963. By today's costs this would probably approximate something on the order of 250 million dollars to accomplish everything that we thought was then necessary.

Another factor was the number of existing naval shipyards. I had the deep conviction that we had more naval shipyards than we needed. I also felt the same about the private sector. In the private sector it was difficult to play god and decide which shipyards you'd give business to. We did have latitude under the system prevailing, and the authority then held by the Chief of Buships, and to assign ships to some yards to the exclusion of others, which then possibly dry up and disappear. In the naval shipyard area I did have responsibility for making specific recommendations about closing shipyards. Fairly well into my term, approximately midterm, I proposed the closing of three naval shipyards. This was endorsed as appropriate by the line side of the Navy and by the secretariat of the Navy. I went into great detail, reviewed the shipyards' capabilities and made my recommendations based on belief in shipyard capability. I proposed the immediate closing in 1961 or 1962 of the Boston Naval Shipyard, the Philadelphia Naval Shipyard, and the San Francisco Naval Shipyard. This received endorsement all the way through the Defense Department. Somehow or other, before the normal steps that should be taken to prepare people for such drastic treatment, the word got out that Boston was on the block. This was just about when Kennedy came into office, and the fur began to fly. I recall that it was Ken Belieu, who was then the assistant secretary, who was my biggest supporter. He was called up to McNamara's office one day to explain, "why Boston." It seems that Congressman McCormick - John McCormick - had learned of this threat, and boy, he really raised cain. Jack Kennedy was in on this by this time. McCormick is reported to have found Jack swimming in the White House pool when he came in livid with the prospect of losing the Boston naval shipyard. He got a commitment that it wouldn't be closed from the President, while Kennedy was swimming and not studying his homework. With the elimination of Boston from among the shipyards to be closed, the conviction of the need to close yards still remained in the Defense Department. Shortly after I left office McNamara picked up the ball and went through the motions of carrying on a personal investigation himself. He came to the conclusion that Portsmouth naval shipyard, New York Naval shipyard, and the amalgamation of San Francisco with Mare Island should be accomplished. Portsmouth, however, was to be given a ten-year breathing spell before the closing.

Then it was to be Portsmouth, New York, and San Francisco. New York was directed for immediate closing and subsequently was closed. San Francisco was merged with Mare Island, which did nothing to reduce the number of shipyards. It simply eliminated one separate command from the list of naval commands, but all the facilities, all the manpower, and all the scramble for assignment of work continued. Just to follow this through to conclusion, as I said, finally the New York yard was closed. Just last year the

San Francisco yard was again separated from Mare Island to become a separate command. I think this is at least the third time it has gone through this same abberation, and recently the present administration announced that Portsmouth would not be closed. I believe this was a ploy used by President Nixon to try to get Margaret Chase Smith's vote for the SST a matter of months ago. He didn't get the vote and in the meantime he's committed himself to keep Portsmouth open. Portsmouth was not one of the yards that I would have closed and I still don't think it would have been the right yard to close, even today, but I do believe that Boston has little usefulness and very ancient facilities. Philadelphia has marginal usefulness because the fleet no longer finds it convenient to make that long haul up the Delaware River to Philadelphia. San Francisco - there might be more argument for keeping it than for keeping Mare Island in actual fact. But this is a matter for the future.

My effort to close three shipyards and the effort to conserve administrative costs of maintaining more yards than there was any need for and to stretch our modernization program across a fewer number of shipyards with a better final result didn't get very far. I don't believe the shipyard-closing matter is a closed book by a darned sight. With the continued reduction in fleet strength, the need for the shipyards is ever diminishing and I would say that today, while we have lost one out of the original eleven, there's probably need to lose about four more before we shake down to the condition that would be required to maintain the fleet size that we have today. Also the fact that the ships of the future are going to be different from those of the past and they will have specialized equipments requiring new overhaul facilities. For example, the DD-963 class, the new class of destroyers, is coming along with gas-turbine propulsion systems. The PF program that Admiral Zumwalt is advocating of about 50 ships, will also have gas-turbine propulsion systems. We don't have gas-turbine overhaul and test facilities within the Bureau of Ships or the NavShips Systems complex. The Bureau of Aeronautics or the Air Systems Command I guess do have gas-turbine overhaul capabilities at some of the Air Stations. But these are things that must be taken care of in the future at naval shipyards.

And then there's one more thing that I'd like to touch upon. . .

Q: May I ask in connection with the shipyards and the possible closing of them. Is it not unfortunate that we can't seem to look at the situation realistically and in a practical way, but that political considerations have to enter the picture and obscure it?

Adm. J.: I would say it's one of the great tragedies of our democratic system, that politicians can manipulate things that are useless or unneeded by the military establishment and then turn around and charge the military establishment with poor business management. That is sheer and utter hogwash. We knew that we should have closed the Boston naval shipyard and only the political considerations and a new president from the Boston area listening to the hubbub of the delegation from Massachusetts, kept us from closing a yard that has no reason to be in business today. And Philadelphia is not much better. Both of them were Revolutionary War-built facilities, and many of their facilities are still

Revolutionary War types of equipments. A hell of a situation, one that would not be tolerated in business and yet we were forced to accept this.

That reminds me of a letter I found in my desk when I first took over as chief of the Bureau of Ships. It was a letter from a congressman from Charlestown, Massachusetts, to one of his colleagues in the Congress. They were speaking about the attitude of the Commander of the Boston Naval Shipyard toward certain of the requests that this congressman had made. He went on to say that the situation had gotten intolerable with this individual, whom he identified, and he was going to have to take steps, and hoped his friend would join with him in making it clear to this naval officer in command that the Boston naval shipyard was not being administerd and run by the Navy, it was indeed there to satisfy the requirements of the political exigencies of the incumbents in office from that area. It was shattering, to see such a blatant statement of determination to politically control the yard operation. The curious thing, and the reason it was in my desk, was the date of the letter. The date of the letter of 1868!

Q: What a timely reminder to you!

Adjm. J.: Yes.

Q: The awarding of the contracts for the new type destroyers you mentioned, the gas-turbine types, was obscured also, was it not, by political considerations?

Adm. J.: Oh, I'm sure it was, but this is not in my personal field of knowledge, so I'd not want to discuss it too extensively. One of the finer shipyards that should have been in that program, the Bath Iron Works, was squeezed out of position, and I am suspicious enough to believe that it was some sort of a political pay-off because of the relationship of Litton Industries with the then-Secretary of Defense.

However, this subject of the modernization of shipyards is still a matter I'd like to continue with and I want to relate very briefly, although I shouldn't because it's a major topic of its own - I was going to say that I would like to discuss the development of the hydrofoil craft and hovercraft which fortunately it was my privilege to initiate within the Navy. But they are such new and novel technologies and have such a tremendous impact on the prospects of the future Navy that I think it's a subject that deserves more time than I have immediately available this morning. So, with your concurrence, Dr. Mason, I'd like to bring this interview to an end at this point so I may go to the launching of the USS California at Newport News.

James #10 - 325

Interview No. 10 with Rear Admiral R. K. James, U. S. Navy (Retired)

Place: His home in Annapolis, Maryland

Date: Tuesday morning, 25 January 1972

Subject: Biography

By: John T. Mason, Jr.

Q: Admiral, I've been looking forward to this chapter. The last time when we broke off you promised to talk about the hovercraft and the hydrofoil and bring them down to date - the development of these vehicles, if one may term them as such, which started during your regime in the Bureau of Ships and are a matter of real concern to you even now.

Adm. J.: Yes, indeed they are. I think a little of the history of the hovercraft and the hydrofoils will be of interest. Perhaps the hydrofoil, being the older technology, would be the one to discuss first. Actually, it was surprising to me to learn that hydrofoil development had started in the 1890s decade. I had thought it was an up-to-date, relatively modern, invention.

Q: Are you sure Leonardo hadn't thought of it!

Adm. J.: Perhaps he had, but as the American history books record the development of the hydrofoil, they credit Alexander Graham Bell in 1898 as having put the first hydrofoil to sea. The hydrofoil, as I'm sure you're aware, is simply a conventional mono-hulled boat that is lifted above the surface of the water to reduce the drag of the viscous fluid of the sea and increase speed. The device used to lift the boat out of the water is a series of ladderlike appendages that are arranged in different configurations that constitute small aircraft foil-type wings. As the craft develops higher and higher speed, why, these ladderlike affairs, that look like the steps of a ladder, raise the craft above the surface and it flies as an air foil might.

Q: This is a matter of pressure, isn't it?

Adm. J.: It's a matter of forward movement of the ship creating negative pressure on the upper side of the foil and positive pressure on the lower side, which gives you the lift of the craft. Now, the so-called surface-piercing-foil concept, which at first was the only prevalent system, did not permit very successful heavy-weather operations with hydrofoils. Generally speaking, they were limited to use in protected waters. The Europeans had done a gre deal in developing this. A German with Swiss citizenship whose name was von Schertel was a principal designer and entrepreneur in the field of hydrofoils. One of the principal producers of hydrofoils was an Italian firm known as the Rodriguez Shipyards in Catania on the isle of Sicily. These craft were all the so-called surface-piercing type hydrofoils.

However, in the Bureau of Ships and some years before my taking over as chief, a concept of a submerged foil - a fully submerged foil, like an airplane wing upside down in the water - had been postulated. The firm of Gibbs and Cox had been employed in the early 1950s - about 1956, I believe - to study this type of foil configuration, and to invent, if they could, a system for control of these foils. A system so the foils could be adjusted in their angle of attack, in order to anticipate the oncoming wave heights and, in doing so, lift the craft to meet the oncoming waves and allow it to slide back as the waves' crest passed under the boat.

Q: In the manner, perhaps, of the wing of an airplane -

Adm. J.: Just exactly in the manner of the wing of an airplane, except it would be a system that would actually rotate the wings so as to anticipate the oncoming wave. Well, this largely was an electronic nightmare and had a standard type of altimeter placed in the bow of the ship. This altimeter would read the height of the bow location to the top of the oncoming wave or to the trough, as it happened, and then by a series of servo-mechanisms adjust the angle of attack of the foil that was submerged below the boat. It proved to be hugely successful. Shortly after I became chief, the demonstration of a little boat called Sea Legs that had been outfitted with these foils and the electronic controls took place. It was so completely successful that thereafter in our Navy we considered it appropriate to go only in the direction of the submerged foil, as contrasted with the surface-piercing foil. This became the configuration that is today receiving great attention from our Navy.

Q: What is its great advantage over the surface-piercing one?

Adm. J.: Largely the immediate response of the craft to the wave form. In other words, you can rise and fall with the waves without the delay which occurs when this motion is dependent on the surface piercing foils that project from the craft down into the water. Also you're able to maneuver the vessel much more efficiently. The seakeeping capabilities are greatly enhanced.

An interesting event occurred when Sea Legs made her initial voyage from New York, where she had been fitted out (I think I said, a 36-foot motor boat) to transit to Norfolk area for conduct of the tests. We arranged to have her escorted by a standard deep-sea tug just for safety purposes. They ran into a storm. The storm was rather violent though brief. The waves and the surface of the sea were greatly agitated and the tug had to heave to, but our little Sea Legs continued to fly (as was the expression used) around as the escort for the tug in this period of severe weather. This one fact alone, I think, convinced many navy people of how effectively the submerged-foil configuration was. It gave the enthusiasm that I later capitalized on in the construction of the first hydrofoil of the submerged-foil class. My dates are a little wobbly, but let me guess this was in 1960, when we offered for construction a Bureau of Ships design of the submerged-foil configuration with the wave-sensing controls. Boeing Corporation were the successful bidder. They, in turn, subcontracted to Takoma Boat Company for the construction of the hull under the supervision of Boeing. Takoma Boat in Takoma, Washington, is not far away from the main Boeing plant at Seattle. I visited there several times to see what was later named the USS High Point, after some town in North Carolina, I believe.

The High Point was a very successful craft ultimately, although in the early stages we had problems in transmitting the power in the craft from the gas turbine engines through 90-degree transmission changes to the propulsors which come out of the struts that carried the submerged foils. This development of drive system caused quite a long period of trial and error in improvement of the mechanics of that propulsion system, but ultimately it was overcome. When the success of the High Point was reasonably well established or assured, we postulated a much larger hydrofoil craft, and laid down the design in the Bureau of Ships, of the ship that later became known as the USS Plain View.

The detailed design of the Plain View was offered for competitive bidding. The Grumman Corporation on Long Island won the design contract. They received the contract plans of the Plain View from the Bureau and converted them into a detailed design, with working plans. They came in with their finished design and it looked like a very successful one. With it, we advertised for bid, the construction of this craft - no, let me back up a bit. It had been our intention at the time of awarding the design contract, that the successful bidder of that would also build the first craft -

Q: May I ask you, Sir, what was your over-all objective in producing this craft? What did you intend it to be used for?

Adm. J.: Well, if I may finish this one thought on the awarding of the Plain View contract, I will then answer your very appropriate question. As I said, we had anticipated that the winner of the design contract would also be the builder of the first craft. I think Grumman took advantage of the fact that they were on the inside track, and they came in with a very much higher price tag for the Plain View than was within our budget and even within the realm of reasonableness. I had to cancel the previous tentative commitment to award the construction of the craft to them. It was later offered out/to a number of aerospace companies and was ultimately won by Lockheed Company.

Now, your very appropriate question as to why hydrofoils. We had envisioned many applications of the hydrofoil because of its much greater speed potential than the conventional surface ship of its approximate size. I should mention the sizes of these craft, the High Point was on the order of a 75-ton craft and the Plain View was, and is still today I believe, the world's largest hydrofoil ever built at 320 tons. These ships, then, in this range of size had many mission potentials. One was patrol of the coasts for antisubmarine detection. They had search and rescue potential. They had mine-laying capabilities that could be fitted into them. I think, perhaps, at the time, we thought primarily of the ASW problem, which was then and still is a major Navy concern. The configuration of the High Point provided essentially what could be called gunboat-type of armament, with very limited armament. She could be utilized in connection with landings on beaches, amphibious operations, or operations such as Market Time in the Vietnam war, where interception of infiltrating ships could be conducted. It was their high speed, which was in the order of 40 to 45 knots, that gave hydrofoils a greater potential than the conventional boat type, even a planing type hull. So these potentials were envisioned as we designed these ships. Of course, with the Plain View on the order of 320 tons of ship we could put on a much larger weapon suit and this added greatly to their potential application.

Q: May I interrupt again? You say the Plain View was 320 tons. Is there a maximum conceived as the limit for this type of craft?

Adm. J.: The maximum is a matter of further and continuous development. There has been none bigger built to date and largely for the reason that in order to build a hydrofoil you have to lift the total weight of the boat up on your foils. Therefore, the design of the foils, the materials used in their construction becomes a major factor in establishing the limiting size of the craft. I used to speculate that about a 500-ton maximum limit of hydrofoil design would evolve. To date, I have knowledge of the fact that Boeing Corporation are postulating a 1,000-ton craft. If that can be built within the technology now existing, I would say that is certainly reaching the outer limits of hydrofoil potential. Because of the fact that the foils eventually lifts all this weight out of the water and must have a foil structure to do this, even with our more exotic-strength materials, high-tensile-strength steels, titanium, nothing has been developed yet to lift any more than 1000 tons. I "hae me doots," as my grandmother used to say, whether it even has the potential of lifting 1,000 tons. But, nonetheless, that size perhaps is the outer limit.

Q: Still another question. Is there any remote resemblance to the German E boat of World War II?

Adm. J.: No. The E boat was strictly a conventional type hull.

It just was a beautifully designed hull form and had a lot of engine power, but it was not in any sense a hydrofoil.

Today with the advent of Admiral Zumwalt, the Navy has gotten rather wildly enthusiastic about hydrofoils. A later design than the High Point, called the Tucumcari, was built also by Boeing Corporation. It has become a favorite of some of the naval line officers. In fact, the Tucumcari was ordered into the Mediterranean last year as a demonstration vehicle, trying to interest the NATO nations in the Mediterranean to place orders for construction of this craft.

Q: What's her size?

Adm. J.: She's about a 60-65-ton craft, rather small, a gunboat type, something that would be useful in the Mediterranean to offset some of the Soviet missile-carrying gunboat types. I am not cognizant of the success of this venture, although I believe it was not as great as its proponents had anticipated. The Tucumcari is undergoing a refit, as, I believe, is the High Point, to incorporate more sophisticated weapon developments. I believe that Boeing is extremely anxious to merchandize Tucumcari-type hydrofoils but I am not aware of any specific orders for additional craft that have been placed.

Now about hovercraft. Actually, many people confuse hydrofoils and hovercraft, evidencing the limited knowledge that exists in the world today about what a hovercraft is. A hovercraft is a relatively recent invention. Some Americans claim responsibility for the invention, but I think it is generally accepted in the marine field that Sir Christopher Cockrell, a Britisher, conceived the idea of a hovercraft from what was a classic laboratory experiment known as the Coffee Can test. Cockrell utilized a standard coffee can partially filled with water and then inserted another one in it. He blew air under the base of the second can and found that he had reduced the friction of the surface of the water to such a point that he had almost a free-floating can. This was in about 1955 or 1956. Westland Aircraft Corporation, a British firm, by one device or another unknown to me, acquired the rights and built the first sea-going hovercraft known as the SRN-1. Shortly after I took office as chief of the Bureau I saw photographs of the SRN-1 crossing the English Channel. It was a spidery-looking vehicle with a large fan that was blowing air beneath the bottom of the craft.

Q: Blowing it down?

Adm. J.: Blowing it downward, and another airplane propeller blowing it horizontally to propel the craft. Perched on this weird-looking vehicle was Prince Philip of Britain along with a chap I later became closely associated with, Mr. John Chaplin then of Westland Aircraft Corporation. They crossed the English Channel in about a fraction of the average time required by conventional craft, amidst a great flurry of spray, and I'm sure arrived at the other side in France thoroughly drenched. However, the concept appealed to me. In BuShips we had been looking at ground-effects machines, as they were then known in our country, during the period from the Cockrell invention until I came into office. In fact, we had a little gem out at the David Taylor Model Basin that BuAir had produced.

It was a tethered, flat-bottom vehicle that flew around on the maypole-like standard, by blowing air under the flat bottom and propelling it by a fan that blew horizontally to give it forward motion. I rode this craft in 1959. I was interested, but it took the SRN-1 photographs to really stimulate my imagination.

By this time Westland had built the SRN-2. I was privileged to ride in that - in fact I rode in two or three hovercraft, for by this time Westland had competition from Vickers-Armstrong. I thoroughly enjoyed this experience and was tremendously impressed with the potential that this vehicle had. At this particular time, all the craft were completely amphibious. They could operate on the sea and on land. The first craft I actually rode in was a Vickers-Armstrong. We proceeded from their building yard in Southampton, down across mud flats into the Southampton River, and out into the Solent. As we started to cross the Solent, which is the open water between the Isle of Wight and the mainland of south England, the seas were very rough, I would say about a State 3, maybe State 4. I asked the pilot on the intercom - I was seated beside him in the co-pilot's seat - how the craft handled in rough water, and I couldn't get an answer. I fiddled and diddled with all the switches that they had briefed me on and still couldn't raise any communication with the man sitting right beside me. The noise in the cabin prevented any voice communication. So, we proceeded across the Solent and it was a rough trip. As we approached the far shore where we were to dock at an abandoned British seaplane base, we started up the ramp onto land, when the intercom came on loud and clear. The pilot, Mr. Colcughoon said, "Admiral, now I can answer your question. You and I both have just learned how this craft handles in rough weather."

Well, I got an awful bang out of that because here was Vickers-Armstrong subjecting me to the hazard of testing their vehicle for the first time in rough water. As it turned out, it was a memorable trip and one I will always remember.

Q: So the air cushion doesn't really save you from the . . .

Adm. J.: No. The theory of the hovercraft is essentially that you can have a variety of bottom forms which we've not fully developed, but largely they have flat bottoms. The craft is equipped with a large fan to produce a downward flow of air into the cavity below the hull. Then an aircraft type propeller gives you forward motion. Control of the craft is by regular aircraft rudders abaft the propellers. Fans raise you off the surface of the sea by varying heights, depending on design.

Q: It's a consistent height, however?

Adm. J.: Yes - well, of course, as you go across the seas you rise and fall, but it maintains a steady gap between the sea surface and the bottom of the craft.

Q: Roughly how high is it?

Adm. J.: Let me come to that after I describe how this is achieved. This then cuts the drag of the water to virtually zero, so your speed potential is tremendous. It is much greater than the hydrofoil which has the foil appendages dragging in the water, but the hovercraft flies above the water with no actual appendage in the water in the fully amphibious versions. I'll talk further about that.

Stimulated by this experience in England, by the developments that were going on in the United States with the ground-effects machine (and there were many in the automobile industry, the railroad industry) and with everybody getting into the act and trying to utilize this technology to minimize surface resistance - I returned and accelerated a hovercraft design within the Bureau of Ships that later became known as Skimmer-1. This craft was designed with the then conventional flat bottom, with two large airplane propellers to drive it, with rudders to give it directional stability, and two fans to give the cushion airlift pressure. We advertised for a finished detail design and craft construction. We advertised it to the aerospace industry with the admonition that they marry themselves with a shipbuilding company to be sure to provide the integration of the marine technology of the hull with the aeroframe technology of the rest of the vehicle and propulsors, to provide the minimum gross weight of craft and hence the maximum payload in a given sized vehicle.

Bell Aerospace, then Bell Aircraft, of Buffalo, New York, won this contract from us in 1960. In the meantime I visited again in England and rode on more sophisticated surface-effects vehicles of Westland Aircraft. At that time I made the suggestion to the management at Westland that they make Bell Aircraft a licensee to give Bell the benefit of the technology which was much further advanced in England at that time than it was in our country. Later, Bell consummated such an arrangement and has become a direct licensee of British Hovercraft, which is the successor agency to Westland Aircraft Corporation.

Well, the construction of our craft proceeded, then it was launched and successfully operated. In the meantime, British Hovercraft, through their own innovations, had developed a scheme of surrounding the entire periphery of the craft with a flexible type of rubber skirt to retain the air bubble under the craft much more efficiently than did the gap between the flat bottom and the surface of the land or sea permit. It increased the height at which the craft then could flay above the sea or land surface. In the early version of the Bureau of Ships design, six to eight inches was the maximum height above the surface that you could fly the craft. With the advent of the skirt, which Bell then fitted to Skimmer-1 before it was finally delivered, you could reach heights of three and a half to four and a half feet above the surface. This added a tremendous new dimension to the whole concept because then it meant that you could go over obstacles of three to four feet in height, at least, and it meant less power for the craft to contain the cushion under the vehicle. It opened up a tremendous potential for the application of this craft into many military areas, such as in amphibious assault, as part of an amphibious assault force. It had the potential of taking troops and equipment right through the surf to the beachhead, through the surf at the beachhead, up on to the land and climb, as has later been demonstrated, about

15-degree slopes, deposit the men and equipment well above the surf, which in World War II was generally the most critical area of a beach landing.

Q: And right over the pill boxes?

Adm. J.: Well, not over, but around them and if the pill boxes were no more than three to five feet high, then you might go over them. Because of the potential of higher and higher speeds, it also opened up the possibility of antisubmarine warfare operations of tremendous advantage. In Skimmer-1 we developed speeds of up to 65 knots. This was greater than any standard naval vehicle had ever achieved. Until quite recently Skimmer-1 was the largest hovercraft ever built in this country. It has been finally overtaken.

The craft was delivered in 1963. I retired from the Navy in 1963. The delivery of the craft and my retirement were almost coincidental. Although I had pressed Bell to deliver it so that I might achieve the privilege of seeing it operate before I did retire I never did see it. Its completion occurred almost the same day that I retired. After exhaustive tests by Bell, the craft was taken over by the OpTevFor of the Navy. For better than a year and a half it was subjected to some of the most rigorous tests over seas, entering the well decks of LPDs, withdrawing from the well deck with a load, going on to the beach, and operating in all kinds of sand and beach conditions, as well as surf and weather conditions. A series of movies made of this two-year-long test have only recently come to my attention. It was just shattering to me to see that this craft that performed so beautifully in all of these OpTevFor tests but it never caught the imagination of our navy line personnel. After the tests, it was laid up and after years of being laid up and kicked around from one naval station to another, it finally was scrapped in the Philadelphia Naval Air Center, just about a year and a half ago.

Q: How do you account for this oversight on the part of the authorities?

Adm. J.: I was the principal advocate of this then exotic craft and I had to almost sell my soul to get the Navy to agree to let me expend around five million dollars on this new technology. Even though we projected the use of it in many naval applications, there just wasn't anybody who responded. When the craft finally came along, I had retired. My successor, Bill Brockett apparently did not share my enthusiasm for it and consequently did not give it the personal attention which I had provided. When I realized this, even though I was no longer active in the Navy, I used to make periodic visits to people in high office - the CNO, the Secretary of the Navy -- and tried to talk up the hovercraft as a vehicle they should not overlook.

In the long period from 1963 to about 1968 there was little development in this country of the hovercraft. There was, however, considerable development in Great Britain, with British Hovercraft producing the five ships called the SRN-4s that are now in service across the English Channel. These ships are delivering about 95 percent continuous service throughout the year, operating on schedules of about 25 minutes for the crossing from Calais to Dover. They've virtually captured the cross-Channel traffic. They can handle about 250 passengers and upwards to 35 automobiles on each transit. They are operating well in the "black." There are two British companies - or maybe one's a Scandinavian company - in the field. There have been many new companies come into the hovercraft building field. Some have already passed through the horizon and gone into oblivion, but others have remained along with British Hovercraft. British Hovercraft has in operation over 70 of their hovercraft throughout the world.

Q: Have the Japanese and Russians been involved in working with them?

Adm. J.: Yes. The Russians have developed a hovercraft. I've seen photographs of it operating. I don't know much about its technical features because I've only seen photographs. Virtually every major country has moved into this field, but it took the Vietnamese war and then Rear Admiral Zumwalt to generate the state of enthusiasm that now prevails in our Navy. I should perhaps give credit, in part, to Nicholas Johnson who was the Maritime Administrator in the period of about 1964 to 1967. Nick thought he had discovered the hovercraft. He devoted some of the very limited funds of the Maritime Administration to development and studies of hovercraft. He began a concept known as the Joint Surface-Effects Ship Program to get the Navy and the Maritime Administration to build a test vehicle. At that particular time I was affiliated with a steamship trade association and had many conversations with Nick Johnson about hovercraft. As I say, he likes to think that he discovered the concept and wasn't particularly responsive to a suggestion that I advanced. I advised him that this was primarily a military vehicle, that it therefore should be developed initially by the Navy, that his limited funds, which as a member of the maritime industry, we wanted to see conserved for something more pragmatic in our problem areas of the maritime ships, would be better spent in other areas than this relatively far-out concept. I commented that I thought it would take close to five hundred million dollars to finally evolve a commercial hovercraft. My advice was to let the Navy do the development for its more short-term needs that could be quickly developed, then let the whole merchant concept be acquired as a peel-off of military developments.

Well, Nick is pretty strong minded person. He got thrown out of the Maritime Administration but ended up in the FCC where more often he's the one commissioner who's "agin' everything."

But his efforts started a hovercraft program perhaps earlier than otherwise might have happened within the Navy. The Joint Surface-Effects Ship office, if I may digress from where Zumwalt got into the act, started their project and contracted with two companies, Bell Aerospace and Aerojet General, to each build a

100-ton surface-effects ship of 80 to 85 knots' speed for developing the uncertainties and unknowns in this field of technology. These particular craft were not amphibious in that they had fixed structures that extended into the water and remained in the water, known as the solid-sidewalls, having a flexible skirt at the bow and stern of the craft to contain the bubble and allow for the minimum air leakage, which is essential in the operation. These craft are reaching full completion at Bell by February of this year, and at Aerojet perhaps a month or so later.

Q: Does this indicate, Sir, that there is some difference in the nature of the air bubble as it operates on sea and/or land?

Adm. J.: Well, because of their solid sidewalls, craft that are being built of this type are not amphibious; they cannot come up on land. They must remain in the water because they have solid structure of the ship that extends deep into the water, and thus cannot be lifted out and flown over the land surface. It's only when you have the complete periphery of the craft ringed by flexible skirts that you can move up over the beachline and onto land.

Q: But I meant, is there any basic difference when it operates over sea from what it is over land without this fixed skirt?

Adm. J.: There are many differences, too many to enumerate in this limited interview. But, for example, power then can be transmitted below the surface by such propulsors as water jets or supercavitating high-speed propellers, as contrasted with the air propeller or fan, which is the only propulsion system you can use when operating amphibiously. The hull structure, of course, is considerably different. There are literally hundreds of differences between what is known as the solid-sidewall craft (the surface-effects ship, SES) and the ACV, the air-cushion vehicle, both of which are in the generic family of hovercraft, or surface-effects vehicles.

Q: Permit me another question, Sir. During this interim time when the U. S. Navy had no interest in the development of the hovercraft, what about Bell Aerospace? Did they continue their association with the British outfit? Did they do anything in terms of research?

Adm. J.: Bell did considerable in terms of advanced research on their own. They expended a tremendous amount of their own capital in facilities to build among other things a model basin or towing tank for testing hovercraft, the first in the world, I believe. They have developed advanced designs, and have accumulated all the available data including that of British Hovercraft which has made available all the data that has been accumulated from the operation of their vehicles.

Well, it's about this time that I think we ought to introduce Bud Zumwalt, who, as the senior U. S. Navy commander in South Vietnam, had under his command three British Hovercraft-built, Bell Aerospace-modified, SRN-5s. They were put into service in the riverine operations in South Vietnam. These craft operated where boats and all other normal waterborne craft of the Vietnamese and our own navies could not operate. In such places as the Plain of

Reeds, up on the marshes, over the swamps, into areas that were heavily infested with Viet Cong and yet inaccessible to anything but hovercraft and aircraft. He saw their potential, saw them operate and obviously he has become a dedicated enthusiast of the hovercraft concept. So, while the Nick Johnson concept of a joint effort (JESPO finally poohed out because Maritime could not maintain their proportionate share of the cost of this development, the Navy with Zumwalt, as chief of Naval operations, took over the full cost of bringing the SES-100 program to conclusion, an event which should occur within about one year from date.

With his enthusiasm for the service of these limited type of ACVs, as the SRN-5s were, he came back to become chief of naval operations fairly enthused with the great potential here and in many other fields.

After I had been six years out of the Navy and having been contacted periodically by Bell to associate with them in one capacity or another, I became a private consultant and Bell became a principal client in this field of hovercraft. Bell has advanced many designs and has seen one of a 2,000-ton hovercraft acknowledged enthusiastically by the Navy and as the follow-on vehicle to the 100-ton craft that is nearing completion both at Aerojet and at Bell. Unfortunately, for the moment, the funding of this one has been held up in Congress who felt that they should see the results of the operation at 100 ton SES before they launched into the broader technology of a 2,000-ton craft - perhaps a very prudent position to take. But Bell and Aerojet are prepared to bid on a 2,000-ton craft as soon as the Navy knows that they have the funds to proceed.

Q: Would these be troop-carrying, or what?

Adm. J.: At the moment, it's simply to be a further extension of the development of the technology, but it is my speculation that these will become fast amphibious support-type ships and/or anti-submarine warfare ships. Because of their very high speed - and these craft will be in the regime of 100 knots or more - the advantage in submarine warfare will be returned to the surface ship. Heretofore in the recent past the speed advantage has been in the hands of the submarine commander who can outrun virtually all present ASW ships in service today - the destroyer types, for example. It therefore has fantastic potentiality here.

SEVs have potentiality for logistic support of remote locations where piers or harbors don't always exist and yet where we maintain forces, like in Alaska. Here you could resupply stations ashore by running in with supplies from outside the ice pack, over the ice, and into the communities to be serviced like in the area of Prudhoe Bay where the tremendous oil discovery was made a few years back and which has not yet reached full development. The potential of the hovercraft to bring in supplies from the air terminals over the tundra and over the ice to various drilling locations exists today. The State of Alaska is looking at this as a means of resupplying the Bethel area, which is pretty much of a large underpopulated delta area on the southewest coast of Alaska. Also in and up the Yukon and the White Horse practically all over in that area. In military applications, in addition to the ASW potential is the amphibious assault vehicle. Four such craft have been ordered by the navy and are being built, two each, by Bell Aerospace and Aerojet General.

So, what was a viable concept with tremendous potentialities as was envisioned with the construction of the Skimmer-1, its tests and perfect performance (I might say with a little bit of pride) went unnoticed until Elmo Zumwalt was exposed to this potential in Vietnam and has created in the Navy and, in fact, all over the country a burgeoning of enthusiasm to bring the hovercraft into full technological development.

Bell Aerospace, perhaps because of being in the program longer and having invested so much in design, testing and development, is way out in front of any other American producer. They have only recently acquired a Hovercraft manufacturing facility in Canada. Just last month, I witnessed the flight of the first of the so-called *Voyageur*-class of hovercraft, much smaller than the hundred-tonner with a payload on the order of twenty tons. It has been demonstrated by flying in my presence over cornfields at Grand Bend, Ontario, where it was built. It has now been moved to Toronto and has successfully operated over deep-water on Lake Erie. It perhaps will be acquired by the Canadian government for use in their northern territories, or by the Canadian coast guard. Our own Coast Guard is tremendously interested in its potential for servicing their net and buoy systems, navigational aids and pollution control. Hovercraft would minimize the number of cutters, tugs and buoy tenders now needed to keep in service for these functions, reducing them to almost 20 percent of the present population. This means a much lesser ultimate total cost because of the speed with which the services could be performed and fewer crews required. Now, I'm sounding like a salesman and not like the chief of the Bureau of Ships, which, in effect, I guess I am with Bell.

It is a great personal gratification, however, as I credit myself at least with having brought this technology to the attention of our Navy, that the hovercraft finally is a "hot item" in this country. It was a great disappointment that it languished so long, until Admiral Zumwalt came on board and had the foresight to see the potentiality. Now, today, when you hear Navy speakers, they talk about the 100-knot Navy and they're talking about the hovercraft Navy.

Q: Admiral, I see that you've looked at the plaque on the wall and I know that this is in a sense an outline of the chief accomplishments of your regime at the Bureau of Ships. So now you're going to talk about one other subject, the Design Work Study effort.

Adm. J.: Most of the Bureau of Ships' initial and conceptual ship design work was done laying out ships of the future and producing what we called "spring styles" for review, consideration, and acceptance by the operating Navy.

Q: Why "spring styles"?

Adm. J.: It was just a nickname that was applied maybe because they came along in the spring of the year, or the springtime of an idea, I presume. They constituted much of the ship design effort of the Bureau. When accepted, these were converted into what were known as "contract designs," drawings that were sent out with invitations to build our ships to the shipbuilding industry.

These drawings largely represented the input of skillful naval architects and marine engineers who had been in the business of warship design for decades. All engineers begin to develop little personal fetishes. You could almost see the trade mark of a given set of engineers who work on a set of plans by these little particular features that they incorporate in the ships they worked on. Some of these patterns grow to be expensive, some of them become unnecessary, some become outmoded, and yet the habits of engineers, as for human beings generally, are to perpetuate those things which they know.

On one trip abroad, I was visiting with the Director General of ships of the Royal Navy in Britain. I was exposed to a program which had been organized by the First Sea Lord called Fleet Work Study. This constituted an effort by a group of selected young men, not all engineers, to go aboard ships that were in service, to examine their various systems and to recommend improvements or simplifications in the systems. For example, one of their major aircraft carriers - I think it was HMS Eagle - was pulled out of service and many of the recommendations of this group were applied to simplifying the means of landing and take-off of the aircraft and the striking of them below. They did, in effect, what would be time studies of every operation aboard ship, and then analyzed these to see if the installed facilities permitted them to do this in the simplest way. If they didn't, then, the group recommended the changes to the ships to bring this about.

While witnessing this program, which I thought was very effective, I also thought it was awfully late to be introducing this kind of critical review of engineering processes into the ship construction cycle. My thought was let's do it at the drafting board, during the initial design of the ship.

Q: No FRAM programs for you!

Adm. J.: No - well, FRAMs, of course, were means of updating and

James #10 - 349

modifying ships years after their initial outfit began to get obsolete. But if these improvements could be identified by seeing systems in operations, after the ship was completed, wouldn't it be better to analyse the system by engineers performing a critical examination before the lines on the drawings were finalized.

I asked the First Sea Lord, Sir Casper Johns - his father was Augustus Johns, a very famous British portrait painter - to loan me the head of his Fleet Work Study group for a year, Commander Keenan. To my delight he acquiesced. I then had a very fine young USN commander by the name of Hal Kauffman who was on duty with the Director General of Ships for the Royal Navy. I sent him to this fleet work study course that Royal Navy was giving their people. I brought the two of them back to the Bureau of Ships and set up the Design Work Study Office. Their project was to select a given ship design that was in the process in Bureau and to redo it, but to redo it with a view to eliminating all the unnecessary and devious approaches to solution of system operations before the drawings were converted into metal. Well, it started off on a very small scale. We recruited more and more people until we had about 25 or 30 people in the project. They demonstrated to me the validity of this concept without having demonstrated in on any one specific ship. They used small sample systems to start off with.

Q: There was no definite prototype, then, that they worked on?

Adm. J.: Not yet, no. Finally I decided if we're going to prove this out that it has real validity, let's take the DE-1032 class, I think it was, and do competing designs - one by design work study approach, and one by the traditional approach that had characterized the Bureau procedures for a long, long time.

Well, to make a long story short, after the usual six or seven months, we began to begin to evaluate the significant differences. We came up with a design of this ship that was about 600 tons less total weight than the traditional design. This meant that we could build a smaller, cheaper ship and perform every military requirement of speed, armament, payload and electronics capability imposed by the CNO in establishing the characteristics for that class ship. So., with some degree of personal pride and with a great deal of enthusiasm, I carried these two competing designs to Admiral Burke and his CNO advisory board and told them we could now build the DE-1032 for 600 tons less weight and I've forgotten how many millions of dollars less cost, and not reduce its capability one iota. I said in passing, of course we could still build the ship to the original design weight and put more military payload on it to the tune of roughly 600 tons. Well, the answer of the CNO and his board was obvious. They wanted the original size ship with all of the extra features on it. That's the way the ship was built. But in the Work Study design, they could have had about a third fewer crew, 600 tons less weight, hence a smaller machinery plant, a lot less fuel for the same endurance and the same speed as well as all the other military features. As was to be expected, and I should have been smart enough to have anticipated what would be the outcome. CNO wanted the big ship with everything else that could be added. However, the concept of design work study was born, its effectiveness was demonstrated, and became a way of life in the Bureau of Ships. In fact, it became such a way of life that the pressures for the application of it became so great that the Bureau couldn't handle the total volume of work.

One day, knowing the proclivities and capabilities of a gentleman by the name of Tad Stanwyck, who had a small operation here in Washington with 30 or 40 people doing sort of marine engineering consulting work, I brought him in and described our project and asked him to participate. To make a very long story short, Stanwyck grew to be a company of over a thousand people performing this function for the Navy in a variety of forms, until it became an accepted pattern. Then, by Mr. McNamara's edict to emasculate BuShips, it became necessary to pull apart this fine engineering body about three years following my retirement. He put the design of ships into the hands of the private shipyards' design groups, who now separately do it each in their own way. They haven't yet embraced these new design work study features unless they happen also to have embraced Stanwyck Company. So now we're going through the old cycle again where all of these fine concepts are forgotten and are not being applied, and Uncle Sam is paying a fantastically higher price for his navy ship designs and not getting as good a product as he might have.

Q: This design work system, could it not have applied elsewhere in the Department of Defense?

Adm. J.: Oh, it could apply anywhere. Actually, there's nothing unique about design work study that if you are a smart, inquisitive, knowledgeable engineer, you wouldn't do for yourself without being stimulated by a specific program. But, as I said in my introductory to this subject, lots of people became slaves to little idiosyncrasies of their own and did not apply that searching, analytical examination to every line that they drew on a new design. The alternative to design work study would be the mock-up, which is a term for building up a model of your system, seeing it in the model form, and then recognizing problems and correcting them at that time. But that's an expensive way to do it. It is followed by a number of companies. Litton Industries, for example, in their LHAs and their DD-963s have done this, to their credit, although it must have been terribly expensive. They might have gone into design work study to carry on the concept and accomplished the same thing for a hell of a lot less cost. But, of course, their profit is made on how much they spend, so I guess they're not particularly anxious to do design studies at the least possible cost.

Q: I'm surprised that an idea like this wasn't taken up by the Secretary of Defense and utilized.

Adm. J.: The Secretary of Defense was not interested in that which he did not conceive, or if he did not conceive it, had embraced. Take SCAP, why it came out bearing a different label and could scarcely be recognized as the same product. I guess you must have assumed through my discourse that I am not one of Mr. McNamara's advocates. I think he was one of the real sad, if not tragic, occurrences that has happened to our Defense Department.

Q: You've got lots of company!

Adm. J.: Yes. Well, I think we've covered quite a bit here, Jack, and might call it quits for today.

Interview #11 with Rear Admiral R. K. James, U. S. Navy (Retired)

Place: His residence in Providence, Annapolis, Maryland

Date: Thursday morning, 17 February 1972

Subject: Biography

By: John T. Mason, Jr.

Q: I looked forward to seeing you today when I looked out and saw that it was a dark day. You help make the day bright, so go ahead, Sir, with your Chapter No. 11.

Adm. J.: It's very kind of you to say so. Occasionally, I find in reminiscing that it even brightens my own day because I remember so many pleasant things that occurred during my tenure as chief of the Bureau of Ships. One of them in particular used to tickle me. These were the various problems that we had launching naval ships. You'd think that with a practice that was almost as old as the world is itself there would have been developed a refined foolproof technique for launching. Every ship, of course, in recent centuries has been sponsored by some lady - every naval ship, that is. This lady is generally thoroughly coached and prepared for the moment when she is the star performer. Yet during my tenure in office there were more glitches, more foul-ups, in launchings than you can shake a stick at! I believe history is replete with these. In fact, my predecessor, Al Mumma, once addressed the Sponsors Society when I was present on this subject of ship launchings. He recited many of the difficulties that the ladies had experienced in the execution of their task. The two or three I experienced, I believe, were interesting enough to record here.

Q: Well, Admiral, there's excitement, of course, attendant upon such an occasion for the sponsor, but also isn't there kind of an aura of mystery that surrounds a launching? I mean, the nature of a ship embarking on a career on the waves.

Adm. J.: Well, of course, there is an emotional appeal that attracts people by the thousand to come to launchings. It is certainly true that while the mystery, from the point of view of the technicians present, may be whether the ship is going to go down the ways or not, from the point of view of the casual audience, I'm sure the mystery of the sea and the naval service are considerations that make it a highly emotional affair.

The first launching I ever witnessed was while I was a postgraduate student on my way to becoming a naval architect. We were on duty at the Philadelphia Navy Yard, young ensigns engaged in learning a little about shipyard practices, when the SS Manhattan was to be launched at the New York Shipbuilding Company. I'd never seen a ship launched before, coming, as I did, from the Middle West. I made it a point to seek out an opportunity to attend this launching, and I witnessed it from a unique point of view. We got a boat out of the Philadelphia Navy Yard and a dozen or more of us went up to Camden where the shipyard was located. We lay offshore while the Manhattan went through the preliminaries. When finally she slid down the ways into the Delaware River we saw her in all of the glory of the occasion. Since then, I guess I have been present at hundreds of ship launchings of all sizes and varieties.

Let me review a few that were particularly interesting. Before I became chief, I was Supervisor of Shipbuilding in the southern California area in addition to being the Long Beach shipyard commander. As such, I supervised the launching of the ships that were being built to Bureau of Ships contracts. One of these was a small minesweeper that was to be turned over to the Danish Navy when completed by the Harbor Boat Company of San Pedro, California. The president of Harbor Boat Company invited Mrs. James to launch this ship. She had launched an LST some years earlier and it was traditional that one lady never launched more than one naval ship.

Q: Does that still hold?

Adm. J.: No, unfortunately. I might have broken the custom so that she could have launched a more impressive ship than LST 11 - as I was later in a position to more or less dictate who launched what. But she was selected to be a sponsor very early in my career. I was a young captain when she was appointed to launch this LST, and that in itself is a funny story. I'm going to digress a bit, perhaps. Mrs. James was delighted to accept the offer, only to find that she had to make a brief speech in the Ingalls Shipyard, Pascagoula, Mississippi. Well, this frightened her to death. She, nevertheless, carried on. We proceeded to Pascagoula by train the day before the launching. On board was a very dear friend of ours, George Hodges, who met us on board as he came through from New York. He decided to help my wife prepare her remarks. The two of them sat in the club car of the "Southern Crescent" practically 'til it was bedtime writing her speech. It started off with an acknowledgment of Mr. Lanier, who was the executive vice president of Ingalls Ship and was to be the master of ceremonies for the event.

Her little speech started off, "Thank you, Mr. Lanier," and then proceeded to other little courtesies she expressed for the privilege of being the sponsor. The morning of the launching dawned. It was pouring rain. Her spirits were low because she was nervous as the devil. She had brought a bouffant, spring-like dress with a big wide-brimmed, garden party type hat for the launching. None of this could be worn because of the foul weather. I was called just an hour or so before the launching to come and see Mr. Monroe Lanier. I went up to his room in the Longfellow House, where we were all quartered, to find him sick in bed with the flu. He reported that he was unable to take part in the launching ceremonies, but his executive assistant, Mr. Guest, would be in charge. I hesitated to tell this to my wife because she was in such an overwrought state that I was afraid she'd want to pick up and head for home. During the night before I could hear her mumbling throughout a very restless night in bed, "Thank you, Mr. Lanier" and then de-de-de-da, the rest of her little speech. I finally had to tell her because of that opening line in her remarks. When I told her that Mr. Lanier was not going to be present, she said, "I'm not going to launch this ship." This was an emotional reaction that expressed her mental attitude of the moment, due to the bad weather and this unexpected development.

We finally went to the launching and to her credit she did a splendid job, including directing her remarks to the master of ceremonies, Bill Guest. I think hers was typical of the state of mind that many of the sponsors are in at the moment of launching.

On one occasion when I was chief, we were launching the USS Lynde McCormick. The widow of Admiral McCormick was the sponsor. The ship yard was in Bay City, Michigan. There they launched ships sideways into a little narrow slough. A side launch is rather a unique operation, as contrasted to the end launch in which the ship sails majestically down the inclined ways. A side launched ship just all of a sudden goes "plop" into the water and the whole of the ship is immersed immediately. It is a tricky type of launching. The control of the launch release mechanism at the Dafoe ship yard was by a series of lines that came together midships, where the foreman in charge of launching with an ax cut all of the lines that were brought together into a single cord. This released all of the sliding ways - perhaps as many as twenty - simultaneously. The ship, thereafter, moved rapidly and quickly moved out of reach of that sponsor who didn't take that precise instant of ship movement to crack the bottle and do their little speech about "I christen thee..."

Mrs. McCormick had been clued in on this. She stood at the alert waiting for the signal to swing, but the launching superintendent failed to punch the buzzer which signalled, "I am now lifting my ax to cut the lines." He cut the lines, then punched the button, and by this time the ship was beyond Mrs. McCormick's reach. The bottle was pulled unbroken out of her hand. It had been suspended from the bow of the ship on a red-white-and blue braided cord. It went sailing off into space, leaving Mrs. McCormick dissolved in tears. Being a Navy wife of many years, she knew the traditional belief that an unchristened ship was an unlucky ship. This distressed her so that she was tremendously overwrought. Realizing that the ship was still unchristened and not completely out of range because it was only a matter of 100 yards away from us as it rocked back and forth in this little narrow slough, I asked the president to quickly commandeer some sort of a small boat. He found an old beat-up work boat, and brought it alongside. We stumbled over all the packing material that goes with a launch and climbed aboard. Tom Dafoe manned the boat with Mrs. McCormick and myself. Mrs. McCormick and I stood up in the bow of this craft like Washington crossing the Delaware and headed out to the bow of the ship where the bottle of champagne, still intact, was dangling from its cord.

When we were about twenty feet away from the bow, some kid on the opposite bank had spotted it and decided that he was going to make a trophy of the champagne bottle. He dove off the bank in his clothes, swam through all the packing material that was floating around in the water, and was just about to reach for this bottle and cut it with a knife when I spied him. Well, I screamed like a drunken longshoreman. The kid almost flipped. He dashed back to the beach, scrambled up the bank, and disappeared. Mrs. McCormick, Tom Dafoe, and I, then, approached the ship, took up the bottle, and she did her bit to christen the USS McCormick - not quite in the authentic and appropriate manner, but nevertheless in a manner to relieve her distress.

We had had a number of failures by the sponsors to break the bottle, cindluing Mrs. Truman who failed to break it on the occasion of whatever ship she launched, also Mamie Eisenhower failed to break the bottle on one of the earlier nuclear submarines at Groton, Connecticut. This prompted me to write an instruction to all of the yards that were building ships, directing that no ship would move, would not be released, until the bottle was broken and the sponsor had said her little piece.

Out in Bremerton, Washington, we were building destroyers. They were not built on inclined ways. Rather, we built them in a large graving dock and simply floated the ship off of the blocks. Then it was brought up to and nestled into the launching platform, where the sponsor had no problem with the ship ever getting away from her. Here, we had one of our most curious failures to break the christening bottle. On that occasion the sponsor was one of the heriditary kin of - let's say David Lawrence - some very prominent naval figure of Revolutionary War days. The sponsor was a little old lady in her eighties. She had been coached by Admiral Bill Dolan, the shipyard commander, on how to christen the ship. The bottle is always scored so as to make it break easier - scored with some sort of a glass-cutting tool. This simplifies the breaking of the bottle. The bottle was encased in a stainless steel jacket, so that this would be the souvenir that the sponsor would carry away with the fragments of the bottle inside. The base of this jacket was a welded disc. Everything proceeded well except that the poor little old lady just didn't have the strength that it took to break the bottle even in its weakened state. She swung twice and nothing happened. Finally, then, Bill Dolan decided that he would have to help her. He put his arms around her shoulders and, together, the two of them swung the bottle like it was a baseball bat. Instead of the bottle breaking, the welded disc broke loose, the bottle slipped out of the jacket and fell into the bottom of the dry dock. This was an occurrence that couldn't have been anticipated!

Getting back to the launching that occurred in the Long Beach area by the Harbor Boat Company, when I was the Supervisor of Shipbuilding, I had told Mr. Rados, the president, that I appreciated the honor of suggesting my wife but she, having done her christening stint, couldn't do another. He said, "Well, how about your daughter?" whom he had met. Our daughter was Mrs. John Withers. I would guess this was about 1956, which meant that Pat was then 26 years of age. She was delighted and came on from her home in Minneapolis, Minnesota, to officiate. Ships there were launched on a marine railway cradle. The cradle actually runs down on rails and the ship is not free of the launching cradle until it fully enters the water and then floats up. In the desire to ensure that the craft would launch successfully, all of the pre-arrangements were made and the launching platform was put in place. The launch was scheduled for the next day -- a Saturday. About 3 a.m. on Saturday morning I was awakened at home by a frantic call from Mr. Rados stating that the ship was already launched. I asked, "For heaven's sakes, what happened?" He said, "Well, we were testing the launching release trigger, a chain cable broke and the ship proceeded to launch itself." I said, "Well, this is a fantastic situation. What do we do now? Call off the ceremony?"

"Oh, no," he said, "we're going to pull it back up on an adjoining cradle, and then we'll launch it once more."

So in this case, this MSB was double launched -- a distinct event. Most of the audience, infact, all of the audience, was completely unaware of the fact that the ship had already been launched once. The second time went off with great precision. Our daughter was privileged to present the ship when it was taken over by the Danish Navy with a photograph of herself. Some years later when I was Chief of the Bureau, I toured Denmark. The people over there knew who I was, of course, and knew that our daughter had christened this ship. I was therefore delighted when they said that they had called it into port so that I might go aboard. With my wife, we went aboard and had a tea with the officers in their very small wardroom. There we saw the photograph of the King and Queen of Denmark prominently displayed on the little wardroom wall, and immediately below was the photograph of our daughter, which, we thoroughly enjoyed seeing.

I was present at another launching in New Orleans at the Avondale Shipyard when the wife of the now Chairman of the Armed Services Committee, Mrs. Eddie Hebert, was the sponsor. Here, again, it was a side launch, with the trickier problems of timing. Unfortunately, Gladys Hebert did not break the bottle. That was the occasion of the launch of the USS Semmes. I don't think he enjoys having this fact publicized.

Q: That prompts me to ask a question. Why was it thought necessary, why did the custom develop, the simultaneous breaking of the bottle and letting the ship slide down? Why was it necessary to do this? Why couldn't it be christened first?

Adm. J.: When you say "why was it necessary," it obviously wasn't, as my instructions to our ship yard commanders and supervisors of shipbuilding clearly indicated, not to launch the ship until the christening had been completed.

Q: One thing and then another?

Adm. J.: Yes. Now, obviously, it had some origin in folklore . . .

Q: That mystique?

Adm. J.: Yes, and the mystique of a ship launching. Some of the other features - one that Al Mumma spoke to - was the reason for the dog shore. This was the last shore removed, before the ship moved down the ways. The dog shore was a prop at the stern end of the ship, under the transom, to a stop on the ground, and in the center of the slipways. They used to bring convicts that had been condemned to death to do the job of releasing the dog shore. If the condemned convicts succeeded in scrambling out from under the ship before the ship crushed them to pieces, he was immediately pardoned of previous crimes. They tell me there were more blood-spattered slipways from convicts that didn't quite get out from under.

The whole story of ship launchings is one that's extremely interesting.

Q: How were the launchings conducted during World War II when sometimes it was expedient to get a ship in commission very fast?

Adm. J.: Well, I'm sure every ship that has ever hit the water in this country has had a formal launching. I'm also sure there were simplified ceremonies during the war that were not the great hubbub and commotion, as was attendant to the launching of the J. F. Kennedy or even the launching of the USS Enterprise, which were both built down at Newport News. There were fabulous social functions that followed each of those occasions, the Kennedy, perhaps, being the most fabulous of all.

Q: You were there for the Enterprise?

Adm. J.: I was there for the Enterprise.

Q: Tell me that story.

Adm. J.: That was more or less a traditional ship launch. It had one unique little feature. As they began to flood up the ship in the building dock, lifting from the stern to the bow, a series of electric lights were activated that illuminated one letter of the ship's name at a time. So as the aft end of the ship lifted the first letter "E" was illuminated. The audience could see these letters illuminate one by one until it got up to the last "E" at the end of the name, when the ship was fully free-floating, then the sponsor did her little bit. Mrs. Bert Francke was the sponsor of the Enterprise. She was the wife of the Secretary of the Navy. As far as I know, she was also the first lady to break the traditional pattern that only one naval ship would be launched by one lady.

The circumstances were that President Eisenhower had directed that Mrs. Francke launch the Enterprise. It was the first nuclear carrier. It had a great deal of attention paid to it, so perhaps the only other logical person that might have launched the ship would have been Mrs. Rickover. Unfortunately, too, I might have had my wife launch it had she not had her stint before, and, of course, that would have been a real feather in her cap.

The story of the launching of the Enterprise has some humor in the events leading up to the actual launching. The president of Newport News Shipbuilding Corporation at that time was Bill Blewett, a fine gentleman, a rough cob, if there ever was one, a shipbuilder of tremendous capability, highly respected by those of us in the shipbuilding fraternity, a former president of the Society of Naval Architects and Marine Engineers, and a humorist without equal. Bill Blewett was frustrated by the fact that in was frustrated by the fact that in the Buships contract that he had signed for building the Enterprise there was the admonition that social festivities of the launching would be limited in the amount that would be paid by the Navy as part of the contract price. This frustrated him because he was a lavish type and wanted to give a very fine launching party. He sent out invitations to attend throughout the country. He had his staff assistant, a chap by the name of Tilford Smith (nickname "Tilly") prepare ten special overprinted invitations, which he sent to, among others, myself, my deputy, Bob Moore, Jimmy Farrin, assistant chief of the Bureau of Ships for shipbuilding, all told ten people in the Bureau. When I got mine, of course, I was tickled to note at the bottom of the letter was a statement approximately as follows:

> "Because of the financial restrictions imposed by the chief of the Bureau of Ships on the expenditure of funds for launching festivities, we will be unable to conduct our usual reception following the launching. We request that all invitees BYOL [bring your own liquor]."

I knew that this had to be a phony. I found an invitation that went to my secretary that didn't have this overprint on it. I charged her with finding out who had received the special prepared invitations. She turned up ten names. I got them all in the office and I said, "Bill Blewett is trying to be funny. He's trying to pull our tail, so let us reverse the tables on him. Now, first of all, don't acknowledge having received your invitation. Just keep it under your hat. Of course, attend the launching, but don't let anybody have the benefit of thinking that you received the special invitation."

Well, about ten days later Bill Blewett came into my office. I opened the subject by saying, "Hey, what's the problem here. I have not received an invitation to the launching and yet my secretary has and so have a lot of other people. Why haven't I had one?" His face turned stern and he said, "You haven't had an invitation! Why, I directed one personally to come to you." I said, "Well, something happened. It didn't get here."

I could see his mind churning, but, of course, that was about the end of the conversation at that moment. Later, I learned that he went back to Newport News that night, promptly called his assistants who had been in charge of preparing these special invitations and just chewed him out to a fare-thee-well for having failed somewhere along the line in getting these gag invitations into the proper hands.

Q: I hope you made amends to the assistant later!

Adm. J.: Well, later on, on the occasion of the launching, I was asked to join Mr. Blewett with Secretary and Mrs. Francke at the head table, along with other distinguished guests. I waited deliberately until the whole group were seated. Then, rather majestically and certainly with an attempt to call attention to myself, I walked in with a small picnic basket hanging on my arm. In the picnic basket I had brought several of these vulcanized sandwiches wrapped in wax paper. I'd gotten three or four little two-ounce bottles of liquor and had these prominently displayed in the basket. I took my seat at the table, which was groaning with the food and then started to open my sandwich and open my own liquor! Of course, Bill Blewett just about flipped his lid and the whole of the table had to have an explanation of what this ridiculous performance was all about. And, instead of him enjoying a laugh at my expense, I enjoyed one thoroughly at his. His wife, however, after the laughter had subsided, said, "Jimmy James, look out. Nobody, but nobody, ever finally tops Bill Blewett." So I had to be alert to his response at some later time.

Q: Did it come?

Adm. J.: Yes, it did, but it was rather anticlimactic because only he and I knew about it.

Well, that perhaps covers the interesting launchings I have attended, or rather events at launchings that were different. I attended many other launchings that went off in the traditional manner, although on the occasion - I've just been reminded of this - on the occasion of the launching of the nuclear submarine up at Groton, I was there when Mamie Eisenhower almost did the honors. Following that ceremony, there was a large luncheon in a local armory. I was seated at the table with the VIPs. The young waitress that was serving the coffee was being questioned by the lady to my left as she held the coffee pot poised over my glistening white service uniform. She didn't hold it horizontally and shortly thereafter I began feeling a warm trickle down my back which grew to be quite a stream. She was pouring hot coffee down my back as I was seated at the table.

This was the second such event that occurred to me in my uniform that same day. Earlier that morning, having spent the night with a dear friend of mine and his lady, Al Dunning, who was an employee of the Electric Boat Company and also a retired Navy captain, we were having breakfast in their dining room. They had a very lovely antique dining table with little openings between the leaves of the table. I think Admiral and Mrs. Pyne were present at the same occasion. Either he or I, I can't recall which, knocked over a pitcher of cream. Well, the cream ran over the table top, down through a crack in the table, and onto my shoes and socks. I had only one pair of white shoes and white socks with me. Fortunately, Schuyler Pyne had two pairs of socks so I was able to wash off my shoes, change my socks, and proceed to the launching. I guess that day I was a marked man. I had no spare uniform after the coffee incident, so I had to go aboard the special train that had brought us up from New York and change into civilian clothes to return for the remainder of the festivities.

So, sometimes, the office of chief of the Bureau gave many pleasant experiences, some of which I've recounted here.

Q: The Emoluments?

Adm. J.: Yes, indeed.

Let's see - from here, perhaps we might take a brief look again at the so-called Dollar-Stretch program. This had its basic foundation in the SCAP program which we've discussed and I believe you have a copy of the full SCAP report. One of the features of the SCAP program which I thought was vital and which I thought would be a major means of conserving the Bureau's funds was the re-organization of the ship yard management. In the various ship yards, the basic artificer functions, the trade functions of the ship yard - were carried out in a separate shop for each of the major trades. For example, there was a ship-fitting shop, there was a plumbing shop, there was a sheet-metal shop, electrical, and so on. Each shop had its own organizational structure. The head mechanic was generally the master mechanic of that trade and he had foremen and quartermen beneath him who carried out the various tasks of the shop. In some yards there were as many as thirteen different shops and some of them were perhaps no more than fifty men total, in a given shop, while others could be as many as 500 or 600 in a given shop. Nonetheless, each had its own separate structure such as I've outlined.

I proposed as a result of the SCAP program to re-organize the shops of comparable services, comparable trades, I should say, into a group and have a master of a group, rather than a master for each of the shops. Each of the shops, if not headed up by the group master, then would have a foreman. This would take off many of the key top-level people, and reduce the number of people reporting directly to the Production Officer from an unmanageable number of individuals to a manageable five or six group masters. Obviously, this was met with much resistance by the entrenched organization of masters and foremen. A chap who was the national president of this organization was also the master of one of these very, very small shops, the ropewalk at the Boston Navy Yard. I can't recall his name at the moment. In any event, they resisted strongly my proposed simplification of management, but finally I bulldozed it through. Today I'm gratified to find it working, working well, and working to the best interest of the Navy yard as well as the shops themselves. There were a lot of annoyed people, one or two of whom threatened to institute suits against me for forcing them to take a secondary role, but no key individual was released or discharged. Many of the billets were never to be refilled when the incumbent retired or otherwise left.

I predicted it would take about six years to shape up the organization, but it took a little bit longer than that. I saw it through the first three years of the agony. Some few people - in fact, one did try to institute a suit against me for taking away his perquisites and privileges, which wouldn't have gotten off the ground because it was an exaggeration. He just lost prestige more than anything else.

Q: It would hardly stand up in a federal court!

Adm. J.: It wouldn't have and he never did carry it to that extent, although he wrote me and told me he was going to. Curiously enough, my daughter, who now lives in Santa Rosa, California, found herself back door to back door with this individual, who resigned from the Navy yard in Long Beach in a huff, moved up to Santa Rosa, and there he is perched. Whenever we visit our daughter I have the opportunity, which I seldom exercise, of calling on Larry Luhman, who hasn't done anything since he resigned in fury from the Navy yard.

However, this program of SCAP went into many areas. I happen to have a clipping before me where it was reported that by 1960, in October, we had recorded a $150 million saving as a result of the program that had, then, only been in being a little over a year and a half. Many of the savings were achieved after a longer term, and began to approach a considerably higher number. But the production planning and control programs of the ship yards were modified significantly. We centralized job planning that facilitated the responsiveness to the ships that came in for overhaul and also minimized the cost of getting ready for their overhaul. There were so many things that it's hard to identify them, but, let me say, I think it was one of the more successful programs that it was my privilege to launch. While the concept was originally that of Al Mumma, my predecessor, I was the SOB that had to execute the specifics of the SCAP program, a system I and my team had generated.

Q: This leads me to a question. How widespread is this conscientious effort at dollar-stretch within the vast Department of Defense?

Adm. J.: I'm sure that it is widespread, very widespread. It receives a lot of lip service, perhaps more than actual hard work and effort, because dollar-stretch is a term that attracts people. It has to be buttressed by specific programs of all sorts of detail as to how to proceed to stretch a dollar. That's wherein, I believe, SCAP was unique, because we took the trouble for about six or eight months to spell out precisely how to proceed and how to achieve these savings. Then when it was my privilege to execute the program, we put in follow-ups to ensure that the actions were being taken. Now, many people are conscious of the importance of achieving results at the minimum in cost. I think one of the tragedies of the re-organization of the bureau system forced upon the Navy by Secretary McNamara was that it took away from the technical experts the ability to recognize the areas where a dollar might be stretched and took away their authority to execute them. This is part of the problem we are witnessing today where we see a lot of bright operating line officers filling technical billets, generally only for brief intervals without time to become knowledgeable enough to execute a sound program of dollar-conservation because they just haven't been trained in this type of duty.

Also, the dismembering of the bureau system by McNamara forced most of the basic research and development and design effort of the technical bureaus into the hands of industry. Industry is plain not going to work for free. They're going to take every project that they do and add their profit, and properly so, but this adds to cost even if it were only modest profit say in the range of not over ten percent. This does not characterize basic development or research or design type of contracts. Profit generally is much higher than that. But these extra costs are added to basic design and, of course, the desire to have many companies or groups participate on a competitive basis means each has to have its own engineering and design and research capability. So we see a proliferation of engineering talent that used to be concentrated under a single roof, under a single technical bureau. Now, for example, in the shipbuilding field we've got Litton with a fantastic ship systems company of people working in ship design and developments. You have the same thing at Newport News. You have the same thing, to a lesser extent, at Bath Iron Works, and so on around the entire shipbuilding industry. Each one has to have its own little Bureau of Ships. The cost of this to the defense production must be fantastic. I've never seen it added up, but I was overwhelmed when I had a visit with Admiral Sonenshein on a plane that we were taking up to Buffalo, New York, last summer. I asked him what the population of the Naval Ships System Command was, which was the major residue of the Bureau of Ships as organized in my day. He said he had about 3,100 or 3,200 people in the headquarters. This compared with about 3,400 to 3,500 people that was the population of BuShips. But BuShips had been broken up into Naval Ships System Command, the Ships Engineering Center, the Naval Electronics Systems Command, and all of the research and development of significance was moved over into the Office of Naval Research. When, together, we tried to total up the population of these elements that had comprised what the Bureau of Ships was, we came to the conclusion that it was something in excess of 4,500 people to do what had been done by some 3,500 people on a program that was comparable in size to that which he was then charged.

This just shows how these various government structures can be expanded, proliferated, and you can have more people churning water rather than accomplishing and producing the ultimate product. This is just one more reason why I think that Mr. McNamara's desire to standardize the form of approach within the Army, Navy, and Air Force to have a central military material command was an ill-considered venture that I'm sure he didn't fully comprehend the impact of when he directed that it be done within the Navy. This is water over the dam, however, and I don't think we'll ever see it re-structured the way it was most effective.

I understand you're about to take off to Hawaii, Dr. Mason, and I understand you're going to interview Admiral Felt. I will always remember Admiral Felt with respect and consideration for his tremendous job that he did as commander of the Pacific. That was it, wasn't it?

Q: Yes, CinCPac.

Adm. J.: We had many contacts during my tenure as chief of the Bureau and all of them extremely pleasant, except one. During the time of his command of the Pacific Fleet, the Navy was setting up an over-all command control center on Hawaii. I had a very knowledgeable young woman who was a mathematician at the David Taylor Model Basin who got involved in the development of these various electronics control systems. Her name was Ruth Davis and she was involved in the study of what would best serve the requirements of the commander of the Pacific Fleet in this particular installation. I had her go to Honolulu on occasion to discuss the matter and she had several audiences with Admiral Felt. She came up with a solution which later, after a very detailed examination in the Bureau and review by Captain Ed Svendsen, who was in charge of command control functions was disagreed with rather violently. The issue was finally brought to my attention. After taking considerable time to study it, I completely supported Captain Svendsen at the expense of the proposals made by Ruth Davis. She was quite a determined female, a bachelor girl, and made private representations to Admiral Felt that he was being short-changed in the proposed Bureau installation. It was a question of which major electronics supplier did the hardware production and installed the system. My own belief after thorough study of this was that the Control Data Corporation, then a relatively new company, was the right company to award this contract to. Davis was sponsoring another group which I prefer not to mention. It became an emotional matter where she violated all of the proprieties of her position as a participant in the study phase of this program to inject her opinions and, in fact, convince Admiral Felt that only the company which she was endorsing was ever going to deliver him the appropriate kind of hardware and a system that worked.

Well, at this point, I get called to task by Don Felt for trying to foist off on him something that he, I'm sure sincerely, believed was not appropriate for the task. It took all my effort and persuasion to try to convince him to the contrary and I don't believe I ever did. However, it was my ultimate responsibility and I proceeded to install the Control Data Corporation's system in this Hawaiin facility. Ruth Davis kept my feet in boiling water all the time by unauthorized visits to Hawaii, to whip up enthusiasm by Don Felt to challenge my decision. Finally he laid it on the line, cold turkey, that he was opposed to what I was doing, that I had the right to persist, but in doing so, I was sacrificing his military readiness and that he would hold me personally responsible when the failure of this system became evident.

Notwithstanding all this claptrap, we persisted because we were just as convinced that he had been misguided and that this project would be carried forward successfully so we proceeded. Well, it was carried forward successfully, and on time - carried forward in a manner that even exceeded our own evaluation of the situation. In the meantime, our friend, Dr. Ruth Davis, found it uncomfortable to be under my command and she slipped out from under.

Q: I would think so!

Adm. J.: She found it uncomfortable to be under my command because I made it uncomfortable for her, and to this day I don't know whether Don Felt has ever accepted the fact that the results were what he wanted and they were achieved following a route different than he was led to believe was the only appropriate route.

Q: You weren't dragged up for high treason!

Adm. J.: No, I never was dragged up for high treason. I was never dragged up by him for failure to produce what he wanted. I must assume, therefore, that he, too, was satisfied with the system. But it was one of those unpleasant little things that don't have to happen unless people believe you're trying to hoodwink them rather than to help them. In his case, of course, there was nothing more important than to satisfy him with a system that would do his job, and that, I believe, he got by a route different than was his female advice.

Toward the end of 1961, the Australian Navy took great interest in the destroyer escorts that we were building up at Dafoe Shipyard and wanted to have some built for themselves. I believe they wanted three such ships. The arrangements were finally brought to a head in discussion with the Australian naval attache and other representatives of the Australian Navy. It was decided that I would go out to Australia to sign the final papers to get the construction of these three ships under way. The Australians had accepted the design of the destroyer escort but they wished to install a missile system that they had devised themselves - Ikara - in lieu of the Tartar air-surface missile which we projected for the destroyer escorts for our own Navy.

I had a very pleasant trip to Australia. It was the first time I'd returned there since the wartime days when I had a two-week rest and recreation period in Sydney and Brisbane. I went to meet with the Australian chief of naval staff, an Admiral Burrell. We negotiated a contract for these three ships to be built in the United States and to be turned over to Australia when they were completed.

Q: Was this a departure for the Australian Navy?

Adm. J.: A very significant departure. They had generally had their ships built in Great Britain. They were looking for a particular ship type. We were pleased, of course, to have them seek out our particular ship because of the fact that, as I say, they customarily leaned on British ship design to outfit their Navy. We set up an organization here in the United States where they came to supervise the construction of the ships under the general guidance of our own resident supervisor. The ships were delivered after I retired, but one of these days I hope to have the privilege of seeing them. I'm kind of rambling here because I'm reminiscing as I'm reminded of things.

I think this was the first major ship construction for a foreign nation that was done in this country, other than submarines that were built by Electric Boat Company on private contract with other nations. But this was a U. S. Navy agreement direct with the Australian Navy.

Q: Admiral, could one hazard a guess that this practice won't grow appreciably because of the expense of fitting out a ship in the U. S.?

Adm. J.: I'm sure that it will not for that very reason. You've put your finger right smack-dab on one of the amazing features of this sale of three ships. The Australians were so eager to get them that they were willing to pay the higher price for a U. S.-built ship. Their study team which had gone around to several different places, including Britain and Japan, concluded that they could have the ships built for the lowest possible price out in Japan, but it meant delivering to the Japanese many of the military techniques and systems and secrets that were incorporated in the ship. They therefore elected to come to this country in spite of the higher price. They sent an Admiral Urquhart, who was the head of the mission, to study the problem of where to build ships, He was able to convince his superiors that they should build them in the United States. I think we were gratified from a military point of view in having more ships of the same general class in being in the world in the hands of allies. We did not do any more of these, except small minesweeper types and patrol boat types, which we did build under lend-lease programs and some of them were built here in the United States during my tenure. I described the minesweeper for Denmark, which was one of several such ships. Then we also supervised the building of ships to our own U. S. Navy designs in foreign countries, like in Italy and West Germany and Norway. But as far as actual construction of major combatant ships in the United States, I think this group of three ships represented the first of that approach. Later, I believe, they ordered two additional ones to be built here, for a total of five.

I made this visit to Australia as part of a trip that I had scheduled to Japan where I went out to launch a U. S. Navy-constructed destroyer for the Japanese Defence Forces, that was built with our funds, with our supervision, but to their design. Obviously, Japanese ships are considerably different than American-designed ships because of the physical stature and height of the Japanese sailor. He's considerably smaller than our Yankee bluejacket. Consequently, the ship design can reflect much different type of accommodations for the crew. I remember going through this brand-new ship at the Mitsubishi plant in Nagasaki, and I had to stoop to go through the living spaces and out of passageways because the average Japanese is only slightly over five feet and I'm a six-footer, as are many Americans. So the design had to be done in Japan, but the construction was approved and financed and overseen by the Bureau of Ships supervisors.

The actual launch of the ship, which was to be the occasion of my visit, did not occur when I was in Japan. They, too, were having the beginning of labor strife at that time, and the shipbuilders went out on strike about a week before I arrived so the event could not be brought off on schedule.

Q: Did you, at the time of your Australian trip, visit the scene of your earlier trials and triumphs, Manus?

Adm. J.: No, that would have been an interesting excursion, but, no, I did not. We flew out of the Philippines directly to Darwin and then down to Canberra, where the new capital for the government of Australia was being erected. I was never so overwhelmed by the ordinary houseflies as I was in that area. There were literally billions of flies flying around the city even then, in 1962, when I was there. It was a beautiful potential capital city. It was then only partially constructed. I would like more to go back and see Canberra than I would to see Manus. In Manus, happily, I lived aboard ship most of the time and there wasn't much ashore to stimulate one's enthusiasm for a return visit.

Q: Do the Australians maintain a base there for their Navy?

Adm. J.: The Australians did have a base in the days preceding the war. I don't know whether they've moved back in there or not. It had, of course, all the tremendous potential with the facilities that we put into Manus that were abandoned. Maybe, they have. I just plain don't know.

I think at this point, Jack, I've just about exhausted those things that readily come to mind about my term in office, except some of the really serious and tragic events which occurred during my tenure. One was the fire on board the USS Constellation, which was building in the New York Navy Yard. The next was the loss of the submarine Thresher. I think these deserve more time and attention than the remaining time available this morning. So, with your forbearance, we will make these the subjects to start off our next session.

Q: All right, Sir. Thank you very much.

James #12 - 383

Interview #12 with Rear Admiral Ralph K. James, U.S. Navy (Retired)

Place: His residence in Providence, Annapolis, Maryland

Date: Tuesday morning, 18 April 1972

Subject: Biography

By: John T. Mason, Jr.

Q: As usual, it's good to see a fellow Welshman this morning. We're going to have Chapter 12 and I think you want to talk about the disaster which occurred to the <u>Constellation</u> while she was in the Navy Yard in New York.

Adm. J.: That was really a serious disaster. Ultimately, through deaths that occurred from injuries sustained in the fire, it claimed fifty lives, all civilian employees of the Navy Yard. The fire occurred late one afternoon as the ship was under her final stages of construction. A gasoline tank had been placed on the hangar deck for servicing the various forklift trucks and other automotive equipment that was used aboard in the construction of the ship. It had been decided to move a large tank - I would estimate it must have been about a 500-gallon tank - from its position on the hangar deck where it was beginning to interfere with work in progress to some more suitable location also on the hangar deck. To do this, they directed a forklift operator to pick up the tank and relocate it. For reasons known only to the man himself, he brought in his finger lift, went underneath the tank and, in doing so, severed a main drain line of the tank itself and gasoline began pouring out on the hangar deck.

Of itself it could have been a contained casualty. However, the elevator well for the main elevators - the main aircraft elevators - were being worked on and were only a matter of a few feet distance from the location of the tank and gasoline began pouring down into the well of the elevators where a welder was at work. To make a long story short, he ignited the gasoline and the flames engulfed the tank that was continuously being fed by the ruptured line and there was a real holocaust.

The city Fire Department was, of course, called in and with the Fire Department of the Navy Yard struggled valiantly and in reasonable time for that kind of a fire, it was extinguished.

Q: What was "reasonable time?"

Adm. J.: It took about five hours, as I recall. I happened to be watching the television in Washington and got a flash of the incident on I believe the six o'clock news. Of course, I kept the TV on continuously and went to the phone about the same time that Admiral Pyne, who was then the commander of the shipyard, was trying to reach me to advise me of the disaster.

Shortly afterwards the chief fire marshal of the city of New York came on the air, all dressed in his fancy rain gear and firefighter's helmet and looking very official -

Q: Was that Mr. Cavanaugh?

Adm. J.: Mr. Cavanaugh. He began to explain how the fire had started, how it was the negligence of the naval shipyard, how the Navy should be chastised for such brutality which at that time had claimed an unknown number of dead. He generally shot his mouth off about things that he was not informed about at the time. This incensed me and I'm sure it did Admiral Pyne who I believe was in the TV picture while these things were being said, although I'm not certain about that.

Well, it was a tragedy of great proportions. There was little we could do except to proceed to reconstruct the ship. We needed, of course, to survey to assure ourselves that there was no major damage that could not be repaired, and having established that fact we proceeded with reconstruction. My recollection is that because of the many pieces of hardware that went up in flames or were melted down or at least made unserviceable, it took a long period of time to re-acquire all of the equipment, mostly electronics gear that was destroyed. The ship structure was not too much of a problem. My recollection is that the ship was delayed about nine months in completion.

Q: How much was added to the cost?

Adm. J.: I don't recall that but I estimate that it must have been close to twenty million dollars. In fact, I think that was the figure that we had speculated about. As a matter of fact I believe we brought it in for somewhat less than that in the final accounting.

One of the more unpleasant tasks of my tour as chief of the

Bureau of Ships occurred as a result of that fire and the deaths of those many fine civilian employees. Needless to say, I was anxious to demonstrate the great concern of the Navy for the bereaved in their various homes. After discussing this with the chaps at the shipyard dealing with personnel, it was decided that I should come to New York to participate in a Memorial Service but also to make personal calls at the homes of some five or six selected families who had lost a member of the family in the fire.

Q: These were civilian employees?

Adm. J.: These were all civilians. A selection of the families to call upon was made and it included an Italian, of which there was a large population in the shipyard, a Jew, a Negro, a Protestant, and a Catholic. During the agonizing experience of visiting these people I learned a great deal about the different customs of the different ethnic groups and was truly drained emotionally of any fiber that I might have had.

Q: Did you take Mrs. James with you?

Adm. J.: No, no. I went in a small group with the Director of Personnel of the shipyard and the President of the Employees Association. We went about and extended the sympathy of the Navy and tried to comfort these people, which is almost impossible to do at that sort of a time. I recall that when we called on the Protestant family, we were courteously received and I believe gratefully received. The same was true at the Catholic Family. When we called on the Italian family, the body of the deceased was in a mortuary surrounded by grieving relatives, all emotionally overwrought and all carrying on at a great rate. When it penetrated the gathering that I was there to extend my sympathies to the widow and the rest of the family, why, bedlam broke loose in the emotional reaction of the women, at least, and I thought that I had done more harm than good by intruding on their sorrow.

We next went to the mortuary where the colored person was lying and I got a bad time from the blacks. They virtually made me feel as though I personally had been the assassin. I don't know whether I ever saw the bereaved wife, mother, or immediate family or not, because I was literally surrounded by a group of blacks who while not threatening were pressing me in a manner that today is accepted as more or less routine conduct. Ten years ago, however, frankly I was a little frightened.

The last call we made was on a Jewish widow whom I never saw more of than that which is visible through the crack of a door. My staff who had set up this visit had neglected to recollect the Jewish practice of interring the deceased almost instantly after death. There was no corpse, there was no funeral, no nothing except this distraught wife who peered out through a crack in the door while the chain held it. I conveyed my message of sympathy rather inadequately, I'm afraid, and departed.

Putting it all together, I don't know whether it was a smart maneuver or not, but at least it did demonstrate to these saddened people that their husbands' sacrifice, because truly that's what it was, had not been unnoted by the top brass. Whether it gave them any comfort or not I'll never know.

Well, the Constellation went on to be commissioned and into service. During the interim of reconstructing the damaged portions of the ship we were able to upgrade some of the systems that earlier had been deferred because of the need to get her out of the shipyard on the earlier schedule.

Q: You had scheduled her for May of 1961?

Adm. J.: Yes.

Q: Was there a board of inquiry on this?

Adm. J.: Yes, there was. There was no direct responsibility placed on any of the management of the shipyard, although there were admonitions about where to locate/such construction equipment. I think one of the requirements was that hereafter nothing like a tankful of raw gasoline would ever be placed in a ship. It would be retained on the pierside and cans would be carried in the quantities needed to refuel these various automotive vehicles.

Q: Was there not some discussion about the use of wooden staging also, which was ignited?

Adm. J.: Well, of course, all inflammable material came under scrutiny. Why do we have this? You just don't build ships without having some wooden material for various purposes temporarily installed in the ship during the construction period. I don't believe any major lesson was learned except the relative stupidity of having an explosive bomb, so to speak, right in the middle of the construction area. I'm sure that if any of the shipyard management had sat and thought about it two seconds they would have realized this in advance. But actually I believe the poor chap who was responsible for it was among the deceased, so there was never any clear-cut explanation as to just why he did what he did. However, when you realize that you're dealing with a relatively low-grade employee, a not too highly educated individual, it's not hard to understand that somebody can make a goof like that without realizing he had.

The next tragedy that affected my administration, and a terrible one was the loss of the nuclear submarine Thresher. She was lost with all hands. It has subsequently been located, as I believe you know. I don't know whether we've ever recovered any of the pieces of the ship, as she was located after I retired. However, in order to understand what I postulate as the reason for her loss, you have to understand some of the problems we were having with the construction of the nuclear submarines.

These submarines were fitted largely with special piping systems utilizing silver solder to make joints between sections of piping. We were having difficulties in all yards, both private and naval, in assuring ourselves of completely satisfactory soldered joints in every instance where there was high-pressure water or other services. We had recognized the problem and we had recognized it through several earlier casualties that were generally not severe, except in one instance. I don't recall the name of the submarine but she was a newly constructed boat, operating down in the Caribbean. One of the silver-soldered joints let go and the service that it was on, I believe it was the ballast system, although I could be wrong about that, and water poured into the boat. The crew was exceptionally well trained. The captain and his crew responded immediately to the casualty and the boat did not suffer serious damage. However, it was one of the major factors why we took extreme caution thereafter in examining all joints using x-ray treatment and every conceivable other means to determine the adequacy of a joint made up with silver solder. I'm sure we achieved a significant increase in the quality of the installation.

Q: What was the alternative to silver solder?

Adm. J.: There wasn't a hell of a lot of good alternatives because you had to join these pipes together, they were generally in very tight locations, which is characteristic of submarine hydraulic systems. In some instances they were poorly installed in that they were put in almost inaccessible spots for making up a joint which precluded getting around the periphery of the joint to ensure a completely sealed system. The alternative was - well, we just plain didn't have one, except to ensure the integrity of the work we were doing.

A great many additional man hours were expended, first, in determining what to do, and then, directing that it be done, and, finally, in doing it, as all these new boats were being brought along.

When the <u>Thresher</u> went down, of course, there was a great hue and cry because she took with her one hundred and some people. A court of inquiry was immediately convened with Vice Admiral Count Austin as the senior officer. I was among many witnesses called and, of course, so was Admiral Rickover.

The theory that I have about the accident may or may not have any validity, but at least it's what my feelings are. I expressed this to the board and as I have later learned from Admiral Austin, unless he is putting me off, they never reached a conclusion as to what caused the casualty. So I guess if that's true then my postulation of cause is just as valid as anybody else's who was as intimately involved as I was.

Q: Without seeing the evidence it's pretty difficult?

Adm. J.: Yes, indeed it is. It's almost impossible. However, in the background of this silver solder failure problem, with the ship operating as it was by specific intent at almost maximum collapse depth of the boat, which in those days was around 1,200 feet (a considerable depth for a submarine in those days). I have a feeling that she suffered a silver solder pipe joint failure in the nuclear power control area. With water pouring out of even a two-inch pipe, a tremendous volume and weight would be added to the boat in short order. I speculate that this water, in one way or another, either by the water level in the compartment rising or the flow from the pipe itself impinging on the control panels that regulated the nuclear power plant, caused the nuclear power plant to Scram, meaning loss of all power on the boat. With the ship at or near collapse depth she needed all the power she could get to blow tanks to rise. She had air blow systems that she could operate even with power off, but she needed power on to maintain the forward motion of the boat and particularly an upward forward motion to overcome the weight of water coming into the boat. She didn't have power to operate and began to settle and finally went through the collapse depth, collapsed, and that was the end of the Thresher.

Now, part of my reasoning is based on changes that were instituted immediately thereafter by Admiral Rickover in his full and complete responsibility for the nuclear power plant. That was a reduction of the interval of time that it normally took for a nuclear power plant Scram to be overcome and power put back on the line. As I recall it, ten seconds had been considered a reasonably short interval of time to allow the restoration of power after a power plant Scram. In normal operating conditions without any extraneous load coming into the boat, such as flooding, this probably would have been very adequate. In the emergency situation that faced the crew of the Thresher without power for ten seconds could have been the difference between losing the boat and not losing it.

Q: Pressure? The element of the pressure?

Adm. J.: The inability to remove the water and its weight, to blow it out or otherwise adjust your trim, occasioned by the flooding which was literally pouring tons of water in every two or three seconds. Submarine balance is so tender that at that depth and with virtually no speed on the boat, why, this would create an extremely dangerous condition.

The reason I go to this approach is that, as I started to say, Rickover instituted a drastic change in the nuclear plant controls immediately after the event. The event occurred within three months of my retirement. I did not stay aboard to learn all of the changes but I did learn through hearsay that the interval between a scram plan and the restoration of power had been reduced to four seconds. In other words, almost a sixty percent reduction of the time interval, and this was ordered into all our nuclear submarines. It appeared to me and still does that this was a recognition by Rickover that his power plant as designed had a major fault for handling a situation such as confronted the Thresher.

I could be completely in error in this analysis. I have informally expressed it to Admiral Austin fairly recently, long after his report was submitted. He's a very astute gentleman and he gave me no clue as to whether or not the board had any similar feelings. I do not know what the conclusions of the board were. I do know, however, that there have been these major changes in the nuclear system of the boat. If my theory of a broken pipe is correct, changes ordered could have also included a rerouting of all piping out of the area of the nuclear control room, if indeed there were any.

A tragedy of that sort has to be the basis of learning some important lessons and unfortunately the evidence will never be available to examine to insure ourselves against a repeat incident.

Q: I take it that the conclusions of the board were never made public?

Adm. J.: I have never seen the conclusions of the board. I must conclude that they have not been made public because if they had been I surely would have been apprised of them. I was deeply involved.

Q: And you didn't know the gist of Rickover's testimony before the board?

Adm. J.: I never did know of his testimony. The board was very cagey. Yet Rickover very clearly indicated that, of course, as chief of the Bureau of Ships, I was responsible for the submarine in its entirety. He was simply responsible for the power plant. This was a fact, indeed, but it scarcely is the impression that Rickover has managed to sow around the nation which believes that he invented, designed, built, and operates the nuclear ships and submarines all by himself.

Q: Is silver-soldering still the means that . . .

Adm. J.: I would not know, but I do not know of any development that has come down the stream to change that. There have been many mechanical improvements in the method of making up a joint. In other words, filling your piping so that at the butt of two pieces you install silver solder in grooves inside one fitting and outside the other to ensure that when you heat it, it flows and makes a good joint. Also all sorts of mechanical improvements have taken place which, if they accomplish their purpose, I'm sure would suffice for ensuring against defective joints.

I have pondered other possible solutions to the loss of the Thresher and I don't come up with any. To me, what I have recited here seems to be as reasonable a theory as any that I can imagine. I do not for a moment maintain that this is what actually happened to the Thresher. Needless to say, it was a blight on my administration because indeed we had built the Thresher during my watch, including the nuclear power plant. There must be some answer somewhere but I don't know how one finds it under the circumstances.

Q: There were many others of the same category built at the same time, weren't there?

Adm. J.: Yes, without similar incidents. The only other submarine accident to boats built in my era was to the Scorpion that was lost in the South Atlantic. We located the Scorpion rather quickly, primarily through the help of the Russians, which leads you to ponder whether or not they didn't have a hand in her destruction. That's a possibility but, here again, we'll never know unless indeed it was a Russian incident and some day we are able to unearth in the archives of the Russian Navy an admission to this effect. We would have to be victors in a major cataclysm, however, in order to accomplish that.

Those two events, I think, were perhaps the most tragic things that happened during my four years of service as Chief. While There were many other incidents and accidents they were all of relatively lesser import because in the art of building ships there is no guarantee against human error, witness, the most recent submarine casualty occurred alongside the pier at Mare Island Naval Ship Yard. One of my former aides and perhaps one of the most intelligent of the young naval officers in those days was commander of the shipyard at the time of the incident. Frankenberger, Rear Admiral Norvell Frankenberger. It was also the occasion of an assistant SecNav visit to Vallejo. Frankenberger was at a city luncheon honoring this VIP when he received the report that the submarine had sunk right there at the pier. An inquiry was conducted on the sinking and it revealed that the people at one end of the boat didn't know what the people at the other end were doing and both were pumping water in until finally she just sank. Later, of course, she was raised, pumped out, rebuilt and put back into service. But Frankenberger's career went down the drain. He was the principal individual responsible for ensuring that shipyard workers don't pump water in both the bow and the stern end of a submarine under repair without knowing what the other is doing. It's a long-established practice of the Navy to assess responsibility in those terms, but sometimes it's a little hard to justify. Frankenberger is now out of the Navy and the Navy's deprived of the services of a terrific guy. Some school down in Tennessee, I believe, is now enjoying his services as a member of the faculty.

One other item, I think, Jack, that would be of concern - I know is of concern to me, and would be of interest to whomever might chance to read this biography at a later date. It's a problem which affects the specialist personnel of the Navy.

Did I review the circumstances that led to the amalgamation of the naval constructors and engineers?

Q: Yes, you did that in the fourth interview.

Adm. J.: Well, with that as a backdrop - I believe that was the backdrop for events that occurred subsequently, that to me, have undermined, if not destroyed, the engineering capability of the Navy. As I mentioned at that time, the ultimate outcome of the merger of the construction corps and the engineer officer of the Navy of itself was a good idea, but the fundamental faults with that effort, which occurred in late 1941, was the restoration of the star, the line star, to the sleeve of the naval constructors. All of us at one time had been line officers, and had voluntarily given it up. All of us were required by events in 1941 to put it back on but with the concomitant stigma of "engineering duty only" attached.

The EDO symbol was intended to isolate the alleged brainy specialists from the run-of-the-mine line officer. To me it was insulting. I graduated sufficiently high in my class that I might have achieved the position of CNO if I had elected to remain on in the line. That's something nobody will ever know, but it was an option that I elected to give up, and then much later to be tagged as an "engineering duty only" type was galling. It was also galling to the linfe officer that we had our star put back on. There was no distinguishable difference between the line and the engineer type while in uniform.

Q: It was only in the written name with the "EDO" after it?

Adm. J.: Right. As a very young lieutenant I had opposed the restoration of the star. I thought that these engineers who joined the Constructors and who had been wearing it all the time, should be happy to come into a specialist corps where we might have an independent esprit and might achieve some of the enthusiasm for our specialist service, as the Supply Corps had so successfully achieved. It became galling enough to the line officers that we were again wearing the star - and I say "line officers" in general. There must have been a handful of senior ones, that they went out of their way to invent what I call the sheriff's badge, a little circle with a star in it to indicate command capability. Well, command capability is no more than an individual's intellect and I think that I could command any bloody thing that exists in the Navy today, as could most of the naval constructors.

But along about 1945 or 1946 they began issuing these little sheriff's badges to be worn on the breast of the line officer who had command or who was in command or who was capable of command, "capable" meaning he wasn't an EDO. There also was a sop to the injured feelings of the EDOs in changing the designation from "engineering duty _only_" to "engineering duty officer." If it had happened that way in the beginning I don't think there'd have been generated the ill feeling that this "engineering duty only" bit did. I had served as senior watch officer on two Navy ships. I was a line officer for two years, so the mystery of what it is that makes one a command jockey is not very great in the minds of those of us who have been there.

However, I'm digressing quite a bit, except that I believe it's important to get to the background of what later became known as the Keith Board. Roger Taylor Scott Keith, a very delightful southern gentleman, a classmate of mine and one I consider a dear friend, was in Washington in late 1961 or 1962 - I guess maybe it was 1961 - and he was put in charge of a board to examine the Navy's requirements for specialist technical officer personnel.

I'd never seen his precept. I must conclude, however, from the results that he more or less had an established objective given to him, which was to reduce the number of engineering duty officers, to maximize the number of straight line that were to receive some sort of technical training in an effort to achieve minimization of dependence upon the pure technical specialists.

At the time we had a population of engineering duty officers of roughly 1,100 persons. The Keith Board reviewed all of the functions that were being fulfilled by the engineer types, management of shipyards, management of laboratories, research and development, design of ships, production of ships, maintenance of ships and engineer officers afloat. I think in the design area there was a belief that he who did not go to sea could not very well understand what the seagoing man required, and that there had to be some better way to do it. I don't subscribe to that idea, but I've heard it mentioned repeatedly. I've been unable in my years of ship design and construction to find more than two Navy line operating types who could agree at the same moment on what they needed, where to put it and how to operate it. So they needed an independent arbiter who, if he was intelligent and skilled enough and could listen to the requirements of the seagoing personnel and ought to be able to put it together that way. I think we EDOs were hugely successful in the over-all.

The Keith Board's conclusions were that we should reduce the strength of the specialist technical officer, the ED group, from 1,100 to about 950, a rather significant reduction. It also recommended a minimization of the type of duties performed. It urged the postgraduate technical instruction for virtually all straight seagoing line officers to become specialized in what were termed subspecialties that could be applied in the various naval fields. This makes sense, except for the general belief of the operating line officer that he shouldn't be besmirched by engineering type duties so to assign him to some technical duty was to him more or less like being sent to Siberia, an attitude that prevailed for generations, not just something that happened with the Keith Board.

Consequently, you saw people endeavoring to avoid assignments in subspecialties, even though they were operating line officers. So the gap between requirements and available personnel began to widen as we went downhill, as we reduced the EDO intake from the fleet of young line officers. There was also a general attitude of discouragement by those who passed along requests for transfer to the EDO corps. Many senior officers in many instances would stifle a young fellow's ambition to become a specialist, discourage him and finally disapprove it in the desire to retain him in the line I was one who had this peronsal experience when a young ensign

So you began to get a lesser and lesser quality input into

the full specialist field. You also had a bunch of unhappy people who constituted the residue, if I may call it that, to the point where some of the smarter ones were getting out of service early. The whole situation, in my opinion, became, and is today, highly undesirable, most unhealthy. Because of this trend and also because of other such idiosyncrasies, regarding specialization by top naval officers, McNamara concluded that the Navy should not do its own ship designing any more, or its own aircraft designing, which it did to a lesser extent than ship designing, and that we should farm this work and responsibility out to private industry.

Well, we've talked about this in a past interview. The cost of this to the nation is fantastically high. I don't think the quality of our ships is the least bit better in fact I think it is poorer. I have to focus on the LHA program designed, in part, maybe almost in full detail, by Litton Industries, which is in grave trouble today, costwise, equipment-wise and delivery-wise. Litton or any other company that now suddenly is forced to accept the responsibility of designing ships just doesn't have the experience or the reservoir of trained qualified engineers. They've hired virtually every available ex-EDO as soon as he left active duty and put him into a position of responsibility. Industry, therefore, has recognized the importance of specialist training and is using it to good advantage. Concurrently the Navy's paying about four times what they could have had it for if they had kept a good, stimulated group of engineer specialists.

Q: Kept them in the family!

Adm. J.: In the family. A tragic situation. The ancillary results are, of course, the abandonment of the bureau system for producing combat hardware. Instead we have the various Systems Commands, putting into the key control positions, unadulterated, and maybe even very competent seagoing line officers to administer technical programs. I hear of the goofs, the outright boo-boos, these line types who are trying to run the Navy's technical functions have pulled repeatedly. I'm appalled. I'm fearful for the future of the Navy's technical capability. I may exaggerate, but I believe that we have dissipated not only the enthusiasm of the young officer to come into the engineering specialty, but we have reduced to a bare minimum the standards of performance that we can expect from outside industry sources that now are almost exclusively doing the very complicated task of ship design.

There is no greater complexity of system engineering than exists in a ship design, not only today, but almost from the days of the Ark. These beliefs have been more or less discarded as being vital and the Keith Board, in my judgment, was the basic instrument at which this deterioration began to set in.

Q: Who instigated the Keith Board?

Adm. J.: I would have to assume it was the chief of naval operations, operating through the chief of naval personnel. I did know, I'm sure, at the time, I've forgotten. Now, let's see who was the CNO at that time? I'm quite sure it was right after Arleigh Burke, which was Goerge Anderson. The Keith Board proposals have since been reversed by awareness of some of the Navy's own top personnel people of the importance of recruiting more specialists to keep abreast the exploding technology. They have restored the number, in fact, have increased the number of EDOs allowed. They've also increased the number of assignments that have been given to engineer specialists. I do not depreciate the potential of the subspecialist, the seagoing line officer, but to me he's a sort of a "jack of all trades" and master of none type of person and this was what the Keith Board recommended. Also the general feeling of the seagoing line officer was that he has to follow a certain career command pattern or else his career was going to be bobtailed at an early date.

I think the Keith Board did great damage to the Navy. I think that whoever ordered it did the initial damage and Taylor Keith in his enthusiasm to do the job either the way he was instructed or, perhaps, as he saw it, drove the last nail into the coffin of the Navy's in-house technical competence. We now will be dependent, as is the Air Force (and, to some extent, as was the Bureau of Aeronautics) on what is dished up to us by industry representing what the Navy can have.

By contrast, the Russian Navy has gone the exact opposite direction. The engineer training of the Russian Navy has become fantastically accelerated. The British Navy Never did have much of a uniformed technical corps, but they did have a highly capable, highly trained, highly skilled civilian technical corps which was an integral part of their Navy. So integral, in fact, that their so-called naval constructors while laboring at home were in a civilian status, but if they went overseas they put on a uniform of a British Royal Navy regular officer and were acknowledged and received as such abroad.

These things, I feel, cannot be restored to their early - let me restate that. I don't believe that the situation that gave us the greatest navy in the world for generations by the inhouse capability of its own Navy-trained engineer ship specialist group can ever be restored. The dismembering of the bureau system and placing of it under the Chief of Naval Materiel, a line officer, has brought about the dissipation of the finest engineering capability of the former Bureau of Ships organization both civilian and military. I find more former BuShip-ites, both military and civilian, in positions of prominence, importance, and responsibility in industry today, and, to a degree, therefore, we're receiving their services, but not in the manner in which it was and could have been administered and at a fraction of present cost.

Q: And the source will dry up in another generation!

Adm. J.: Sure, it will. The input may be numerically higher than when I was - than the Keith Board dictated, but it is into a group who now have no real close-knit independent organization and the esprit de corps of the past. If the objective was to subjugate the engineer, the results have been amazingly successful. I'm fearful that they've also been disastrous for the national good.

Well, that ought to wrap that up.

Q: Admiral, in the first interview you said this: "In the course of becoming chief of the Bureau of Ships, which is the top position in the engineering field, I found more and more feelings of disrespect from line types that resulted in some stupid, if not tragic, decisions," and I take it that what you've said this morning is implementation of this statement?

Adm. J.: I think the Keith Board and all the subsequent dismembering of the bureaus was a stupid, disastrous occurrence.

My induction into office as the chief of the Bureau of Ships occurred in April of 1959. At the conclusion of my four-year term in April of 1963, it became necessary, of course, to identify and swear in my successor. I was called in to discuss my successor with the Secretary of the Navy, Fred Korth, and later, after he had discussed it with the Secretary of Defense, we further reviewed it with the chief of naval operations, George Anderson. I had in mind a very capable officer whom I knew extremely well as my successor, but he was in the group that had just then selected to flag rank. I did not believe that there would be any problem of his ultimately achieving the position of chief of the Bureau and felt that because of his relative juniority it might be well to nominate someone whom I did not know nearly so well, to succeed me immediately and hopefully to be followed by the first person I mentioned.

The first person I mentioned was Rear Admiral "Red" McQuilken. The second person that I did nominate was Rear Admiral Bill Brockett. Bill Brockett was someone I had only relatively recently come to know. I respected his performance and his capabilities. So I made the nomination of Brockett with the expressed hope, as I mentioned to both Anderson and Korth, that as the successor to Brockett, a hot-running candidate to be considered had to be "Red" McQuilken, who was really my initial choice. He was a gung-ho type who was more concerned with these personnel problems that I've just recently commented on, knew all of the background, having been an Engineering Duty Officer, initially a naval constructor, back from about 1936 or 1937, Brockett entered this group about 1944. Brockett was appointed and carried on the normal functions of responsibility. I know that he had a greater rapport with Admiral Rickover than I was able to achieve, more, I believe, because he was willing to yield to Rickover more than I was, or better, he was less able to prevent Rickover from walking over him. This need not have been a hazardous situation and, by and large, Bill Brockett was a good candidate. He also got highly exercised over these changes in personnel that were being forced upon the engineer specialist as a result of the Keith Board.

The establishment of the Chief of Naval Material as his immediate senior instead of the Secretary of the Navy as in my case, led Brockett to resign from office before the expiration of his four-year term. The press story on his retirement stated it was for a personal reason that he got out and I'm sure that it was, but it was also motivated to a large extent by his dissatisfaction with the circumstances that were being brought upon the Navy by the dismembering of the bureau system and by the reduction of the engineer duty personnel. So Brockett went out of office and along with him went his deputy, Charlie Kurtze, both of whom did it over their disgust with those developments. I felt they would have done better for them to have remained on active duty and fought vigorously to prevent the occurrence of some of these things which I have lamented in earlier comment, but out they went and with them virtually went the Bureau of Ships and all its technical competence. The finally dismembering happened under Brockett's successor, Admiral Ed Fahy, who served the last few months as chief of the Bureau of Ships and then became the first of the Naval Ship Systems Commanders.

However, I perhaps should leave it to Brockett to express any of his opinions of this relatively brief period of his tenure, and go back to the circumstances that followed my being relieved as chief of the Bureau. This occurred at the end of April, as I said, 1963.

I had the desire to fulfill my full 35-year term which meant to carry on til June 30th of that same year. I was asked to make a survey of naval shipyards, in part, but particularly the Portsmouth Naval Shipyard, with the objective of trying to improve its performance as part of the SCAP program study had indicated a need for. I organized a study team, bringing into the group some of the senior officers and many of the senior civilians from around the Navy industrial establishment. We proceeded to Portsmouth to spend time considering the problems of the Portsmouth Naval Ship Yard, its personnel recruitment, its difficulties in recruiting labor from the area that was not already historically entrenched in the grandfather, father, and son worker syndrome.

We found Portsmouth to have many shortcomings, mainly because of the worker attitude towards their responsibilities to the Navy. They considered the Portsmouth Naval Ship Yard as their own private province, that the naval officers that came and went were merely fly specks on the window of the time, and they need not really follow management direction too carefully because, given an appropriate interval, the incumbents would be gone and the next man probably would have some other "idiosyncrasies."

Well, for the next two months this was essentially the problem that I labored on with the objective of implementing proposals that I had previously made for closing certain naval shipyards excess to the Navy's requirements. My concern was that this shipyard was most unproductive. We ferreted out what we thought were the reasons and expressed them. We rendered our report to the Navy and concluded that the shipyard either had to "shape up and fly right" or it should be closed. This caused considerable consternation when the results of this were made known in Portsmouth. I can recall my departure conference, to which I asked the shipyard commander to bring all the key military and civilian personnel to receive some of the obvious findings in the hopes that they would recognize the validity of our recommendations and start to "fly right."

As we walked out of the conference after an hour and a half of review of various detailed matters, I can remember walking behind a couple of civilian quartermen or leading men of the yard that had attended the meeting. They preceded me and were unaware of the fact that I was immediately behind them. One of them said to another, "That's the same old crap we've been hearing for years. He's going to be gone in two months' time, so we can forget this one, too." That, I'm afraid, was the attitude of the people in the portsmouth Naval Ship Yard. At no time in my earlier recommendations for closing shipyards had I included Portsmouth. We deliberately didn't include them because they were a submarine-building yard. It was one of the two that we had, only, Portsmouth and Mare Island. I therefore was hopeful that we might stimulate these people to greater achievements, greater productivity, and perfection of performance. Later when McNamara, with Brockett, decided to make his own survey of shipyards to be closed, he came up with the ridiculous recommendation that Portsmouth, New Hampshire, would be one of those shipyards to be closed. However, it was not to happen then but ten years later. I don't know what could have inspired the man to bring forward such a silly recommendation, because who in the hell can regulate what's going to be the attitude of a shipyard ten years in the future. I think it was just a political ploy to suggest the munificence of the Administration in power for the people of Portsmouth. I think that they concluded, and I believe my report was a part of the reason, that Portsmouth ought to be closed forthwith, but they didn't have the guts to do it.

I really don't think it should have been done at all. I think that the steps that we had indicated, how to bring them around to "fly right," would have been useful and could have greatly improved this yard.

That was my last official act on active duty. The next and final official act was, of course, my retirement. For personal reasons and because of my responsibility for the then David Taylor Model Basin, I arranged for this ceremony to be held at Carderock on the wide open parade ground with the guns booming, the parade of the troops and the speeches and the medals and all of this in the standard pattern.

Q: A highly exciting event!

Adm. J.: I couldn't have picked a hotter day for the occasion.

The one thing we failed to do was to have the ambulance standing by to carry off people who nearly went berserk with the heat. We had a little reception afterwards on the grounds in the cafeteria area. This was air-cooled of sorts, but the logistics did not permit the people waiting in line to shake hands to come indoors while waiting, they stood out in the boiling sun. Most of them will never forget that one retirement ceremony, and neither will I!

Well, with great pride in accomplishment, but also with a feeling of frustration for lack of accomplishment, with personal gratification for a life of excitement and achievement, and a reasonable financial remuneration for what I considered yeoman service to our government, I left the Navy after thirty-five years of commissioned service and four years as a midshipman, with a feeling, essentially, of pride and deep affection, affection for the service and affection for the individuals who make it up.

Q: The date of your departure was?

Adm. J.: The 30th of June 1963. I think, then, Jack, that constitutes the end of the interview this morning.

Interview No. 13 with Rear Admiral Ralph K. James, U.S. Navy (Retired)

Place: His residence in Providence, Annapolis, Maryland

Date: Tuesday morning, 16 May 1972

Subject: Biography

By: John T. Mason, Jr.

Q: Admiral, now we come to a supplementary-type chapter in which you are going to relate your activities in retirement, and some of them have been very important indeed.

Adm. J: I think it would be appropriate this morning, Jack, to not give you a detailed review of my post-retirement activities, but rather to pick out those high points that have a direct bearing on my prior naval service.

In the first place, my retirement came under a then newly enacted law that was extremely discriminatory. A little background, perhaps, is appropriate.

Sometime prior to my retirement, perhaps as much as a year before, there was a bit of a flap in the Norfolk area because of some retired officer who, having been an officers' club manager, was employed by a brewery or a brewer's distributor. He promptly secured long-term contracts for that brew in places where he had been serving while on active duty. This provoked a lot of reaction from the disappointed distributors of beer in the area. They took the matter up and finally got a bill introduced in Congress known as the Conflict of Interests Bill. It was passed to assure that those military people who had served in positions involving procurement of commodities from civilian markets would not, in effect, have the opportunity to "feather their nests" before retirement and leap into the nest upon retirement, there to find a cushy set-up which, by their indiscretions while on active duty, they had engineered in anticipation of retirement.

The Bill, as it was finally enacted, was a brutal thing for a very few people. Fundamentally, it served the over-all problem well. It required a period of cooling-off after retirement before you entered into sales with the military activities. I believe the period was three years of isolation from direct sales to Navy agencies or personnel. In the main, I'm not complaining about this, but they also wrote in a provision and I don't think anybody at the time realized the impact it would have upon a handful, a very small handful, of key people retiring from the Navy, including myself. There was a provision that stated that with any company that you had signed a contract, for the life of that contract you might not be employed by that company in a position involving sales.

As chief of the Bureau of Ships, I had been the Navy's sole agent for signing all the shipbuilding contracts . . .

Q: Excluded you from the whole field!

Adm. J.: . . . which had a life span that averaged about six years. Some of those that I signed are still active, nine years later. Because of possible contractor controversy, and because of the long interval of time needed to contract for a ship, to get it built, to get it delivered, to run it through the warranty period, and finally to deliver it to the Navy, normally at least six years elapsed. Then for the contract to be finalized (closed out), paid off, and put on the shelf as much as another ten years could elapse.

The effect of that law was to exclude me from the industry in which I was a specialist, the industry I had been trained by the Navy to serve, the shipbuilding field. Oh, I could have been employed with a shipbuilding company in one capacity or another, but I would be excluded for the duration of any existing contract from direct contact to sell ships to the Navy. I was offered the presidency of a medium-sized shipyard. The people who made the offer said, "Oh, you won't have to sell to the Navy," but what the devil does the president of a company do? He's the head salesman in virtually every industry that I know anything about. So I deliberately decided not to enter the field where my accumulated years of experience would have been useful, not only to the company that I affiliated with, but to the Navy and the country as a whole.

Instead, I cast about for other opportunities, and I might say without an attempt at modesty that they were numerous. However, I concluded that anything in the shipbuilding and major equipment field was out as far as I was concerned. Perhaps this was partly out of pique as I guess I could have arranged for some sort of an accommodation that would meet the specifics of the law. It irked me to see that I of all of the people in my specialty, because I had been privileged to serve as the chief of the Bureau and had the responsibility of signing virtually every shipbuilding contract of any size, that I was singled out, not deliberately but accidentally, by a law that had not been carefully drafted. The same was true of all other specialists in the Navy who served as chiefs of the other bureaus.

So a handful of us were penalized for the indiscretions of this warrant officer who had caused the bill to be passed. The bill was appropriate, for most situations I say again, but I feel sure it was not intended to have the impact that it did upon me and a few others like me.

Q: I would think people in Supplies and Accounts would be excluded from many things?

Adm. J.: Supplies and Accounts contracts generally run their lifetime in two to three years max. Only in the weapons field and, principally, in the ship field do contracts have a normal lifetime in excess of six years and a potential lifetime of as much as two and sometimes three times that much. I can think of one that ran at least fifteen years. Newport News challenged the Navy on the price of building a number of LSTs back in the mid-fifties. When I came into office they were seeking to have an increase in price allowed under the contract. If I'm not mistaken it was about an 11-million-dollar increase that they claimed the government owed them. I lived through a four-year period term of office opposing their position and got decisions from a series of different appeals boards supporting my position. I left office.

Two and a half years later, my successor left office. His successor finally saw the whole thing reversed in some court. Some civil court awarded Newport News something approaching 11 million dollars. Now, that contract, to my personal knowledge, had a life of at least fifteen years. So you can see the nature of the problem.

Having made the decision not to seek employment in the marine engineering field, I cast about and was invited to consider an opportunity to join with the subsidized steamship companies in running an association known as the Committee of American Steamship Lines. The acronym was CASL. The operation was in Washington, where I wanted very much to continue my residence. This position gave me an opportunity to get into the ship-operating field, that is, the merchant side of it. I always am tickled when I think of how the seagoing line never credited an engineer specialist with the ability to do anything in ship operations. Here I was pursuing a very interesting new career in the ship-operating business, while many of my line associates rushed madly to associate with industrial companies producing weapons systems, electronics, and the like, an anomaly that is amusing but not important.

After examining the opportunity with CASL, I accepted this offer and started to serve with them in the capacity of executive director with a relatively small office in Washington. The committee consisted of the presidents of fourteen subsidized American-flag lines that operated on prescribed trade routes - trade routes prescribed by the Department of Commerce - which then qualified these companies to receive as subsidy the differential in cost between foreign and

American operation of similar ships on the same trade routes. The major difference of costs being the labor costs which in America, because of our extremely high standard of living, were significantly higher than our foreign competitors. Take one of the extreme comparisons - a foreign ship with a Chinese crew, and a U. S. flag merchant cargo liner operating from West Coast ports.

When a ship flying the American flag operated on an assigned trade route and received subsidy, its operating costs were periodically compared with a foreign ship operating on that same trade route. Applying many technicalities, restrictions, and qualifications, Uncle Sam annually paid the difference between the American operating costs and those of the foreign competition. The purpose of this was to allow American-flag operators to operate on the high seas at essentially comparable cost to that of their foreign competitors, hence, making the opportunites for competition a matter of performance and efficiency rather than differential of labor cost, which largely was brought about by the high American standard of living.

Q: Isn't the gap getting narrower in that area?

Adm. J.: Today the gap is narrowing considerably, particularly in another aspect of the subsidy known as the shipbuilding subsidy. American ships, at the time I entered CASL, were costing about - well, let me draw the comparison differently. The cost of an American ship we'll call 100 percent. The cost of an identical ship built abroad could be as little as 45 percent of that American cost. The Merchant Marine Act of 1936, which provided for subsidy, allowed the U. S. building yard to be paid the differential between the foreign cost and the American cost of the ship. Again, this is a reflection of the higher shipbuilding labor costs in this country as contrasted with the lowest world market, which at the time I entered CASL was alternately West Germany and Japan. It later became Japan almost exclusively because of their very low wage rates.

The point you just made is a very good one. Subsequently, as inflation has hit these other countries and under pressure often from our Maritime Administration, the American ship costs have closed that gap so that now instead of the shipbuilding subsidy being somewhere between 55 and 60 percent of the total American cost, it is down around 40 percent with a target of about 35 percent being set as foreign costs continue to rise.

The Committee of American Steamship Lines headquarters, as I mentioned, was relatively small. I had under me a total of about thirteen people. My function was to monitor legislation on the Hill, to propose legislation for consideration by the merchant marine committees of the House and Senate, and to maintain daily contact with the Maritime Administration. In effect, I was a registered lobbyist who performed in behalf of the thirteen member lines. I said there were about fourteen steamship companies under subsidy. Very shortly after I came on, as a result of pique with another company, one of the fourteen members dropped out. About a year later still another one dropped out. We operated, however, with the principal U. S. steamship companies, including U. S. Lines, Farrell Lines, Moore-McCormack, American Export, Grace, Prudential, Americal Mail Lines, American President Lines, Pacific Far East Lines, Lykes Brothers,

Delta Steamship, Gulf and South American, and one other whose name escapes me.

My association with this group was a very exciting experience. The presidents of these lines were delightful gentlemen. I had no trouble with any but one of them who was more a politician than he was a steamship president. After a very violent blow-up between him and me we got along and I did his business. This was the president of American President Lines, George Killian. George Killian concurrently while heading APL was chairman of the Democratic National Finance Committee. His interests seemed to be more along that line than they were in the steamship company. He didn't take the necessary time to learn his lessons about CASL business before he uncorked his feelings. He acted as though he wanted to be treated as the première danseuse of the group rather than as one of the twelve.

One thing that bothered me when I had been aboard about six months was the proliferation of steamship trade associations, all allegedly performing the same task. There was the American Merchant Marine Institute, the Pacific Steamship Association (a West Coast group), there was the Labor-Management Association. Oh, there were at least a total of seven that the various members of CASL also belonged to. After I'd been aboard about a year I wrote a memorandum to the CASL presidents and said I thought this situation required a great deal of serious thought. I said I thought we might find value in merging some of these groups into a stronger association representing more of the steamship industry than any one of us, at that time, did. CASL, with its subsidized steamship companies, represented about a third of the total of the American-flag merchant marine, which at that time numbered around 1,100, as I recall.

We had slightly over 300 ships in our groups. The American Merchant Marine Institute had a few more. Some had considerably fewer.

The executive directors, or presidents, of these several groups all strove to represent our clients generally on the same subjects and, by and large, with the same general position on the matters before Congress and the Maritime Administration.

Q: Did they reflect regional interests and specialized interests?

Adm. J.: They reflected specialized interests and to a lesser degree regional interests. The PSSA membership was strictly West Coast steamship companies. With one or two exceptions they were the same ones that were in my association. There were six companies out there. Matson was not a member of either group. The other associations, however, represented tanker groups or bulk cargo groups, or the inland waterways carriers, or tramp carriers. In CASL's case, our lines operated cargo liners and passenger liners in the foreign trade. The only affluent segment of the merchant fleet was the subsidized lines - affluent in the sense that they were running in the black most of the time, except for the passenger service, and with newer ships. The passenger service when I joined up consisted of thirteen major passenger liners. By and large they were being subsidized heavily because they were staffed by such tremendous numbers of crew, all out of proportion to the need.

Q: Did this reflect feather-bedding?

Adm. J.: This was feather-bedding at its worst. The labor unions had a very dynamic set of presidents. The Seamen's Industrial Union was headed up by a man named Paul Hall, who is still a very major factor in labor circles. I believe he aspires to succeed George Meany one of these days. The other was Joe Curran of the National Maritime Union, NMU. They hated each other's guts. If one got an inch, the other wanted two inches before he would settle.

The labor problem, in my opinion, was what has just about killed our merchant marine. It positively has killed the East Coast passenger liner service. There isn't a single American-flag passenger liner operating on the East Coast today. There are only four in the country, and these are under the aegis of the Pacific Far East Lines, which bought the <u>Matsonia</u> and <u>Monterey</u> from the Matson Line, and the American President Line which is running the <u>President Cleveland</u> and the <u>President Wilson</u>. This constitutes the total American-flag passenger service. At the same time the demand for passenger travel by ship has gone up tremendously, largely on pleasure cruises where people are embarked at a given port and taken out for a week to four months and brought back to the same port. It's largely an American trade. Many foreign flag ships come into U. S. ports and load up with Americans, and they make money doing it. Our labor groups feather-bedded our passenger ships to the point where when the maritime labor contract came up for renewal in 1965 our people took a 78-day strike trying to resolve this matter with the labor unions. They got nowhere. The White House finally stepped in and ordered a settlement which was most unfavorable to operators. At the time, during the course of the meetings, it was expressed that the doom of the passenger service would be sealed if we signed the labor agreement that was being pressed upon the operators. This came to pass in less than four years time.

The labor unions were adamant about the crewing of these ships. They were told "if you don't cut the crew size considerably, if you don't take a lesser increase in wages which generates a very high differential over foreign ship operating costs, why, there would be no more passenger service." Subsequently, we've seen the Argentina and Brazil of the Moore McCormack Lines laid up. We've seen the Independence and the Constitution and ...

Q: The United States?

Adm. J.: Yes, but I was taking them by steamship company. I can't think of the name of the third one of the American Export-Isbrandtsen Line; the United States. The Prudential-Grace steamships, the Santa Paula, Santa Rosa, all the Santa Margarita class, and Delta Lines Del Sol and Del Mar - all of them have gone down the drain. A bill has just been enacted in the Congress and is awaiting signature by the President today that would permit these ships, but not the United States, to be sold off to foreign countries so that the money can be re-invested in building more U. S. merchant cargo shipping.

Q: Have there been no regrets on the part of the labor people?

Adm. J.: There has been very very much opposition to the sale of these ships from the unions. They've suddenly decided that maybe what we told them in 1965 was true. They've now offered to reduce the crew sizes and take lesser wages and fringes. By this time, however, the goose is dead, and there's little likelihood - well, there is no likelihood of the ships going to sea again under the American flag. The bill simply awaits the President's signature to start the companies selling off these ships.

After I retired from CASL, I took a trip around the world on the American President Line President Roosevelt. After we'd been embarked a couple of days, the captain announced that the ship had been sold to the Greeks and at the conclusion of our trip the Greeks would take her over. Well, the Greeks boarded our ship in Southampton a handful of the crew including the captain and the chief engineer and others in the key officer billets. They rode the ship around to San Francisco. Two days later, after the passengers on the round-the-world cruise had departed from the ship, the Greeks painted out the name on the stern, painted on the name Atlantis of Piraeus, and sailed her to Greece. This past summer they brought her back to the United States, having moved the crew out of the separate staterooms, which American crewmen had required, made passenger staterooms out of these spaces, reduced the crew size from something approaching 700 down to about 400. They have increased the number and size of community rooms, the lounges, the bars, the dance floors, the dining-rooms, and the like. She's now back in service, operating out of New York alternately to the Caribbean and to the Mediterranean, and making a potful of money.

This just saddens me, because here are potential naval auxiliaries that at one time we did have. When the Soviets made their threatening moves in Cuba in 1963, CASL members with passenger liners were alerted they recalled the passenger ships and got ready to load troops to move to Cuba. That potential has gone, and all because of the inordinate and unreasonable demands of labor for privileges, for perquisites, for wages, and for numbers of people on board. A man works eight regular hours aboard ship and then he's paid overtime. If it's Saturday and Sunday he's paid double time - one of the things that aboard a ship just isn't reasonable.

When there is a maritime strike on, an American shipper has to ask, "How am I going to get my product abroad?" He looks and sees foreign-flag shipping still coming into our ports in great numbers. After receiving certain inducements, which many foreigners practice, in other words rebates and cutbacks, and the likes, the American shipper picks a foreign line to move his goods. When the strike is over, the American manufacturer has been receiving satisfactory service, so why should he change back to the unreliable U.S. flag line? Consequently, you see our American flag-lines carrying a very minor part of the total American overseas trade. In dollars, the subsidized lines carry roughly a third of the value of the total U. S. export cargo. However, in tonnage, they carry only about twenty percent, and if you take in all the tankers, the bulk carriers as well as the cargo liners, why, we are carrying only about four to five percent of American overseas trade in U. S. vessels.

A major part of my concern with the industry, as I started to say, was the proliferation of Associations allegedly representing them. However, my proposal to study the problem got nowhere. I made a second attempt about a year later. I analyzed the cost that my members were paying to join all these different associations. I pointed out that they were paying about three times what they were paying for membership in CASL alone, and if there were a single larger association it might be not over fifty percent more than what they were paying to CASL, and would embrace a great number of ship companies and ships, and pack a bigger Congressional whallop. I still got nowhere.

Q: Admiral, what were the principal impedimenta to joining forces?

Adm. J.: Tradition, and then later, (and I was going to mention this a little further on) there was the belief that apparently grew up amongst some of my president members that I was trying to build an empire, that I was looking out for R. K. James rather than for the welfare of the industry. I was shocked when I realized this. I could understand it, however, because I had made no overtures or explanation of purpose other than the importance of improving the face of the industry to the Congress, to the Administration, and to the Maritime Administration.

Q: Was this the first effort in this direction, the one you initiated

Adm. J.: No, there had been an association that had been organized in the early fifties, a confederation of sorts. It all fell apart within about two years. That also was in the back of their minds, that it was an unworkable approach. Well, in the fifties they'd brought in too many diverse groups, and maintained diverse control within the over-all umbrella, which didn't work too well in the so-called American Confederation of Merchant Shipping.

These factors all added up to the reluctance on the part of my members to do anything about it.

Well, I was determined that what I had in mind was useful to the country, to the companies, and to the industry, so I persisted, but this time I attached a proviso: when and if any such merger was brought about, my resignation was guaranteed to be available on the day that the new agency came into being. That prompted some serious thought.

American Export Isbrandtsen headed up by Admiral Dutch Will who was variously the president and chairman of the board, & had gotten out of CASL. The real power in the company was Mr. Jakob Isbrandtsen, who was the owner and who called the tunes. He pulled American Export out of CASL and about two years later I guess they wished he hadn't done so. Being the kind of people they were they didn't have the guts to walk in the front door and say - we goofed, we want back in. They took up the cudgel of this merger of associations idea to give themselves a smooth re-entry into an association.

I joined the CASL in 1963. It wasn't till 1968 that this merger began to take shape. In 1969, on the 1st of January, I resigned. I was kept on for an additional five months just as a consultant. This was their idea, not mine. The merger took place and, as of now, the groups are joined together in an organization known as the American Institute of Merchant Shipping. I had a small hand in formulating AIMS. I had a large hand in staffing it, and they're doing just what I had speculated could be done. There are not just thirteen steamship companies members, they have over forty lines affiliated. They all work together but with separation of their specialized interests. The tankers have special interests, the dry-cargo liners have special interests, bulk carriers, and so forth, but they're pulling together on basic Maritime policy issues.

Our merchant marine in the meantime has been slipping downhill rapidly. The Merchant Marine Act of 1936 was engineered by Joseph P. Kennedy back in the days when he was Maritime Administrator. It provided for paying subsidy only to the dry-cargo liner fleet and the passenger liner fleet, which was a mistake. It should have embraced all American-flag shipping, including tankers, bulk carriers, tramps, and the likes. Now we've got a new type of ship coming on in a big way - the liquid natural gas (LNG) tanker - to take care of our national energy requirements in the future. They will actually transport liquified gas from the oilfields of the world and bring it to this country to provide fuel, which we will be desperately in need of in the future.

When they finally got the AIMS merger going, the bill, which had virtually been drafted in my office by Ad-hoc committee groups that we used for these sort of things, was offered to Candidate Nixon in 1968 for his maritime policy and it was accepted. Well, Nixon's been in office since early 1969, and it wasn't till the fall of 1970 that the bill virtually as drafted by CASL has become the Merchant Marine Act of 1970, now known as the Nixon Bill. This provided for including many other ship categories other than liners under the subsidy provisions. So far, the act hasn't produced many new ships.

Although it provides for the construction of thirty new ships a year under shipbuilding subsidy, the various steamship companies have not responded as expected. The liquid natural gas people have joined in and are trying to get a number of ships under construction of the LNG tanker type.

One of the problems in getting a revitalized and vital merchant marine act before the Congress in my early CASL days was the Defense Department. When McNamara, who seems to be my whipping boy from time to time, got into office, he was approached and asked to determine the requirements of the military for merchant fleet support. The merchant fleet, at least the subsidized lines, under regulations that provided them subsidies were committed to release their ships to the Defense Department in a time of an emergency. This was a consideration that was of great importance to the Navy for the lift of cargo and troops, because, no matter how many airplanes they fly and no matter how fast they fly it's a demonstrated fact that in Vietnam and all other theaters, over ninety-four percent of the total military cargo arrives by ship. Therefore, the need for an adequate and viable merchant fleet is tremendous.

McNamara had a study made, and he concluded that the Reserve Merchant Fleet, which was a bunch of old crocks (Liberty ships, a few Victory ships, and a few miscellaneous newer ships), with the fleet in being was all the Navy ever needed. Well, this was a kick in the pants, because the merchant ships in service were all getting older and older. I had made a study when I was still active, showing that the number of merchant ships under twenty years of age by 1973 would drop to just about two hundred in the United States merchant fleet, from something over 1,100. We had something over 6,000 new ships build during World War II, and here we would be down to less than two hundred ships less than twenty years old. We still have a few old crocks, the tramps, they're still running Liberty ships, some of the old Victorys, and some of the ships that the subsidized lines, when they replaced their ships, sold off to American operators. That's how the trampers got their ships, by buying up the old discards of the subsidized lines.

Q: Many of those old World War II ships weren't very good to begin with, were they?

Adm. J.: The old Liberty ships were spewed out like sausage from a machine. They were anything but sophisticated ships or anything suited for the trade of today. One development that you can say is a bright spot in our merchant ships, and here almost exclusively our subsidized operators, is the innovation of the container ship, which became, and is today, the hottest thing on the high seas. One container ship can perform the service of two, and sometimes three conventional ships, depending on size, by carrying great numbers of containers (800-1500), which are much better for purposes of moving cargo from an inland city to a foreign port. You load the container at the shipping dock of the manufacturer's plant. There it is locked and sealed, then delivered overseas, where it's unlocked and emptied. The opportunity to pilfer, which is a disease of the waterfront, is significantly reduced.

This caused another labor problem.

Q: There were desperate fights against it!

Adm. J.: Oh, the labor unions, the longshoremen's union, fought like mad to have the right to open up at dockside <u>all containers</u> packed inland and re-stow them. This, of course, opened up pilferage as was the custom. Containers were fought bitterly -- I don't recall the details. In the meantime, the waterfront was struck. Of course, a longshoremen's strike affects foreign-flag shipping as well as American-flag shipping, all shipping stops, so it is a disastrous strike in that it takes up potential time for moving cargo and affects the U. S. balance of trade. It does not discriminate against the American-flag operator, however, as does a shipboard maritime union strike.

But the container development is coming on strong, and finally being accepted in all quarters. We have to pay in extra premiums to the funds of the longshore unions to cover things - well, let's call a spade by its right name, to cover the loss in pilfering opportunity. This kind of thing is just a tragic situation, and it confounds our merchant marine today.

Q: Are the shipping companies demonstrating any greater ability to deal with the unions since they organized into one group?

Adm. J.: No, because the labor negotiations are generally undertaken company by company, or at least coast by coast, The maritime unions are the most segmented of all labor groups. When you negotiate a labor contract with a seagoing union, for example, you don't solve the problem even with that one union. Some companies had as many as nine different unions with whom they would have to reach wage agreements - the Seamen's Union, the Officers' Union, the Engineers' Union, the Radio Operators' Union, the Stewards' Union, the Electricians' Union, and so on ad nauseam. Each union would take its position chronologically in line. If any one got a little bit more than the predecessor, then the next one got that much plus whatever else he was able to negotiate independently for his union. By the time they went around the circuit, say an average of about six different unions, then the first one wanted to come to bat again because he'd been shortchanged by what the last one got.

This was the vicious circle that went on with the trade unions and the merchant marine operators. The ability to negotiate with the unions is a specialized field, and the steamship company presidents are generally "babes in the woods." They hire tough labor-educated attorneys to fight their fights for them. It's only when you get a situation such as where the passenger ship service is all scrubbed and ships are readied to be sold abroad that you get any recanting of unacceptable positions by the labor unions.

I seem awfully anti-union in my comments here, but I think that, fundamentally, the unions have been the cause for the demise of much of our once-valiant merchant service.

Q: Admiral, do you honestly see any hope that the Congress will come to grips with this problem?

Adm. J.: No, absolutely none. Many congressmen get financial support from these labor unions. It even broke out so crassly when the SIU, Paul Hall's union, went about dropping fifty thousand here and ten thousand there in different congressmen's baskets and thumbing their nose at the laws which prohibit this sort of thing. The laws have been strengthened and tightened, but the congressmen, at least many of them on the Merchant Marine Committees, are certainly inclined to be favorable to the trade unions' position in realization of the fact that unions exercise a hell of an influence over the votes in their home communities. Most members on the Merchant Marine Committees are from coastal cities.

I don't know what the answer is. The same fundamental problem exists in industry throughout the entire nation, not just our steamship industry.

But getting back to the ship types. The container ship is a tremendous improvement in the capability of our merchant ships. Many of the older ships are being modified by lengthening them and making them capable of carrying containers. We're seeing the ability to carry more cargo in fewer ships very positively represented by the actions of the steamship companies.

Then, too, the barge ship has come on the scene, an idea that was first generated down in New Orleans by an extremely capable naval architect known as Jerry Goldman who heads up the company of Friede and Goldman, outstanding naval architects. He developed what's called a lighter-aboard-ship concept whose acronym is LASH. We've seen a couple of dozen of these ships under construction here and in Japan. The concept is that a LASH ship comes into port, it discharges a bunch of small lighters - really not small in that they carry upwards to four and five hundred tons of cargo. These are lowered over the stern on a tremendous gantry crane that drops them into the water, after picking them out of the holds of the ship. These barges are then towed to various inland ports, up rivers, through canals, and the like, where they are exchanged for loaded barges which are towed back down to the basic port, the barges are picked up on the ship, and the ship departs.

One of the extremely expensive things in ship operation is the time that has to be spent in port unloading. Some cargo ships take as long as nine or ten days to unload, and you're not making any money while she's tied up and unloading, with the full crew all being paid. The barge ships, of which there are two versions, the LASH ship and one invented by Lykes Brothers called the Sea Bee - fundamentally the same concept but a different approach to how barges are loaded aboard. The Sea Bee lifts larger barges on a hugh 1,000-ton stern elevator and then translates them off of the elevator into stowage in the hold of the ship. This version, named after the Seabees of World War II, was invented by the president of Lykes Brothers, Frank Nemec, who is a very imaginative, every effective, very impressive guy. Presently, he is also president of Youngstown Steel, which Lykes Brothers bought up, and I guess that now they wish they hadn't.

Q: Youngstown Sheet and Tube?

Adm. J.: Yes. These barge-type ships are a really significant innovation. Many of the owners are going for the LASH, because the LASH was invented outside of the industry by a naval architect concern, while the Sea Bee is a Lykes Brothers patented ship. These type ships have added greatly to our U. S. carrying capacity, but our ships are not being built in the numbers that are being retired, or even in proportion to their ability to carry cargo.

I started to talk about McNamara and his inability to judge the requirements for the merchant marine, which had a very unfortunate impact on the attitude of the Congress toward the requirements of the steamship lines to build more ships and get larger shipbuilding subsidies from the Congress. He, in effect, said, "We don't need any more merchant ships than those we've got." Well, he just plain didn't know what he was talking about, because what he had in the reserve fleet were all old ships that had been put in the reserve fleet because they were less than satisfactory. During Korea we did call a number of them back and at the outset of Vietnam we called back a number also, simply to have some U. S. bottoms to carry the cargo in. Since then, those ships have again been laid up, many of them have been scrapped and some have been sold abroad.

Our merchant marine is in a hell of a state of affairs. The Nixon Act of 1970 will go a long way to improving that, but even it has technical difficulties which keep steamship lines from moving in this direction. It would have aided immeasurably if the Defense Department had come out and said - we must have a viable merchant marine. McNamara's attitude was - we'll fly it there, we'll also build a bunch of ships, (which he called FDLSs, Fleet Defense Logistic Ships) preload them with cargo, station them round the perimeter of the world, and therefore we won't need the merchant marine. We can do it all ourselves.

Well, the clamor within the shipping industry over the FDLS, and the clamor within the Congress finally shot that project down. And I think I'm perhaps as much a moving spirit in shooting that down as anybody. The concept really was something, from the point of view of the international relationships of our nation -- how would you feel if you were, shall we say, a Far Eastern country and suddenly fifty miles off one of your ports came a hugh American ship to just fool around waiting for the time to come when you got mad at us and started making threats. Then we move ashore with the pre-loaded military cargo, and we'd be right on your doorsteps. The concept was ludicrous. It was McNamara's idea that with the C-5A and the FDLS he could move all of his military cargo -- how many of these would be shot out of the water before they had the opportunity to discharge their loads, to my knowledge, was never weighed. These are the rather ridiculous attitudes that came out of the Defense Department under McNamara's administration that went a long way to keep the Merchant Marine Act from being revised, and it was desperately needed as much as fifteen years ago. We desperately needed to update the old Merchant Marine Act of 1936, which was known as the Magna Carta of the merchant marine, but McNamara personally prevented it from going anywhere. Some of his testimony before the Merchant Marine Committee is the most ridiculous testimony I've ever read, and showed ignorance that is so utterly colossal that it scarcely justified him holding the position he did at the time. Any man that took as little time to understand the problem, and took so positive a position on the problem as he did, just is beyond me to comprehend.

Well, I could ramble on with the merchant marine, but let me say that I found it a fascinating field. I found a crying need for the Navy personnel to understand the role of the merchant marine. In this area only one naval person stands out as completely understanding this problem, and that's Rear Admiral George Miller. In his Op-9 position in the Navy defining the long-range planning of military logistics, George Miller quickly realized the importance of the merchant marine. He joined with me on ocassion in trying to influence others in the Navy, and on the Hill, to move in and upgrade our U. S. flag merchant marine. I'm sure that his current position as the liaison officer for maritime affairs with the Department of Commerce and the Navy is a direct result of his full understanding of the importance of the merchant fleet to the Navy.

Q: Is making some progress?

Adm. J.: George is making progress. George is that kind of a quiet guy that insinuates himself, in such a scholarly fashion that he is scarcely ever challenged on the conclusions that he reaches. He doesn't yet demonstrate the ability to make too many people get up and cheer and run to join his band wagon, but he is a hard worker in this vinyard, and so long as he continues in the Maritime Administration he will move things forward. I still take limited opportunity to collaborate with him on merchant matters, including, for example, the installation aboard the Sea Bee barge carrier of hovercraft as lighters to offload these tremendous ships in places where the Army needs logistic support ashore, in such places as the Alaskan areas or other areas devoid of proper ports and harbors. One of these days I think we'll see the marriage of the Sea Bee and the hovercraft, but that's a side issue.

With the advent of the American Institute of Merchant Shipping I resigned from the group with the best wishes of all of its members, had a relatively pleasant concluding five months at full pay, which I might say was somewhat more generous than the Navy paid for my services in an area where I was an expert. These people paid me better where I was an amateur. It makes you wonder about the pay scales that the Navy suffered under for years. Now, to a great extent, these have been corrected. Those of us who were born too early didn't get the benefit of the increases in pay, and I'm sure the Recomputation will never take place.

Well, I don't want to end up my oral history with a lament. I think that the importance of the merchant fleet to the Navy has to be recognized. I spend some time addressing the midshipmen on this subject. I voice it every time I have an audience of Navy types because, to a large extent, they haven't been exposed to the importance of the merchant fleet and its dilapidated state. It wasn't until after I retired from the Navy, and into it, that I realized how vital this is to the wellbeing of our Navy in whatever operations are performed.

From CASL I went into independent marine consulting work, hoping to recover a little of that lost association that I had enjoyed as an active naval officer with the shipbuilding world. This has not occurred because I guess I'm just an old fuddy-dud now. I am, however, involved with an aerospace company which is into the shipbuilding field of hovercraft. This keeps me alive and interested. I've already recited much about my association with hovercraft, so I won't repeat it.

Well, as of this moment, Jack, I believe that I've covered about all that might be useful to future readers or listeners to the tapes on this transcribed oral history, and what it has been like to be associated so long with the Navy, and briefly with the merchant marine, two vital elements in our national defense. I would think, therefore, that having run out of steam on anything that I believe would be valuable, maybe we can conclude this record with the thirteenth interview.

Q: It was tremendously interesting and tremendously valuable, and I thank you for all your effort and the time you've given me.

Adm. J.: It's been a great deal of fun.

INDEX FOR

INTERVIEWS WITH

REAR ADMIRAL RALPH KIRK JAMES

U. S. Navy (Retired)

Aerojet General: 341-342, 344-345

AIMS (American Institute of Merchant Shipping): 425; grew out of CASL but with 40 lines affiliated, 426; method of dealing with labor unions, 429-430

Ainsworth, VADM Walden Lee: commander, DDs, PacFlt, 164

Aircraft Carrier Desk: jeep carriers, 121; role of FDR in development, 122-123

ALCOA: use of Alcoa representative for work with new fittings, 59

Alden, Professor C. S.: 4-5

Alderman, RADM John C. (Bill): innovations with repair job on DD, 129

Algiers: visit there to report to Gen. Eisenhower, 102

Aluminum: use of in shipbuilding, 59

Anderson, ADM George: Institutes Keith Board, 402, 405

Anderson, Paul R.: 13

USS ARGONNE: Headquarters ship for ServRon 10, 142-143, 148

Armour and Company: 2

Armour Institute: 3-4, 6-8

USS ASTORIA, CL: 45

SS ATLANTIS (ex PRESIDENT ROOSEVELT): of the Greek Line, 422

Austin, VADM Bernard L.: 391; chairman of Board of Inquiry on SS THRESHER, 391, 393

Badger, Admiral Oscar C.: 153

USS BAINBRIDGE: 306

Barnes, The Hon. Maynard: State Department representative in N. Africa, 77

Bates, Capt. Rafe: 59-61

Behrens, Captain Bill: 144; captain of USS HOUSTON, 150

Bell Aerospace: 336, 338, 341-345; develops VOYAGEUR Class (hovercraft), 346

Bell, Alexander Graham: 325

Biosson, Gen. Pierre: Governor of Dakar, 79-80, 82

Blair, Clay: role in career of Admiral Rickover, 225

Blewett, RADM William: President, Newport News Shipbuilding Corp., 365-368

Boak, Commodore Jimmie: 126; naval base commander at Manus, 142; explosion of ammunition ship, Mt. Hood, 146-147

Boeing Corp.: 328, 331-332

Boos, Allen and Hamilton: consultants, 65-66; onlocation of Shipbuilding Scheduling Control Center, 195

Boston Navy Yard: recommendation for closing, 319-320, 322-323

Bremerton Navy Yard: 37, 41; assigned to Planning Division, 41-42; role of skipper of ship in effecting repairs, 43; development-design work, 46; 47; ship maintenance, 48; docking officer, 48-49; ghost writer for shipyard manage, 50-51; labor relations, 52-53

British Hovercraft: successor to Westland A/C Corporation, 337; continues development of idea, 339-340, 343

Brockett, RADM Wm. Alden: successor to Adm. James in BuShips, 339; 405; retires early from BuShips, 406, 409

Broshek, RADM Joseph J.: 74-75

Brown, Admiral Charles R. (Cat): 179

Brown, Captain Moose: named to SCAP panel, 267

Bureau of Construction and Repairs: duty for maintenance and operation of shipyards work on DDs, 63; merger attempt with Bureau of Engineering, 64-65 ff.

Bureau of Ships: birth as a Bureau, 65 ff; Adm. James named as Asst. Chief, 265-66; proposes and heads panel to study costs of shipbuilding and ship repairs, 267; James named as Chief of Bureau to succeed RADM Mumma, 273-274; problem of aging fleet that comes to fore, 278-279; adopts policy of full and final pricing of ships at time of initial authority to build, 279; FRAM program for modernization of DDs, 280-283; increases made in shipbuilding program, 282; nuclear powered ships, 283-284; program of offshore shipbuilding for NATO countries and Japan, 293-294; Polaris submarine, 299-302; method of acceleration displeases SecDef, 301-302; discussion of Polaris and relation to announced missile gap, 303-304; James suggests arming merchant ships with Polaris missiles, 305-306; first three nuclear surface ships delivered, 306-307; discussion of costs of nuclear powered ships, 308-312; concern with physical state of shipyards - effort at modernization, 313-314, 318-319; attitude of private ship builders, 314-316; discussion of bidding on contracts, 316-317; recommendations for closing naval shipyards, 319-323

Burke, Admiral Arleigh: member of SecNav's Advisory Committee, considers suit against oil companies operating at Long Beach, 238; 280; on cost of carrier ENTERPRISE, 309

USS CALIFORNIA, BB: collision with BB TENNESSEE, 127-128

USS CANBERRA: damaged in Formosa Strait, 143-144, 146, 149-150;

taken out of dock to accommodate BB IOWA, 151-152

Cap de Palm: French frigate, 137

Carney, Admiral R. B.: 143, 146

Casablanca: Haven for BB JEAN BART, 78; 80, 94, 99, 103; near tragedy enroute to, 103; RADM Sullivan in Casablanca, 113

Casablanca Conference: FDR enroute, 97-98; Admiral James invited to report on ships in Dakar harbor, 98; 107

CASL (Committee of American Steamship Lines): James becomes Executive Director, 415; discussion of its purposes, 415-417; duties undertaken by Adm. James, 417; list of member steamship lines, 417-419; 423-425; earlier effort at uniting, 425

Chaplin, John: with Westland Aircraft Co., 333

USS CHICAGO, CA: 48-49; story of battle damage repairs at Manus, 158-161

Chinbloom, The Hon. Carl: 7

Church, RADM Albert T.: 50-51

Churchill, The Rt. Hon. Winston: Prime Minister of Britain - party at British Consulate in Marrakesh, 109-110

USS CLARK, DD: 59

Clark, The Hon. Ramsey: 241

U. S. Coast Guard: interested in VOYAGEUR Class of hovercraft, 346

Cobb, VADM Calvin Hayes: in command of Service Fleet, SoPac, Adm. James made member of fleet maintenance staff, 124

Cochrane, VADM ED L.: Chief of Bureau of Ships, 136; visit to Sydney, Australia, where James serves as aide, 140; gives James assignment to Mechanicsburg Depot, 168-170; at London meeting of Naval Architects, 187

Cockrell, Sir Christopher: inventor of hovercraft, 333

Collinet, VADM: 82

USS COMMENCEMENT BAY, CVS 105: largely a concept of President FDR, 123

Comptroller of the Bureau of Ships: James is named to post and learns that 'the fuel of BuShips is money,' 204-205; appears before Congressional Committees, 206-208

Coney, RADM Charles E. (Yen): 134-135

Conflict of Interests Act: 411 ff.; ramifications for Adm. James, 412-414

USS CONSTELLATION: story of fire on board at New York Navy Yard, 383-389

Container Ships: an important innovation, 428-429

Control Data Corporation: 376-377

Cowart, VADM Kenneth: Chief Engineer, U. S. Coast Guard, 186

Cowdrey, RADM Roy T.: E.D.O., 121, 124, 126

Craig, Captain Edward C.: 125-126

Cranston, The Hon. Alan: 248

Cunningham, Admiral Sir Andrew: Commander, Allied Naval Forces in North Africa, 101

Curran, Joseph: President National Maritime Union, 420

USS CUSHING, DD: 45

Dafoe Shipyard, Bay City, Mich.: launching of USS LYNDE McCORMICK, 358; Australian Navy contracts for three DDEs, 377-379

Dakar, French West Africa: 75, 78; interned ship in harbor, 79; American landing at Dakar with simultaneous departure of Germans, 80; initial attitude of French towards Americans,

81-82; change of heart after Darlan assassination, 85-88; French Naval Forces in harbor, 91; attitude of dockyard commander, 92-94; merchant shipping, 94-95; additional help needed in dealing with ship captains, 95-97; Giraud in Dakar, 102; interest in developments shown at Casablanca Conference, 109; return to Dakar after Casablanca Conference, 117-118

Darlan, Admiral: French Admiral assassinated in North Africa, 83; repercussions, 83-85, 88

David Taylor Model Basin: Carderock, Md.: retirement ceremony for Adm. James held there, 409

Davis, Dr. Ruth: mathematician at David Taylor Model Basin, tangle with BuShips, 375-377

De Gaulle, General Charles: his role in assault on Dakar, 89-90

Design Work Study, BuShips: 347; origin of idea in BuShips, 348-349; development, 349-351; demise of system under Secretary McNamara, 351

Di Raymond, Captain: French skipper of BB RICHELIEU, 79

USS DIXIE, Repair ship: 127

Dolan, RADM Wm. A., Jr.: shipyard commander, Bremerton, Wash., 360-361

"Dollar Stretch": term applied to effort of BuShips to get more "bang for buck," 312-313; part of SCAP program, 369-371; discussion of changes resulting from McNamara reorganization, 372-373

Doyle, The Hon. Clyde: member of Congress, heads committee to investigate the Long Beach situation, 247

Dumont, American Vice Consul in Dakar: imprisoned by French, 84, 93

Dunning, Captain Al: Electric Boat Co., 369

Early, Captain Elx: skipper of CANBERRA, 150; strain of personnel on bomd damaged ships, 150-151

Eccles, RADM Henry E.: 181

Edison Power and Light Co.: 231-232

EDO Officers: comments on, 397-402

Eisenhower, General Dwight D.: 98-100; 274; quote from final State of the Union Message, 279; 303

Eisenhower, Mrs. Dwight D. (Mamie): launching of SS NAUTILUS, 360, 368

Eleventh Naval District: James serves as Industrial Manager, 255-257; the "65-35 fight" of the private shipyards lobby, 255; Supervisor of Shipbuilding, 257-258; daughter of Adm. James christens Danish M/S, 258

Engleman, Captain Christian Levin: in charge of recruitment for Shipbuilding Scheduling Control Center, 197-199

USS ENTERPRISE, CV: 306; incident involving elevator in island structure, 308; escalation of costs, 308-309; launching ceremony, 364-365

Espiritu Santo: U. S. Supply Base in WW II, 124-127; repairs made to BBs CALIFORNIA and TENNESSEE, 128; 129-130; salvage operations, 130-137; spareparts, 137; merchant ship repairs, 138-139

USS ESSEX, CV: 123

Fahy, RADM ED: last Chief of BuShips, 406-407

FARRAGUT Class, DD: 58; the 'gold platers,' 58

Farrin, RADM James Moore, Jr.: 273; controversy with Adm. Rickover, 287

Fay, The Hon. Paul B., Jr. (Red): Under Secretary of the Navy, 301, 303

Fee, RADM John Jerome (Jack): 142; later in charge of conversion of SS QUEEN MARY at Long Beach, 143; 148; named to SCAP panel, 267

Felt, Adm. Harry D.: incident involving Dr. Ruth Davis and the Chief of BuShips, 375-377

Fenard, Admiral: 101; makes an issue of guns from JEAN BART, 106

Flanders, The Hon. Ralph: Senator, 286

Fleet Defense Logistic Ships (FDLSs): a McNamara concept, 434

FRAM program: for modernization of destroyers of the Fleet, 280-283

Franke, The Hon. Wm.: member of Secretary's Advisory Committee, 238

Franke, Mrs. Wm. Birrell (Bertha): wife of SecNav, sponsor of CV ENTERPRISE, 365, 367

Frankenberg, RADM Norvell: Commanding Officer of Mare Island Naval Shipyard, 396

French Camel Corps in Atar: 116-117

French Naval Mission in U.S.: 101

French West Africa: 74 ff.

Furrer, Clint: member of Chamber of Commerce Navy-Military Affairs Committee of Long Beach, 262

Gannon, RADM Sinclar: 16-17, 22, 28

Gates, The Hon. Thomas S.: Secretary of Defense, 215-216; 238;

Gates, The Hon. Thomas S.: Secretary of Defense, 215-216; 238; 250; interviews Adm. James before appointment as Chief of Bureau, 273-274, 285

GEORGES LEYGUEZ, French Cruiser: 91

Gibbs and Cox: American firm involved in early work with hydrofoils, 326-327

Giraud, Gen. Henri: 101-102

Glassford, VADM Wm. A., Jr.: 75; diplomatic handling of French invitations at Dakar, 86-88; FDR's visit at Dakar, 97-98; in Marrakesh, 108; at Anfa Hotel in Casablanca, 108-109; Adm. James's estimate of Glassford's ability, etc., 111-113

Graham Chalmers: in charge of reactivating merchant shipping in Dakar, 118-119

Gray, William: Attorney for the Navy in preparing the suit against the oil companies at Long Beach, Calif., 239; oil company defendants offer settlement out of court, 243

Grumman Corp.: 329-330; failed to receive contract for hydrofoil PLAIN VIEW, 330

Gustaf VI Adolf, King of Sweden: awards to Admiral James the Order of the Royal Sword for aid in shipbuilding program, 296

Haig, Captain Wesley: deputy Fleet Maintenance Officer, 163-164

Hall, Paul: President of Seamen's Industrial Union, 420; 431

Hanson, Capt. Ralph T.: 52

Harbor Boat Co.: San Pedro, California, 356

Harrison, Comdr. Bill: shipyard modernization specialist, 317-318

Haven, Captain Benny: 77-78, 91-92, 98, 119-120

Hebert, Mrs. Edward: ship sponsor at Avondale Shipyard, New Orleans, 362-363

USS HECTOR, Repair Ship: 143, 145

HIGH POINT: first hydrofoil designed by BuShips, 328-330, 332

Hodges, George: 357-358

Holderness, RADM George: 158-161

Holloway, Admiral James: 153-157

Holmes, Col. Julius: adviser to General Eisenhower, 77, 103, 114

Holtzworth, Captain E. C. (Ernie): in charge of BuShips effort
     to maintain records and photographs of ship repairs at
     various bases, 139

Honsinger, RADM Leroy Vernon (Mike): named as Assistant Chief of
     Bureau to succeed Swart, 222; 228-230; in running to succeed
     RADM Mumma, 273; becomes Commander of shipyard at Mare
     Island, 276

Hoff, Captain Wayne: collaborated on paper Admiral James delivered
     at International Conference of Naval Architects, 185

USS HOUSTON: damaged in Formosa Strait, 143-145; 149-150; 163-164

Hovercraft: 40-41; discussion on development of craft, 325-347

Howard, RADM Wm. Eager: 71

Hunt, RADM Danny: 9-10

Hydrofoil: discussion of development, 325 ff.

Ihrig, Commodore Russell M.: 20-21

IKARA: Australian Missile System installed in U.S. built DDEs, 378

Ingalls Shipyard, Pascagoula, Miss.: 356-357

International Conference of Naval Architects: report on battle
     damage repairs effected in South Pacific, 157; 184-192

USS IOWA, BB: Docking for repairs at Manus, 151 ff.

Isbrandtsen, Jakob: owner of American Export-Isbrandtsen Lines, 425

James, RADM Ralph K.: early data, 1-4; interest in M.I.T., 4-5, 21; meets future wife, 22; courtship and marriage, 37-38; Post Graduate school life in Annapolis, 37-38; data on children, 47-48; efforts to gain weight, 51-52; return from Pacific, promotion to Captain, 166-167; private code for communicating with family, 165; account of daughter's wedding, 217

James, Mrs. R. K.: ship launching at Pascagoula, Miss., 356-358

JEAN BART, French BB: 78; inspection of, 104; failure of shells from US BB MASSACHUSETTS to explode in her, 104-105; Adm. James' plan to remove guns from her for benefit of BB RICHELIEU, 105-107

John, Sir Casper: First Sea Lord, 349

USS JOHN F. KENNEDY, CV: launching, 364

SS JOHN PAGE: merchant ship at Dakar, 88

Johnson, Nicholas: Maritime Administrator who becomes interested in hovercraft, 340-341

Joint Surface Effects Ship Program: 341-344

Jones, RADM Frank: 196-197; named to SCAP panel, 267

Kauffman, Captain Hal Adam: one of two officers named to set up Design Work Study Office in BuShips, 349

Keenan, Commander: Royal Navy, head of Fleet Work STudy Group, 349

Keith, VADM Roger Taylor Scott: 399, 403

Keith Board: chaired by Roger Taylor Scott Keith with purpose of examining Navy's requirements for specialist technical officer personnel, 399-404

HMS KELLY, DD: 109

Kennedy, President John F.: action on recommendation to close Boston Navy Yard, 320, 333

Killian, George: President of American President Lines and chairman of Democratic National Finance Committee, 418

King, Fleet Admiral E. J.: 61-62; 100; approves plans for transfer of guns from French BB, JEAN BART, 106; at Anfa Hotel in Casablanca, 108; accepts the Glassford recommendations on French Naval Units, 110

SS KING EDWARD: first passenger turbine-driven steamer, 189

Knight, The Hon. Goodwin (Goody): Governor of California, 248

Koehler, Eric: Scoutmaster, 3-4

Korth, The Hon. Fred: Secretary of the Navy, 318, 405

Kurtz, Captain Germany: story of repairs on the CHICAGO in Manus, 158-161

Kurtze, Charles: 406

Labor Unions and the Merchant Marine: discussion of relationships, 420-421; list of steamships that have been laid up due to labor demands, 421-422; further problems, 429-431

Lanier, Monroe: executive vice president, Ingalls Shipbuilding Co., 357

LASH: the barge ship, 431-432; two versions, 432-433

Leary, Alexander M., Jr.: 12

Leggett, RADM Wilson Durward, Jr.: 137; incharge of ship repairs at Brisbane, 140; Chief of BuShips, 204; 219

Litton Industries: acquires Ingalls Shipyard and constructs West Bank yard, 316, 352, 401

LNG Tanker (liquid natural gas tanker), 426-427

USS LONG BEACH: nuclear powered cruiser, 306

Long Beach, Calif.: attitude of citizens towards naval personnel in the area, 261; Navy Military Affairs Committee of Chamber of Commerce, 262

Long Beach Naval Shipyard: 219-250; subsidence battle, 221-223, 228; withdrawal of crude oil from subsurface causes problem, 228-229; city blames disaster on excavation for graving dock at Navy Yard, 231; description of oil lake beneath surface, 232; danger to city and reason for inaction, 233-234; creation of Hard Core Committee, 234; proposal for pumping water underground to replace oil extracted, 235-236; building of dikes at naval shipyard, 237; James advocates Navy suing oil companies in order to force program of water injection, 237-239; appearance before SecNav Advisory Board, 238-239; attorney hired to take Navy case before Federal District Court in Los Angeles, 239; Justice Dept. prepares to drop case because of opposition, 240-242; James marshalls support from community - preparations for suit go on, 242; settlement out of court, 243; terms of settlement for Navy, 244-245; analysis of Dept. of Justice attitude, 248; interest of State of California, 248-249; The Shipyard, 250; background history, 250-252; volume of work, 253; liaison maintained with other West Coast shipyards, 259

USS LYNDE McCORMICK: launching ceremony, 358-360

Mass, The Hon. Melvin: Congressman involved in battle over merger of Construction Corps with EDO, 67

SS MANHATTAN: launching in Delaware River, 355-356

Manseau, VADM Bernard Ed.: 220 (Benny)

Manus: U. S. Naval Base in WWII, 125; James serves as repair officer for ComServRon 10, 141; merits of location of base, 141-142; naval constructors on staff, 142; incident involving BB IOWA, 150-151, 381

Mare Island Naval Shipyard: life at Mare Island, 182; duties, 183; wartime experiences translated to shipyard, 183

Marrakesh, 107-108

USS MASSACHUSETTS, BB: failure of her shells to explode in French BB JEAN BART, 104-105

McCandless, Commodore Byron: 56-57

McCormack, The Hon. John W.: Congressman, 320

McMillan, RADM George: Postmaster of Long Beach, story of shipment of pheasants from North Dakota, 263-264

McNamara, The Hon. Robert: Secretary of Defense, 213; reviews programs of military branches using cost effective approach, 213; directs acceleration of POLARIS SS program, 301-302; impressed with 'dollar stretch' program of BuShips, 312-313; action on recommendation for closing Boston Navy Yard, 320-321; comments on as Secretary of Defense, 351-353; McNamara reorganization and what it has done to 'dollar stretch' program, 372-374; recommendation for closing Portsmouth Navy Yard, 409; McNamara on subject of military requirements for merchant fleet support, 427-428; 433; proposal for Fleet Defense Logistic Ships, 434

McNeil, RADM Wilfred James: Comptroller, U. S. Department of

Defense, 209; funding of ship construction, 209-212; 215; 279; 311

McQuilkin, RADM John H. (Red): 405

Mechanicsburg, Pa., Naval Supply Depot: 131, 133

Merchant Marine Act of 1936: 426, 434

Merchant Marine Act of 1970: 426-427; 433

Miller, RADM George: 144-147; story of crippled HOUSTON, 163-164; his role in bringing greater appreciation for importance of merchant marine, 435

Milne, The Hon. Cecil P.: Assistant Secretary of the Navy for Material, 270

USS MINDANAO: repair ship, damaged in MT. HOOD explosion, 147-149

M.I.T.: 4-5, 21; life at MIT, 25-26, 29-30; discussion of various aspects of training at MIT, 30-31; graduation from MIT, 35-36; thesis - holding power of anchors, 39-40

Mitsubishi Plant: Adm. James inspects U. S. constructed DD for Japanese Defense Forces, 380

Moore, RADM Robert L.: named Deputy Chief of BuShips, 277; exhcange with Admiral Rickover, 287

Moore, Comdr. Tex: 142-143; 148

Morris, Lt. Allan: aide to General Glassford, 108, 114

Mountbatten, Admiral Lord Louis: 109-110

USS MT. HOOD: explosion, 146-147

Mumma, RADM Albert G.: Chief of BuShips, 219-223; persuades James to take Long Beach assignment, 223-224; 227-228; 267, 269; 273, 275-276; becomes President and later Chairman of Board of Worthington Corporation, 278; his efforts with

Polaris SS, 299, 354, 363, 372

Murphy, The Hon. Robert: 77, 102

USS NASHVILLE: repair of battle damage at Espiritu Santo, 134; inspired need for a riveting school, 135

NATO shipbuilding program: 293-294

USS NAUTILUS: nuclear powered submarine, 287; RADM Moore and Rickover in exchange over NAUTILUS, 287

U. S. Naval Academy: first interest, 4-5; attempts at appointment, 6-12; picking a roommate, 11-12; class activities, 13; editor of LUCKY BAG, 13-15; demerit difficulties, 16-17; midshipman cruises, 18-19

Naval aviation: early interest of Adm. James in, 21-23; takes indoctrinal flight training course, 23

Naval constructor: 23-26; opposition of others to classification, 26-29; training abroad, 29; James sworn in as Naval Constructor, 32-33; struggle over merger with EDO corps, 65-73

Naval ship launchings: 354-369

Naval Supply Depot, Mechanicsburg, Pa.: 168 ff.; Ships Parts Control Center established, 170-171; effort to catalogue materials, 173-175; James reappointed, 176; Sears-Roebuck interested, offers job to James, 177-178

Naval War College: 176, 178-179; James invited to join staff, 179; discussion, 180-181

Nemec, Frank: President of Lykes Bros., 432

Newcastle-on-Tyne: 190

Newport News Shipbuilding Co.: controversy over contract involving LSTs, 414-415

USS NEW YORK, BB: 22, 31, 43

Nixon, President Richard M.: 321

Noumea: development of base as advance repair facility, 124-125

OpTevFor: takes over testing of SKIMMER - 1, 338-339

Otten, Dorothy: Secretary to the Chief of BuShips, 276

Pacific Far East Lines: operates four passenger liners, only
    U. S. passenger liners still operating, 420

USS PERKINS, DD: 45

PLAIN VIEW: second hydrofoil design by BuShips, 329-331

Philadelphia Navy Yard: 319, 321-322

Polaris submarine: see entries under BuShips and VADM W. F. Raborn

Portsmouth Navy Yard: recommendation for closing, 320-321;
    special study undertaken by Adm. James in 1963, 407-408

POSEIDON missile: 304

Post Graduate year, in Annapolis: 33-34, 38-39

SS PRESIDENT ROOSEVELT: final cruise under flag of American
    President line, 422

SS PRESIDENT WILSON, troop transport: 129

HRH Prince Philip: 333

Prudhoe Bay: 345

Pye, RADM Wm. S.: 55, 61; death of his son, 61

Pyne, RADM Schuyler: 384

Queen Juliana of the Netherlands: awards Adm. James Order of
    Orange-Nassau for aid in shipbuilding program 296

Raborn, VADM Wm. F., Jr.: 254, 302, 306

Redman, VADM John Roland: Commander, 12th Naval District, 227-
    228; 254

USS RENO: damaged in Formosa Strait, 143; 146; at Manus, 149

RICHELIEU, French BB: 78-79, 88; account of British and Free French attack on her in Dakar Harbor, 89-91; problem of getting main battery in condition, 100; plan to take guns from JEAN BART, 105-107; sails for New York, 110

Rickover, VADM Hyman George: 221, 224-226; Secretary GAtes queries James on his rapport with Rickover - as a preliminary to appointment as Chief of BuShips, 273; nuclear powered ships, 284; dealings with Congressional Committees, 286-7; exchange with RADM Robert Moore, 287-288; strength gained from expertise in nuclear power, 289; observations on attitude of various line officers, 291; example of his exclusion from an important discussion on ships, 293; tries to put an SS officer in command of ENTERPRISE, 306-307; called to inquiry on loss of SS THRESHER, 391; institutes change in nuclear plant controls after loss, 393-394; 406

Rivero, Admiral Horacio: 60

Robinson, Adm. S. M.: role in merger of Construction Corps with EDO, 69-72

Rock, RADM George H.: 63

Rodriguez Shipyards: Italian producer of hydrofoils in Sicily, 326

Roosevelt, Col. Elliott: 103

Roosevelt, President F. D.: at Casablanca, 103

Rotary International: 86; dinner in Dakar, 87; membership value to Commander of Shipyard, 260-261

Roth, Captain Edward Ellsworth: superintendent of shipbuilding in New York, 195

Royal Australian Navy: contract for three DDEs in Dafoe Shipyard, 377-379

Russell, Admiral James S.: 293

St. Nazaire, France: port from whence BB JEAN BART escaped to North Africa, 107

San Andreas Fault: 242

San Francisco Shipyard: 219-223; James' flag as Rear Admiral first flown in San Francisco, 254; 319-321

SCAP (Ship Cost Analysis Panel): James, as Assistant Chief of BuShips, proposes and heads a panel to study costs of shipbuilding and ship repairs, 267; scope and work of panel, 268-270; Secretary of Defense implements program department-wide, 270; general objectives of SCAP, 272; 312

USS SCORPION: SS lost in South Atlantic, 395

SEA LEGS: prototype of submerged foil-type hydrofoil, 327-328

Sears-Roebuck: interested in Ships Parts Control Center at Mechanicsburg, Pa., offer job to Admiral James, 177-178

Sharp, Adm. U. S. Grant (Oley): 68

Sheppard, The Hon. Harry R.: Defense Appropriations Committee, House of Representatives, 206-207

SHERWOOD FOREST: name given missile battery in Polaris submarine, 300

Shipbuilding Scheduling Control Center: 194-195; efforts to set it up, 197-198; discussion of procedures, 198-200; reflections on success of program, 201-204

Ship construction, total funding: 209-212

USS SIERRA: 155

Sierra Club: 246

Sims, Captain Harry: relieves James in Manus, 158-161

SKIMMER-1: U. S. version of SRN-1, 336-339, 345

Smith, Birg. Gen. Cyrus R.: 77

Smith, Admiral H. P. (Page): 291

Smith, RADM H. Travis: Fleet Maintenance Officer, Pearl Harbor, 163; secures orders for James, 163-164

Smith, Mrs. Margaret Chase: U. S. Senator from Maine, 321

Smith, Tilford (Tilly): general manager of Newport News Shipbuilding Co., 307-308; in charge of arrangements for launching of ENTERPRISE, 366

Snyder, Admiral Peck: 71

Solent: open water near Isle of Wight, scene of trial run of SRN-1, 334-335

Spring styles: as applied to ship design, 347

Sprung, Captain Emmett, E.: 251; Long Beach Shipyard Commander, 251-252

SRN-1: designation of first British hovercraft, 333-334

Stanwyck, Tad: involved with Design Work Study of BuShips, 351

Steamship Trade Associations: discussion of, 418-419

Stillman, Fifi: 182

Strand, Ivar: senior merchant ship captain at Dakar, 95-96

Stroop, VADM Paul David: 291

Subic Bay: Naval Hospital under aegis of BuShips, 297

Sullivan, RADM Wm. A.: (Sully), salvage efforts in North Africa, 99; 113-115

Svendsen, Captain Ed: 375

Swart, RADM Robert Lee, Jr.: 220-222

Sweden: hidden shipyard, 295-296

Sylvester, RADM E. Wallace: 194, 198

Tacoma Boat Co.: constructed hull for HIGHPOINT, the first
    hydrofoil designed by BuShips, 328

Taffinder, VADM S. A.: 43-44

TARTAR: air-surface missile, installed in DDEs of U. S. Navy, 378

USS TENNESSEE, BB: collision with BB CALIFORNIA, 127-128

THE SEA BEE: LASH ship version as invented by Lykes Bros., 432

Thomas, The Hon. Charles: Secretary of the Navy, 222, 255

USS THRESHER: nuclear powered SS, loss of, 288-289; 389-395;
    discussion of subject of-silver solder, 389-390 ff.

Tumbuctou, N. Africa: 84

Tooke, Capt. Charles M.: 69-70

TORCH: North African operation, 75; detailed plans available, 76-77

Train, Miss Gladys: 63; reaches retirement age as Adm. James comes
    in as Chief of Bureau, 274-275

TUCUMCARI: new version of hydrofoil, 332

Tulagi: journey to with fleet of landing ships, effecting
    repairs, overhaul enroute, 161; James receives orders for
    return to U.S., 162-163

Turney, Captain Wm. L.: Commander of San Francisco Naval Shipyard, 220; 226-227

Ulithi: 143, 148

Upper Clyde Shipyard: 189-190

USS UTAH, BB: 31-32

Vichy French: 83

Vickers-Armstrong: British shipbuilders, 334-335

Vinson, The Hon. Carl: Member of Congress, 208

Von Schertel, Herr: principal designer of European hydrofoils, 326

Wallin, VADM Homer N.: 194; indifficulty over Adm. Rickover, 225

Westland Aircraft Corp: British firm that produced the first hovercraft, 333, 336-337

Wheelock, RADM Charles: Deputy, BuShips, 186

USS WHITNEY: duty as hull repair superintendent, 54-55; internal rebuilding of Whitney, 55-56

Wigglesworth, The Hon. Richard B.: Member of Congress, 207

Will, Admiral John M. (Dutch): President of American Export-Isbrandtsen Line, 425

Wilmington (Cal.) Oil Field: 231-232; 237-238; 245

Wilson, The Hon. Robert: Member of Congress on Committee to investigate Long Beach situation, 247

Withers, Mrs. John: (daughter of Adm. James) - ship sponsor at Harbor Boat Yard in Long Beach, California, 361

Wolfson, Louis: New York Shipbuilding and Drydock Co., 317

Wright, Admiral Jerauld: 101-103; 114

Youngstown Sheet and Tube: 432

Zumwalt, Admiral Elmo: 322, 332; responsible for current enthusiasm for hovercraft, 340, 343-344, 346-347